Field Guide to the
Birds
of Britain & Europe

Paul Sterry

**Photographs by
Nature Photographers Ltd**

The Crowood Press

First published in 1994 by
The Crowood Press Ltd
Ramsbury, Marlborough
Wiltshire SN8 2HR

Artwork by Paul Sterry

British Library Cataloguing in Publication Data
A catalogue record for this book is available from
the British Library.

ISBN 1 85223 793 7

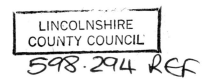
Edited and designed by
D & N Publishing
DTP & Editorial Services
Crowood Lane, Ramsbury
Marlborough, Wiltshire SN8 2HR

Phototypeset by FIDO Imagesetting,
Witney, Oxon

Printed and bound in Great Britain by
BPC Hazell Books Ltd., Aylesbury

Typefaces used: body text, Gill Sans; headings, Gill
Sans Extra Bold; folios, Gill Sans Condensed; Latin
names in species headings, Sabon.

Contents

Introduction

This book covers all the bird species that regularly occur in Europe as breeding species, regular non-breeding visitors and passage migrants. The geographical range covered by the book includes Britain, mainland Europe and Iceland, as well as the Mediterranean islands. A few species that occur on the fringes of Europe, in North Africa and western Asia, are also given reference. It also deals with rarer migrants and vagrants to the region from Asia, North America and even further afield. In a book of this size, the emphasis is, of course, on those species most likely to be encountered. However, because of increasing interest in unusual birds, particularly in Britain, and advancing identification skills, it was felt appropriate to include a few species of extremely rare occurrence since these often attract particular interest among the birdwatching community. In a few cases, species are included that are hot contenders for the British list, having occurred in Europe but not Britain. It is hoped that their inclusion may inspire continued searching.

In the past, field guides to birds of Europe have tended to be illustrated *either* with artwork *or* with photographs. This book breaks with this trend. The bulk of the illustrations are photographic but around 100 artwork illustrations have also been included. These are intended to complement the photographs and, in some cases, they feature aspects of particular bird species that are difficult to demonstrate photographically. All the artwork has been drawn specially for this book. Many of the photographs were also taken for the book and the images were selected with the species' most important identification features in mind.

Although this book is intended primarily as an aid to identification, the photographs also serve as a visual celebration of the wealth of Europe's rich

Birdwatchers at St Ives, Cornwall. This can be a superb place to sea-watch, especially in autumn.

and varied bird life. It is hoped that the photographs will also serve as a record to birdwatchers of birds already encountered and also as an inspiration for the hundreds of bird photographers in Britain and Europe.

How to Use this Book

The birds of Britain and Europe can be organized into a number of groups – families – the members of which share characters; when learnt, these family traits can be easily recognized. It would be inappropriate in a book of this size to dwell on bird classification in too much detail. However, distinct families of birds are described at the beginning of each group and the species list is organized in an order considered conventional and followed by most birdwatchers and other birdwatching books. For each bird, the descriptions are divided in the same way throughout the book for easy comparison between different species. These sub-divisions are as follows:

ENGLISH NAME
The most commonly accepted name is used in all cases. For a few of the transatlantic vagrants included in the book, the North American name and spelling is adopted.

SCIENTIFIC NAME
All species have a unique scientific name comprising two words, the first being the name of the genus combined with the second to create the species name. The name of the genus is sometimes abbreviated to the first letter if the context is clear. Some birds occur as a variety of different races or subspecies, invariably separated by geographical range. In these cases, the scientific name of the bird would comprise three words, the third one applying to the race or subspecies. As an example, the subspecies of Barn Owl found in Britain has the scientific name *Tyto alba alba*, *Tyto* being the genus name and *alba* being the name of both the species and subspecies. The European subspecies has the scientific name *Tyto alba guttata*.

SIZE
Most sizes are given in centimetres. Length (L) is the measurement from the tip of the bill to the tip of the tail. With groups of birds such as birds of prey, measurement of wingspan (W) – from wingtip to wingtip – is also given. These measurements are useful in their own right but also when comparisons are available between species.

MAIN DESCRIPTIONS
These cover the most important markings, coloration and features used in identification. Reference is made, where appropriate, to plumage differences between the sexes, breeding and non-breeding plumages and age differences.

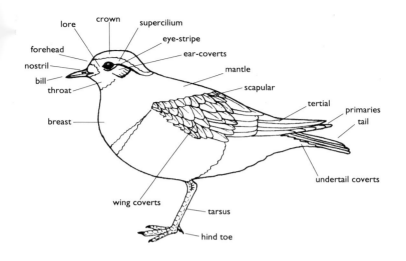

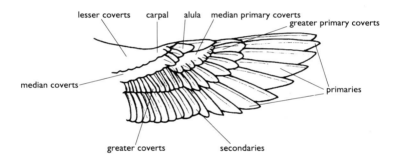

The illustrations of a typical bird, shown above, give details of the various anatomical features and plumage referred to in the text.

Birds of the same species may have radically differing plumages according to their age and so different ages are often referred to in the text. **Juvenile** plumage is acquired when a young bird fledges. Because most European birds breed during the period from April to August, juvenile plumage is usually seen in late summer or early autumn. It is retained until the bird moults, which usually takes place in the autumn. **First winter** plumage is seen during the first calendar winter of a bird's life. The plumage may differ from that of an adult in winter. Some birds take several years to acquire full adult plumage and during this time they may be referred to as **immature**. **First summer** plumage is seen during a bird's first summer, roughly one year after hatching. Adult birds often have very different plumages during the **breeding** season compared with non-breeding periods. The differences are often most marked

The warbling song of the Dunnock is a familiar sound in gardens across much of Europe.

in males, colours and patterns often being important in display. Lastly, the drakes of many species of duck moult and acquire **eclipse** plumage during the summer months, when they resemble females of the same species.

Voice

Voice can be an important aid in identification. Most passerines have unique and colourful songs, delivered during the breeding season. With experience and confidence, most of the common species can be identified on song alone. Many birds, including many passerines, also have distinctive calls uttered, for example, in alarm or in flight. In the text, both songs and calls have been described phonetically. Many birdwatchers may find it useful to listen to recordings of European birds and compare these with their written descriptions. It would be unrealistic to expect to be able to learn the calls of all the birds in this book. However, it is surprisingly easy to become familiar with the more common ones. Armed with this knowledge, it is then much easier to pick out an unfamiliar call or song and then locate the source of the sound – perhaps a new bird for the observer!

Habitat

Most birds are highly adapted in terms of the food they eat and their feeding methods and habits. As a consequence, most are, generally speaking, extremely habitat-specific. This rather obvious generalization applies both to breeding and non-breeding birds and to scarcer passage migrants which may only stay for a few days in one location. Wetland migrant birds invariably occur in wetland habitats and arboreal ones often in woodlands. Knowledge of a bird's adaptations and behaviour can help birders keen on finding unusual vagrants search in more productive sites.

Distribution

Without the aid of maps, this book tries to give as much information as possible about the distribution of birds within Europe. Breeding and wintering ranges are described together with details of migration routes where appropriate.

Occurrence

The status and period of occurrence of each species is given, whether this be as a breeding species, a winter visitor or a passage migrant. For particularly unusual species, a few likely locations are given, together with clues as to weather conditions or times of year during which they are most likely to occur.

Status Chart

An easy-to-refer-to chart indicates the status of those species that are seen in Britain. The following key explains the use of the letters. The numbers refer to months of the year. **R** = resident in Britain, remaining in the same location throughout the year. **T** = seen throughout Britain, but may occur in different habitats at different times of the year. **S** = summer visitor. **W** = winter visitor. **M** = passage migrant. **V** = vagrant. Where no months of the year are given for this category, the species occurs on an irregular basis. For species breeding in Britain, the months in which they breed are given preceded by **N**.

Flocks of migrating **White Pelicans** may be seen in northern Greece.

Migration and Movements

Many of Europe's bird species are year-round residents, some moving only a few kilometres during their entire lives. However, many more are migratory, occurring in completely different geographical ranges while nesting and during the non-breeding period. Some of these migrants occur in Europe during the summer months when breeding takes place. In the autumn, they fly south

The Puffin can be seen at breeding colonies around the coast of north-west Europe.

to warmer, food-rich winter quarters that may be as far away as Africa. Other species are non-breeding visitors to the region, their breeding grounds lying outside the region. Many of Europe's waders and ducks fall into this category, the high Arctic being their summer haunt.

The above two categories are, of course, oversimplifications. Considerable movement of some bird species occurs within the range of this book, some of which is related to breeding seasons and some to weather conditions. Other species occur either partly or wholly as passage migrants to the region. Numbers of these species peak in spring and autumn. These are exciting seasons for keen birders, not only for regularly encountered species but also for the more unusual species – rare vagrants to the region which add spice to most birders' lives.

The occurrence of birds outside their normal range often reflects problems encountered during their normal migration. Transatlantic vagrants, which appear mostly in the autumn, have probably been caught up in westerly weather systems while migrating south down the coast of North America or across the Caribbean. Species normally associated with the Mediterranean often appear as vagrants in northern Europe after overshooting on migration, frequently during periods of southerly winds. The autumn occurrence in western Europe of birds whose ranges lie in eastern Europe and Asia may be due to incorrect navigation – so-called reverse migration. Easterly and south-easterly winds greatly influence the numbers and distribution of this category of vagrants.

Migration periods are important times of year for the keen birder. Watching from coastal headlands at the appropriate times of year and during suitable weather conditions can reveal large movements of seabirds. Many other birds migrate at night, and cannot, therefore, be observed actually migrating. However, visit any estuary during spring and autumn and you will find evidence of their movements – migrant waders and wildfowl from far afield will be resting and feeding after long flights.

Going Birding

EQUIPMENT
In order to get maximum enjoyment from birding, a pair of binoculars, and perhaps a telescope, are vital. There is a bewildering choice of binoculars available on the market, with a price range to match. A reasonable pair is likely to cost you from around £100 but you could pay up to £1,000 for top-of-the-range models. The specification of a pair of binoculars is given by two figures, such as 8×30 or 10×40. The first is the magnification and the second is the diameter of the objective (larger) lens, in effect a measure of the light-gathering capacity of binoculars; the higher the second number, the brighter the view. No one make or model can claim to be the best. Visit a large optical

cal equipment showroom and put several to the test before deciding which pair suits best your vision and your pocket.

FIELDCRAFT

There is no substitute for experience. However, identification of unusual species or of birds seen in challenging situations can be greatly assisted by knowing what features to look for and by being aware of certain pitfalls. Factors such as size, colour, lighting, behaviour and voice all need to be taken into account, as does most birders' subconscious urge to find unusual species: blinkered observation can all too easily transform a common species into a more unusual one!

Size is obviously an important factor in bird identification but gauging it correctly in a field situation can prove difficult. Try to compare the bird in question with another whose identification, and therefore size, is certain. When making direct comparisons, be sure that you are seeing them at the same range because binoculars and telescopes foreshorten distances and create illusory perspectives.

Markings, patterns and colour are of key importance when trying to identify birds. Bear in mind, however, that colours can appear to vary depending on the intensity of the light and its direction. There are also variations in plumage, and even size, to be found among individuals of the same age, sex and plumage. You have only to look at a group of Dunlins in early autumn to see this clearly demonstrated.

Even in poor light and with distant views, experienced observers can often identify birds on their behaviour, posture and stance alone. Combined, these factors are often referred to as the 'jizz' of a species. When observing a species for the first time, all the above factors should be taken into consideration when making an identification. However, difficult species may defy an on-the-spot decision and it is very useful to make notes about the bird and record a full description, perhaps together with a sketch.

Birdwatchers' Europe

The map shows the geographical range covered by this book. It also shows the region's national boundaries and a number of key birding hotspots. The following list details the main reasons for their importance:

Shetland Islands – seabird colonies.

Fair Isle – migration. Renowned for its British rarities.

Cley – migration and coastal wetlands. Renowned for its British rarities.

Skomer – seabird colonies.

Scilly Isles – migration. Renowned for its British rarities.

Lac d'Orient – overwintering wildfowl, cranes and raptors.

Camargue – Mediterranean wetland species.

Majorca – migration and typical Mediterranean species.

Southern Spain – migration, especially on Gibraltar, and wetland species at Coto Doñana.

Algarve – migration and typical Mediterranean species.

Sierra de Guadarrama – southern European mountain species.

Grossglockner Pass – alpine species.

Neuseidler See – eastern European wetland species.

Falsterbo – migration.

Texel – migration.

Area covered by this book, and some major bird observation points.

DIVERS
ORDER GAVIIFORMES
Family Gaviidae

Superbly adapted to life in water. Swim low in water and dive well for fish. Streamlined head and neck, the shape and angle of which are useful in identification. Powerful legs with webbed feet set far back on body for swimming and almost useless on land. Neck held outstretched in flight. Summer and winter plumages different. Nest close to freshwater. Winter around coasts.

Black-throated Diver
Gavia arctica L 67cm

Elegant summer plumage with grey head and back of neck, black throat and chin, and band of white stripes on side of neck. In winter, blackish above and white below with demarcation well-defined. White 'thigh' patch at water level often conspicuous. Medium-sized bill held horizontally. Powerful flight with shallow wingbeats.

Voice Song eerie and far-carrying *klowee kok-klowee kok-klowee*.

Habitat Breeds on large, northern and upland lakes. In winter, around coasts and occasionally inland on gravel pits. Usually solitary.

Distribution Nests throughout Scandinavia and similar latitudes in N Europe. Rare breeding species in Britain, confined to large Scottish lochs. Winters around rocky coasts of W Europe; locally in Mediterranean and larger continental lakes.

Occurrence On breeding grounds May to August. In coastal waters for rest of year. In Britain, best seen off W coasts. Rare in Ireland. Occasional inland on gravel pits during cold weather. .

T	1–12	N 5–8

Great Northern Diver
Gavia immer L 85cm

In summer plumage, head, bill and neck black with green gloss. Band of white stripes on side of neck. Back black with conspicuous white spots. In winter, upperparts blackish-brown with white underside. Dark half-collar often visible on side of neck

with white wedge above it. Contrast between black and white lacks clear demarcation. Larger in all respects than similar Black-throated and bill proportionately bigger. Head shape also more angular. Bill has dark, convex culmen and usually held horizontally. Deep, powerful wingbeats.

Voice Song eerie and evocative *kee aa-oooh kee aa-oooh* heard on breeding grounds.

Habitat Breeds on large freshwater lakes. Winters around rocky coasts.

Distribution Breeds in Iceland. A few summer on large Scottish lochs and may have nested occasionally. Outside breeding season, found in coastal waters of W Europe as far south as N Spain.

Occurrence On nesting grounds May to August. Around coasts at other times of year. Not uncommon off rocky coasts of W Britain and Ireland. Individuals in summer plumage may linger in coastal waters late in spring or return in early autumn. Occasional on inland gravel pits in winter, especially after severe weather.

W	10–3	—

White-billed Diver
Gavia adamsii L 90cm

Black-and-white summer plumage similar to Great Northern. Best identification feature is huge yellow bill with straight culmen, held tilted upwards. Bill always pale and culmen never dark. In winter, upperparts greyish-brown. Underparts white but neck and cheek stippled with brown. Dark half-collar on lower neck. Eye often surrounded by pale 'ring'.

Voice Song not heard in the region.

Habitat Nests beside large lakes and winters in coastal waters.

Distribution Breeds in high Arctic and winters in northern seas with small numbers reaching North Sea.

Occurrence Rare visitor to NW Europe. Most British records from NE England, E Scotland and Shetland Islands, during late winter. Occasionally, birds linger into spring.

V	11–3	—

Great Northern Diver, summer

White-billed Diver, summer

Black-throated Diver, summer

Great Northern Diver, spring

Black-throated Diver, winter

White-billed Diver, winter

Red-throated Diver
Gavia stellata L 58cm

In summer plumage, grey head, red throat, and black-and-white stripes to back of neck. In winter, back blackish-brown, speckled with white, and underside white. White face and neck extending above eye. Graceful in water with neck usually held straight and bill tilted upwards. Bill slender with culmen straight and lower edge upturned. In flight, looks front-heavy with drooping neck.
Voice *kookor-rooee, kookor-rooee* when nesting.
Habitat Nests beside small, shallow moorland pool close to sea or large lake for feeding. Winters around coasts, sometimes in estuary mouths, and often in shallower water than other divers. Sometimes in loose but sizeable flocks in winter.
Distribution Breeds mainly Scandinavia and Iceland. Rare nester N and W Scotland and Scottish islands, and very rare Ireland. Otherwise found coastal NW Europe and W Mediterranean.
Occurrence On breeding grounds May to August but coastal for rest of year.

T	1–12	N 5–8

Red-throated Diver, winter

GREBES
ORDER PODICIPEDIFORMES
Family Podicipedidae

Elegant fish-eating waterbirds with flattened bodies. Lobed toes for swimming and legs set far back on body. Awkward on land. In flight neck sags slightly. Build floating nests of plant material.

Great Crested Grebe
Podiceps cristatus L 50cm

In summer plumage, head pattern is distinctive with orange ear-tufts, fringed with black. In winter, black cap with white face extending to above the eye. Bill pink with dark culmen. Juveniles similar to winter birds but with dark stripes on face and upper neck. Rapid wingbeats in flight. Two conspicuous white panels on wings. In spring, courtship 'dances' common.
Voice *krek-krek-krek* and other harsh, grating calls.
Habitat Large lakes and gravel pits with reed-fringed margins. In winter, occasionally on sea.

Great Crested Grebe, winter

Distribution Widespread in Europe. Breeds throughout Britain as far north as S Scotland.
Occurrence Resident. Nests March to July.

T	1–12	N 3–7

Red-necked Grebe
Podiceps grisegena L 45cm

More stocky than Great Crested Grebe. In summer, neck brick-red, cheeks and throat greyish bordered with white, and black cap. In winter, neck greyish brown. White on face does not extend to eye. Bill yellow with black tip and culmen. Two white patches on wing.
Voice Pig-like squeal, resembling Water Rail.
Habitat Breeds on shallow ponds and lakes. Prefers dense vegetation cover. In winter, moves to open lakes and sheltered coastal waters.
Distribution Breeds in E Europe, moving west in the winter. Widespread but local along E and S coasts of England.
Occurrence Nests from May to August. Occasional birds linger until late spring.

W	10–3	—

Slavonian Grebe
Podiceps auritus L 34cm

Summer plumage elegant and distinctive. Flanks and neck brick-red, black head and ear-tufts, and conspicuous orange-yellow head plumes. In winter plumage, has white underparts and dark upperparts. Can be confused with Black-necked but has more white on face and flatter crown. Bill dark with white tip, held horizontally. Orange-red eye. In flight, single white wing panel on rear of wing.
Voice When nesting, a trilling *hee-arr*.
Habitat Nests on well-vegetated upland ponds and in bays of larger lakes. Winters on sheltered coasts and estuaries. More rarely on inland water.
Distribution Breeds in Iceland, NE Europe and locally in Scandinavia and Scotland. Winters on sheltered coasts of NW Europe from Brittany to Denmark; widespread around British coast.
Occurrence Nests from May to July. Moves to coastal waters at other times of year.

T	1–12	N 5–7

Red-throated Diver, summer   **Red-throated Diver,** summer

Great Crested Grebe, autumn   **Red-necked Grebe,** spring
         Slavonian Grebe, summer   **Slavonian Grebe,** winter

Black-necked Grebe
Podiceps nigricollis L 32cm

In summer plumage, brick-red flanks and black neck and back. Head shows black except for orange-yellow head plumes and bright red eye. Head shape is distinctive with steep forehead and bill slightly upturned and tilted upwards. In winter appears superficially similar to Slavonian Grebe with dark upperparts and white underparts. White on face less extensive than Slavonian and forehead steeper. In flight, shows a white panel on the rear of wing.

Voice Call is plaintive whistling *oor-eet*.

Habitat Breeds on well-vegetated, shallow lakes, often in small colonies. Winters in sheltered coastal waters and sometimes found on lakes and reservoirs.

Distribution Scattered breeding range in Europe, wherever suitable habitats occur. Rare breeder in N Britain and Ireland. Winters around the entire coast of Europe in small numbers and in Britain, best seen along S coast of England.

Occurrence Breeds April to July and otherwise found on coastal waters. Some birds are year-round residents on larger lakes in central and S Europe.

T	1–12	N 4–7

Little Grebe
Tachybaptus ruficollis L 27cm

Smallest and dumpiest of the grebes. In summer plumage, throat, chin and cheek orange-brown. Lime to yellow gape patches and dark bill tipped paler. In winter, upperparts dark brown, underparts buffish-white and chin white. Often fluffs up rear end revealing pale, downy feathers. Juvenile similar to winter plumage but with dark stripes on face and neck. Generally rather shy and unobtrusive but presence often revealed by call. If alarmed, the bird will sometimes remain partly submerged among vegetation until danger passes.

Voice A shrill, trilling call similar to female Cuckoo but much higher-pitched.

Habitat Nests on well-vegetated ponds and lakes and along lush river margins.

Distribution Occurs throughout most of Europe in suitable habitats as far north as S Scandinavia. Absent from mountain ranges such as Alps and Pyrenees. Common and widespread in Britain except for N Scotland.

Occurrence Mostly resident although some birds may move to coast in severe winter weather.

T	1–12	N 3–7

Pied-billed Grebe
Podilymbus podiceps L 35cm

A stocky grebe, like larger version of Little. Buffish-brown plumage. Thick, stubby bill is distinctive. During breeding season, bill pale with black band. In winter, bill horn-coloured and lacks dark band.

Voice Rattling call not heard in the region.

Habitat Reed-fringed lakes and other well-vegetated water bodies.

Distribution Breeds N America.

Occurrence Rare vagrant to NW Europe including Britain, mostly in winter. Individuals sometimes stay for extended periods.

V	11–3	—

Black-necked Grebe, summer

Black-necked Grebe, winter

Little Grebe, summer

Little Grebe, 1st winter   **Pied-billed Grebe,** non-breeding

TUBENOSES
ORDER PROCELLARIFORMES

Tube-shaped nostrils for secreting salt. Hook-shaped bills. Highly marine. Webbed feet. Stiffly held wings for gliding in albatrosses, Fulmar and shearwaters. Fluttering flight in storm-petrels.

Fulmar
Fulmarus glacialis L 45cm, W 105cm

Superficially gull-like but flies with stiffly held wings, gliding for long periods interspersed with bursts of rapid wingbeats. Mantle and wings grey with pale patch at base of primaries. In light phase, head, neck and underparts white. In dark phase (seldom seen in region) whole of body dark grey. Tube nostrils and armoured beak visible at close range. Dark smudge in front of eye. Swims buoyantly and gathers in flocks to feed on surface fish and offal. Vomits stinking crop oil when disturbed.

Voice Cackles and grunts heard at nest.

Habitat Nests in grassy hollows and ledges on sea cliffs. Feeds and winters at sea.

Distribution Isolated nest colonies along the coast of NW Europe from Brittany north to Scandinavia and Iceland. Common around the W coast of Britain. Otherwise found in offshore waters of NW Europe.

Occurrence Some birds present throughout year in vicinity of nesting colonies. Can be seen off most rocky headlands in W Britain. Numbers have increased dramatically this century.

T	1–12	N 4–7

Manx Shearwater
Puffinus puffinus L 35cm W 80cm

In flight, glides with stiffly held wings, wheeling from side to side alternately revealing dark upperparts and white underparts. Small flocks often appear to be flying in line. Glides interspersed with short bursts of rapid wingbeats. Shuffling gait on land.

Voice Weird chuckling and gurgling calls heard at night at breeding colonies. Calls uttered in flight and by birds in nest burrows.

Habitat Nests colonially in burrows on offshore islands, occasionally on inaccessible mainland cliffs. Otherwise at sea.

Distribution Breeding colonies on offshore islands off W coasts of England, Wales, Ireland. Also on many Scottish islands. Isolated colonies off Brittany and Iceland.

Occurrence Commonest shearwater in N Atlantic. Occurs at breeding colonies from May

until August. Only visits land at night but flocks ('rafts') gather close to land at dusk. Otherwise at sea, most moving offshore and south during winter. Seen from ferries and boats. Sometimes comes close to shore during autumn gales. St Ives in Cornwall and Strumble Head in Wales are likely seawatching spots.

S	3–10	N 5–8

Yelkouan Shearwater
Puffinus yelkouan L 30cm W 80cm

Very similar to Manx Shearwater and previously considered a subspecies. Upperparts browner, underparts more heavily marked and vent darker. W Mediterranean race has buffish underparts. Flight and habits similar to Manx Shearwater but often comes closer to shore during daytime.

Voice As Manx Shearwater.

Habitat Nests in burrows on offshore Mediterranean islands. Otherwise at sea.

Distribution Breeding colonies throughout Mediterranean.

Occurrence Seen from rocky headlands throughout Mediterranean. W Mediterranean birds move into Atlantic outside breeding season and a few reach Britain in late summer. Late summer pelagic trips and autumn seawatching off Cornish coast give best opportunities for sightings.

V	7–9	—

Little Shearwater
Puffinus assimilis L 27cm W 60cm

A much smaller version of Manx Shearwater. Good views reveal white face surrounding dark eye. Flight typical of shearwater but with long bursts of fluttering wingbeats and only short glides.

Voice Similar to Manx but not heard in region.

Habitat Nests in burrows on small islands.

Distribution Breeds Canaries and small islands off Madeira.

Occurrence Seen from inter-island ferries in Canaries and Madeira from May to August. Occasionally reaches further north to British coast. Records

Little Shearwater

from North Sea and Atlantic coasts.

V	5–10	—

Fulmar, adult

Fulmar

Manx Shearwater

Fulmar, blue phase

Manx Shearwater

Great Shearwater
Puffinus gravis L 45cm W 110cm
A large shearwater with distinctive upperparts. Dark cap, white collar, grey-brown mantle and wings, and pale patch above tail. Dark markings on underwing and dark vent. Powerful flight on stiffly held wings. Sometimes follows boats.
Voice Not heard in region.
Habitat Usually far out to sea.
Distribution Breeds in S Atlantic and present in NW Atlantic from June to October on migration.
Occurrence Common at edge of continental shelf during late summer and early autumn and seen from pelagic boat trips. Occasionally passes close to shore during severe westerly gales but appearance unpredictable. St Ives in Cornwall and Cape Clear in Ireland are classic sites.

V	7–10	—

Cory's Shearwater
Calonectris diomedea L 45cm W 110cm
Similar to Great Shearwater but lacks dark cap and white collar. Underwings white and almost unmarked. Vent white. Bill yellow, tipped black. In flight, wings held slightly forward. Glides on bowed wings and soars to considerable heights during strong winds.
Voice Similar to Manx Shearwater. Heard only at nest.
Habitat Breeds on offshore islands. Otherwise at sea.
Distribution Breeds on offshore islands in the Mediterranean and off S Portugal.

Cory's Shearwater

Occurrence Common in the Mediterranean. Seen from rocky headlands during onshore winds and from boats. In late summer, many birds move west and north, reaching the British coast in unpredictable numbers. Distribution linked to Ushant Front, the zone of mixing between Atlantic and English Channel waters. During July and August, Porthgwarra in Cornwall and ferry between Penzance and Scilly Isles often produce records.

V	7–10	—

Sooty Shearwater
Puffinus griseus L 45cm W 100cm
All-dark shearwater except for pale patches on underwing. Long wings and graceful flight. Seldom follows boats.
Voice Not heard in region.
Habitat Usually far out to sea.
Distribution Breeds in S hemisphere. Present in NW Atlantic from July to October on migration.
Occurrence Regular visitor to W coast of Britain and North Sea. Best seen during periods of strong onshore winds at known seawatching sites in August and September.

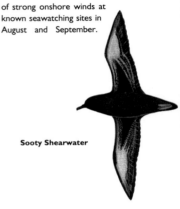

Sooty Shearwater

V	6–10	—

Black-browed Albatross
Diomedia melanophris L 90cm W 240cm
Immense wingspan and effortless flight are unmistakable, but beware young Gannet. Upperwing dark brown. Underwing white with dark borders. Body white except for dark streak through eye and dark tip to tail. Bill yellow.
Voice Not heard in region.
Habitat Open ocean.
Distribution Resident in southern oceans. Rare visitor to N hemisphere.
Occurrence Very rare accidental visitor, seen when seawatching. A few individuals have joined Gannet colonies, staying for several years. Most recent British 'resident' on Hermaness, Shetland.

V	—	—

Cory's Shearwater, adult at nest burrow

Great Shearwater

Great Shearwater
Black-browed Albatross

British Storm-petrel

Hydrobates pelagicus L 15cm W 40cm

Tiny, ocean-going seabird. All-dark plumage except for conspicuous rectangular, white rump. White stripe on underwing. Pale margins to secondary coverts only visible at close range. Bat-like flight with fluttering wingbeats. Follows boats.

Voice Series of purrs and goblin-like chuckles or hiccups heard at night at breeding colonies.

Habitat Nests in burrows and crevices on rocky cliffs. Otherwise far out to sea.

Distribution Colonies on offshore islands on W coast of England and Wales. Also around Irish coast and on many Scottish islands. Isolated colonies off Brittany and Iceland. Wide-ranging feeding distribution in NW Atlantic during breeding season, moving south in winter.

Occurrence Present at breeding colonies May to August but only seen there above ground at night. Responds to tape-lures of song. Driven close to land during autumn gales off W coast of Britain. Seen during ferry crossings to Scottish islands and during pelagic trips from Cornwall.

S	5–10	N 5–8

Leach's Storm-petrel

Oceanodroma leucorhoa L 21cm W 46cm

Larger than British Storm-petrel with more pointed wings, obvious pale secondary coverts, and forked tail. White rump slightly rounded; pale grey central bar only visible at close range. Deep wingbeats and powerful and erratic flight. Dark underwing. Does not follow ships.

Voice Strange series of purrs, chuckles and gurgles heard at breeding colonies.

Habitat As British Storm-petrel.

Distribution Breeding colonies on remote Scottish islands and off Iceland. Throughout offshore waters of NW Atlantic during breeding season, moving south in winter.

Occurrence Large numbers occasionally blown ashore during autumn gales. Regularly seen off Cornish coast in September and October.

S	5–10	N 5–8

Wilson's Storm-petrel

Oceanites oceanicus L 18cm W 40cm

Similar to British Storm-petrel but underwing dark and pale margin to secondary coverts conspicuous. Often glides and patters on water's surface when yellow webs of feet visible at very close range. Legs project beyond tail in flight.

Voice Not heard in region.

Habitat Breeds in southern oceans. Feeds and winters at sea.

Distribution Present in NW Atlantic from July to November but always far out to sea.

Occurrence Common in Bay of Biscay and occasionally further north. Seen from boats crossing Bay of Biscay and on pelagic trips from Cornwall. Very rarely blown close to shores of W Britain during severe autumn gales.

V	7–9	—

Madeiran Storm-petrel

Oceanodroma castro L 20cm W 43cm

Similar to Wilson's but has dark webs. Legs do not project beyond tail in flight. Rump pure white. Gliding flight. Does not follow boats.

Voice Not heard in region.

Habitat Breeds rocky islands. Otherwise at sea.

Distribution Breeds on islands in Canaries and off Madeira. Widespread in oceans surrounding these islands but rare further north.

Occurrence Seen from inter-island ferries in Canaries and Madeira. Very rarely seen in British waters.

V	—	—

Bulwer's Petrel

Bulweria bulwerii L 27cm W 72cm

All-dark seabird midway between a storm-petrel and a shearwater in appearance. Buoyant flight with wings held forward and drooping slightly. Conspicuous pale margin to wing coverts. Long, wedge-shaped tail.

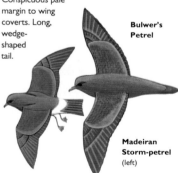

Bulwer's Petrel

Madeiran Storm-petrel (left)

Voice Not heard in region.

Habitat Breeds on offshore islands. Otherwise at sea.

Distribution Breeds on islands in Canaries, Azores and off Madeira.

Occurrence Can be seen from inter-island ferries in Canaries and Madeira, from May to August. Very rare further northwards.

V	—	—

British Storm-petrel

British Storm-petrel

Leach's Storm-petrel

Wilson's Storm-petrel

PELICANS AND ALLIED BIRDS
ORDER PELICANIFORMES

Fish-eating, aquatic birds. Webbed feet for swimming and diving. Colonial nesters. Represented by gannets, pelicans, cormorants and shags.

Gannet
Sula bassana L 95cm W 175cm
Large seabird with long, pointed wings and long, wedge-shaped tail. Head and neck held outstretched in flight. Adult appears conspicuously white in flight with black wingtips. Head and neck buff-orange. Bill large and dagger-like. Legs and feet black but toes marked pale blue. Juveniles mostly brown, speckled with paler markings. Gradually acquire adult plumage over next 4 to 5 years. Powerful flight with glides interspersed with vigorous wingbeats. Usually low over water (often disappearing between wave crests) but rising higher in rough seas. Feeds by plunge-diving for fish from considerable height. Groups of 20 or more often feed together.
Voice Harsh calls at nest but silent at sea.
Habitat Breeds on rocky islands and cliffs. Otherwise at sea.
Distribution Most of world population breeds around British coast. Major colonies off Welsh and Scottish coasts and Shetland Islands. Other colonies on Brittany, Channel Islands, Iceland and Norway. Most birds move south in winter.
Occurrence Present at breeding colonies from April to August. Easily accessible at Bempton Cliffs in Yorkshire and Hermaness in Shetland but most spectacular colony at Bass Rock in Scotland. Often seen from ferries and exposed headlands off W coast of Britain.

S	3–11	N 4–8

White Pelican
Pelecanus onocrotalus L 155cm W 320cm
Large, bulky bird invariably found near water. Plumage white but pinkish tinge to underside often visible. Bare, pink face patch. Huge horn-coloured bill with yellow throat pouch used to catch fish. Often feeds communally, driving fish into tight shoals. Swims buoyantly using large webbed feet. When seen in flight from below, all flight feathers black. Juveniles brownish above and buffish below with yellow throat pouch. Soaring and gliding flight on broad, outstretched wings. Circles on thermals like birds of prey and sometimes flies in 'v' formation. Nests colonially. Migrates in large flocks, sometimes in the company of storks and birds of prey.
Voice Harsh grunting calls at nest.
Habitat Large lakes with vegetated margins and lush river deltas.
Distribution Breeds locally on lakes in SE Europe during summer months. Most birds migrate to Africa for winter.
Occurrence Present on breeding grounds from May to August. Found at Lake Prespa on Greek/former Yugoslav border and on migration on lakes in N mainland Greece and W Turkey. Flocks seen on migration in Israel and through gorges in N Greece.

V	—	—

Dalmatian Pelican
Pelecanus crispus L 170cm W 335cm
Similar to White Pelican but has drab white underwing with black only on wingtips when seen from below in flight. Plumage greyish-white and throat pouch orange. Juveniles similar to White Pelican but paler and with pink throat pouch.
Voice Similar to White Pelican.
Habitat Large, reed-fringed lakes.
Distribution Breeds on a few large lakes in N Greece. Winters on lakes in Greece and Turkey.
Occurrence Now extremely rare and best looked for at Lake Prespa on Greek/former Yugoslav border during summer months or on lakes in N Greece or E Turkey in winter.

Dalmatian Pelican

Gannet, adult

Gannet, juvenile

White Pelican

Gannet, adult at breeding colony

White Pelicans, thermalling

Dalmatian Pelican, nesting

Cormorant

Phalacrocorax carbo L 90cm W 150cm

Dark plumage with brown, dark-edged feathers on back giving scaly appearance. Thick neck and large, dark, webbed feet. Yellow gular pouch and base of bill. In breeding season, British and N Atlantic coastal race has white throat and thigh patches and white streaks on upper neck. Throat duller and loses thigh patches in winter. Continental race has more extensive white on face and neck. Juveniles brown with pale throat and belly. Swims low in water with head tilted slightly upwards and dives well. Perches on buoys and jetties with wings outstretched. Powerful flight with deep wingbeats.

Voice Deep croaking noises at nest. Otherwise silent.

Habitat Nests colonially on cliffs, rocky islands and in trees beside freshwater. Otherwise in coastal waters and sometimes on freshwater.

Distribution Nests locally around British coast and N Atlantic coast from Normandy to Sweden. Also in Iceland, Greece and Turkey. Outside breeding season, occurs around entire European coast.

Occurrence Found in almost all sheltered, coastal waters and estuaries from October to March. Also on reservoirs and large gravel pits, sometimes well inland.

T	1–12	N 4–8

Shag

Phalacrocorax aristotelis L 70cm W 95cm

Similar to Cormorant but smaller with slimmer neck and less robust beak. Bright-yellow gape patches. In good light, plumage has bottle-green sheen, most noticeable on head and neck. In breeding plumage has forward-curved tuft of feathers on forehead. Immatures are brown with pale neck and throat, not belly. Swims low in water and indifferent to rough seas. Dives well, usually jumping slightly out of water. Perches on rocks with wings outstretched. Generally flies low over water.

Voice Guttural croaks at nest, hisses at intruders. Otherwise silent.

Habitat Rocky coasts where nests on cliffs.

Distribution Widespread around rocky coasts of Europe. Mainly W coast of Britain.

Occurrence Present all year around rocky coasts. Less common in other coastal areas and rare inland. Easy to see at most British seabird colonies such as Farne Islands in Northumberland, Skomer in Wales and on Shetland and Orkney.

T	1–12	N 4–8

Double-crested Cormorant

Phalacrocorax auritus L 75cm W 100cm

Similar in appearance to Cormorant but smaller with more slender bill. Facial skin and gular pouch orange. Dark plumage in adult with tufted double crest on side of crown in summer only. Immature has whitish face and breast. In flight, has kinked neck.

Voice Not heard in region.

Habitat Sheltered coasts and freshwater.

Distribution Widespread breeding species in N America.

Occurrence Has been recorded in Britain.

V	10–3	—

Pygmy Cormorant

Phalacrocorax pygmaeus L 50cm W 90cm

Like small version of Shag with proportionately shorter neck and longer tail. Bill short and stubby. Body and wings dark with chestnut head and neck. In breeding season, white flecks on head and neck and green sheen to back. In winter, throat pale. Immature brown with pale throat and belly. Swims low in water and dives well. Often perches on branches and posts with wings outstretched. The flight is direct with rather fast wingbeats.

Voice Croaking calls at nest. Otherwise silent.

Habitat Freshwater lakes with reed-fringed margins. Never on sea. Nests colonially in trees, often alongside other waterbirds.

Distribution Local breeding species SE Europe. Seldom seen outside Greece, former Yugoslavia and Turkey.

Occurrence Year-round resident on many lakes in N mainland Greece and E Turkey. Birds from inland lakes move south to coastal freshwater lakes in winter.

Pygmy Cormorant, summer

Cormorant, adult with young

Cormorant, drying wings

Shag, juvenile

Shag, courtship

Double-crested Cormorant

HERONS AND ALLIED BIRDS
ORDER CICONIIFORMES

Bitterns, herons, egrets, storks, spoonbills and ibises. Medium to large, wading waterside birds. Long legs, necks and bills. Most wade to catch fish and other aquatic life. Many nest colonially.

Bittern
Botaurus stellaris L 75cm W 135cm
Large, heron-like bird. Often stands with hunched-up appearance. If alarmed, stretches body and neck, points bill skywards, and 'freezes', camouflaged among reeds. Plumage straw-coloured with darker markings adding to cryptic effect among vegetation. Pale throat; black cap and moustachial stripes. In flight, broad, owl-like wings are all-brown. Legs greenish-yellow. Shy and retiring and usually detected by call alone.
Voice Loud, deep booming call *uh-boom* repeated from reedbeds in spring and early summer. Heard from dusk to dawn.
Habitat Breeds in extensive reedbeds. Occasionally in other wetland habitats in severe winters.
Distribution Widespread but local in Europe in suitable habitats. Very local in Britain.
Occurrence Year-round resident in W Europe. In Britain, best seen at RSPB reserves at Leighton Moss in Lancs and Minsmere in Suffolk.

T	1–12	N 5–7

American Bittern
Botaurus lentiginosus L 70cm W 120cm
Similar to Bittern but slightly smaller. Streaked appearance on neck and breast. Chestnut crown and long, black moustachial stripes. In flight, broad wings have dark flight feathers.
Voice Not heard in region.
Habitat Reedbeds and marshes.
Distribution Breeds N America.
Occurrence Very rare autumn and winter vagrant to W Europe.

V	10–3	—

Little Bittern
Ixobrychus minutus L 36cm W 55cm
Markings and small size are distinctive. Male has black cap, greyish face and buff underparts. Back and flight feathers black. Pale panel on forewing conspicuous both in flight and at rest. Female similar to male but with subdued colours. Juvenile has Bittern-like plumage. Sometimes clambers up reed stems but generally shy and secretive. Sometimes flies low over reedbeds. Flight distinctive with jerky wingbeats interspersed with glides.
Voice Croaking *guk* repeated every few seconds after dark.
Habitat Reedbeds and marshes with dense vegetation.

Little Bittern, male

Distribution Widespread in central and S Europe in summer. Winters in Africa.
Occurrence Occurs from April to August in European wetlands. Easily seen in Camargue, La Brenne and other French wetlands. Regular visitor to Britain, mostly from April to June. Occasionally stays longer and has bred.

V	4–6	—

Green-backed Heron
Butorides striatus L 45cm W 55cm
Small, rather dumpy heron with thick-necked appearance. N American subspecies *virescens* has dark cap, reddish neck and breast and streaks down front of breast. Feathers on back dark with green sheen. Wing feathers dark with pale margins.
Voice Gruff, barking call when flushed.
Habitat Marshes and lake and pond margins.
Distribution Widespread global distribution in wetlands; absent from Europe as a breeding species.
Occurrence N American subspecies *virescens* has occurred in Britain.

V	—	—

Squacco Heron
Ardeola ralloides L 45cm W 90cm
In breeding plumage, buff-ochre face, neck and breast. Darker buff on back. Long nape feathers. Blue facial skin and base to bill and legs orange-yellow. In winter, buffish-brown mantle and nape streaked dark brown. Underparts paler. Yellow facial skin and base to bill and legs dirty-yellow. Juvenile similar to winter plumage. White wings and tail at all times, making it look mostly white in flight but are hidden at rest. Solitary and retiring.
Voice Call a croaking *kaak*.
Habitat Marshes and water margins.
Distribution Summer visitor to S Europe. Winters in Africa. Declining.
Occurrence In breeding range April to August. Regular but rare spring visitor to Britain.

V	5–7	—

ttern

American Bittern

ttle Bittern, male

Green-backed Heron

Squacco Heron, non-breeding

Little Egret

Egretta garzetta L 60cm W 90cm

Heron-like appearance with all-white plumage. Bill dagger-like, completely black. Black legs. Bright-yellow feet. In breeding plumage, has long plumes on nape and scapulars. Very rare dark phase has plumage all-black. Sometimes stands hunched up. Otherwise has neck extended. Feeds in channels and shallow water by wading slowly and stabbing with beak. In flight, has broad wings with deep wingbeats. Neck held tucked in and legs trailing.
Voice Call a harsh *kaak*.
Habitat Shallow lakes, marshes and estuaries. Roosts and nests in trees, often communally.
Distribution Widespread in S and central Europe.
Occurrence Summer visitor to north of range. Movement south in winter. Regular and increasing visitor to Britain especially in S. Some birds present throughout year.

V	1–12	—

Great White Egret

Egretta alba L 95cm W 155cm

Similar size to Grey Heron but plumage all white. In breeding plumage, bill blackish with yellow base and legs dark with pinkish-yellow tarsus. Long scapular plumes on back. In non-breeding plumage, bill yellow and legs darker (often look black). Yellow facial skin and dark feet at all times. Holds long neck in 's' shape or sometimes fully extended. In flight, deep wingbeats and neck held in loose 's' shape. Feeds in shallow water, walking sedately or standing motionless.
Voice Call is a growling bark.
Habitat Marshes, shallow lakes and river deltas.
Distribution Local breeder in S and SE Europe.
Occurrence Breeds from April to August. Seen at Neusiedler See in E Austria. Disperses to coastal freshwater lakes in winter. Rare vagrant to Britain.

V	—	—

Cattle Egret

Bubulcus ibis L 50cm W 90cm

Appears generally white. Similar size to Little Egret but much more stocky appearance. Thick neck often held hunched up. Feathers on throat and under lower mandible give puffed-up appearance to throat. Bill thick and stocky. In breeding plumage, buff-orange feathers on crown, back and breast. Legs pinkish-yellow and bill yellow. Outside breeding season, legs dark and bill dull yellow. In flight, throat and breast look puffed-up. Often feeds well away from water.
Voice Croaking call.

Habitat Meadows and pastures, usually among grazing animals. Waterside trees.
Distribution Temperate and tropical regions worldwide.
Occurrence Common in S Iberian peninsula. Increasing vagrant to rest of Europe.

V	—	—

Grey Heron

Ardea cinerea L 95cm W 180cm

Size and grey, white and black plumage are distinctive. Adult birds have white neck and breast streaked with black and bearing long plumes on breast. Cap and crest black with long plumes. Back and wings grey, edged with black at rest showing black 'shoulder' patch. Long, dirty-yellow legs and orange-yellow, dagger-like bill. Juvenile has generally more subdued plumage. Lacks plumes on head and breast. Wades in water to catch fish and other aquatic animals. In flight, shows broad, bowed, grey wings with black flight feathers and deep, slow wingbeats. Stands motionless for long periods.
Voice Call a raucous *kraaak*.
Habitat Found in most freshwater habitats, especially lakes and rivers. Also around coasts. Nests colonially, usually in trees.
Distribution Common throughout.
Occurrence Year-round resident in most of Europe. Begins nesting early. Juveniles often disperse in summer, turning up in unusual places.

T	1–12	N 3–7

Purple Heron

Ardea purpurea L 80cm W 140cm

Slightly smaller than Grey Heron with more slender appearance. In poor light or at a distance looks dark. Adults have reddish-brown head and neck with dark cap and black longitudinal stripes. Throat and front of neck paler. Greyish-purple mantle and wings with reddish 'shoulder' patch. Chestnut chest and belly blackish. Juveniles lack dark crown and stripes on neck. In flight, neck held in snake-like 's' shape. Underwing looks reddish. Retiring and often overlooked.
Voice Mostly silent.
Habitat Prefers extensive reedbeds where it nests in small colonies.
Distribution Breeds throughout S Europe to central France and Germany. Migrants overshoot northwards in spring. Winters in Africa.
Occurrence Locally common breeding species, present from April to August in S Europe. Rare spring vagrant to Britain, usually to S and E England.

V	5–8	—

Cattle Egret

Little Egret

Great White Egret

Grey Heron, adult

Grey Heron

Purple Heron, male

Purple Heron

Western Reef Heron
Egretta gularis L 60cm W 100cm

Size and shape of Little Egret but with thicker bill. Legs dark with striking yellow feet. Occurs in two colour phases. Dark phase has blackish plumage except for white throat. Bill mainly dark but paler on lower mandible. (Little Egret also has rare dark phase.) Light phase similar to Little Egret but has dark bill, yellowish-brown at base.

Voice Generally silent.

Habitat Coastal habitats, often estuaries.

Distribution Breeds coastal NE and NW Africa and Arabian peninsula.

Occurrence Very rare vagrant to Mediterranean coasts.

Night Heron
Nycticorax nycticorax L 60cm W 110cm

A stocky heron with thick-necked appearance. Adults have black, grey and white plumage. Bill dark and legs yellowish. White head-plumes at start of breeding season. Immature is brown with large, white spots on mantle and streaked head and neck. Largely nocturnal and generally skulking. Most frequently seen at dawn and dusk. Sometimes flies to feeding grounds from daytime roost in trees. Roosts communally where common. In flight, has broad wings and fast wingbeats. Flies in lines.

Voice Coarse croaking call, like crow.

Habitat Freshwater marshes and swamps. Occasionally by salt water. Nests in trees.

Distribution Widespread summer visitor to S and central Europe. Most winter in Africa.

Occurrence Locally common in suitable habitats from April to August. Migrants regularly overshoot northwards. Recorded annually in Britain, mostly along S and E coast.

V	5–8	—

Glossy Ibis
Plegadis falcinellus L 65cm W 90cm

Long neck and legs and long, pinkish, curved bill are characteristic. In poor light, looks all-dark. At close range, adult has reddish neck, white at base of bill and beautiful green and purple glossy sheen. Juvenile has duller plumage with streaks on head. Has characteristic flight appearance with neck outstretched and bulbous head. Rapid wingbeats with occasional glides. Groups fly in lines. Wades in shallow water, searching for aquatic animals.

Voice Croaking call.

Glossy Ibis

Habitat Feeds in marshes and shallow lake margins. Nests in trees or reedbeds.

Distribution Local in SE Europe especially N Greece and W Turkey. Most individuals winter in Africa.

Occurrence Uncommon summer visitor to region from April to September. Sometimes wanders outside breeding season and has been recorded in Britain.

V	—	—

Bald Ibis
Geronticus eremita L 75cm W 130cm

All-dark plumage with pinkish legs, shorter than Glossy Ibis. Long, pink bill and bare, red facial skin. Long black plumes on nape.

Voice Raucous calls at colonies. Otherwise silent.

Habitat Nests on cliff ledges and feeds in fields and dry, open country.

Distribution One declining colony at Birecik in SE Turkey and others in Morocco.

Occurrence Present at colonies from March to September. Disperses in winter. Has declined seriously this century. Now extremely rare and threatened with extinction.

Sacred Ibis
Threskiornis aethiopicus L 66cm W 120cm

Distinctive black and white plumage. Head and neck bald. Bushy black plumes at base of wings. Legs and curved bill black. In flight, shows broad, white wings bordered black on trailing edge.

Voice Generally silent.

Habitat Shallow, freshwater marshes, lake margins and coasts.

Distribution Normal range throughout central and S Africa.

Occurrence Very rare vagrant to the region. Most records refer to escapes from captivity.

Western Reef Heron

Night Heron

Night Heron, adult

Night Heron, immature

Glossy Ibis, adult

Bald Ibis

Sacred Ibis

White Stork
Ciconia ciconia L 105cm W 170cm

Unmistakable because of large size and conspicuous black and white plumage. Long red legs and red, dagger-like bill. In flight, broad wings are white with entirely black flight feathers. Outer primaries form distinct 'fingers'. Flies with neck extended and legs trailing. Often feeds in small parties, searching for insects, frogs and other small animals. Sometimes follows ploughs. Has a rather stately gait. Migrates in large flocks.

Voice Generally silent except at nest. During courtship and when mate returns to nest, clatters bill, usually with head held over back.

Habitat Feeds in meadows, marshes and agricultural land. Builds huge platform nest of twigs in trees but more usually these days on roof and church towers.

Distribution Common in central and S Iberian peninsula and east of a line between Denmark and Italy. Local in W Europe. Winters in Africa

Occurrence Present in breeding range from March to September. Year-round resident in SW Iberian peninsula. Huge migrating flocks pass over Bosphorus and Gibraltar in August and September. Migrants rarely overshoot northwards in spring.

V	4–6, 9–10	—

Black Stork
Ciconia nigra L 100cm W 180cm

Similar size and shape to White Stork. Plumage mostly dark with greenish-purple metallic sheen. Underparts white. Red legs and bill and red facial skin around eye. In flight, shows broad, black wings with outer primaries forming obvious 'fingers'. Immatures are dark brown with greenish-brown legs and bill. Generally shy and retiring. Tends to be solitary both when nesting and when feeding.

Voice *chee-lee chee-lee* call heard at nest.

Habitat A forest-nesting species that feeds in secluded marshes, swamps and riverside meadows.

Distribution Rare and local with populations in S central Iberian peninsula and E and SE Europe. Winters in Africa.

Black Stork

Occurrence Iberian birds present throughout year but elsewhere in region from April to September. Very rare vagrant to Britain, mostly spring.

V	—	—

Spoonbill
Platalea leucorodia L 90cm W 125cm

Egret-like plumage but with unmistakable long flattened bill. Adults have buff patch on throat and neck plumes in breeding season only. Bill and legs black. Juveniles have pinkish bills and black wing tips. Flies with neck outstretched and legs trailing. Wingbeats rapid, interspersed with glides. Feeds by immersing bill in water and sweeping from side to side.

Voice Generally silent.

Habitat Shallow lakes, marshes and sometimes estuaries. Nests colonially in bushes or in reedbeds.

Distribution Local and uncommon in W Europe, breeding in Netherlands and S Iberia. More widespread but still local in E and SE Europe.

Occurrence Nests from May to July. Disperses outside breeding season, most birds wintering around the Mediterranean. Scarce but regular visitor to S and E coasts of England, particularly the coastal wetland reserves of Norfolk and Suffolk.

V	1–12	—

Greater Flamingo
Phoenicopterus ruber L 140cm W 150cm

Unmistakable with pale-pink plumage, extremely long, pink legs and long neck. Bill is scythe-shaped, pink, tipped with black. Immatures are mottled brown and white, gradually becoming uniformly pale with age. Red wing coverts of adult best seen in flight contrasting with black flight feathers. Neck and legs held outstretched. Feeds in shallow water by wading and bending neck so that bill touches water surface. Bill used to filter tiny animals.

Voice Goose-like calls in flight.

Habitat Saline lagoons.

Distribution Widespread but local around the Mediterranean. Flocks wander in winter.

Occurrence Breeds colonially in Camargue in S France and Coto Doñana in Spain. Regularly seen on shallow coastal lakes in N Greece and on Cyprus in winter. Individual flamingos outside range are usually escapes from captivity, and often not European in origin. Caribbean race of Greater Flamingo has dark-pink plumage while Chilean race has dull legs with bright red 'knees'.

White Stork

Black Stork, adult with young
Spoonbill, adult

White Stork, pair at nest
Greater Flamingo, nesting

WATERFOWL
ORDER ANSERIFORMES
Family Anatidae

This large and varied group comprises swans, geese and ducks. They are aquatic birds with webbed feet, relatively short legs, long necks and narrow pointed wings. Most make simple, down-lined nests and lay large clutches of eggs. The downy young leave the nest soon after hatching.

Swans, Sub-family Cygninae

Easily identified as adults by their large size and all-white plumage. The sexes are similar. The neck is relatively long and often used to feed on submerged vegetation. Juveniles have dull, fawn plumage. Family groups often remain together after breeding and fly in a distinct 'V' formation. Three species occur in Europe.

Geese, Sub-family Anserinae

A group of medium- to large-sized birds with plump bodies and relatively long necks. In winter, they are invariably seen feeding and migrating in often large flocks. All species graze shoots of vegetation for at least part of their diet. All have large webbed feet. The European species are divided into the 'grey' *Anser* geese and the 'black' *Branta* geese. The sexes are similar.

Ducks, 4 sub-families in Europe

A diverse group with feeding habits ranging from dabbling to diving. Sexes have different plumages with the males generally being much more showy. **Sub-family Anatinae** are surface-feeders and use their bills to feed in shallow water. **Sub-family Aythyinae** are diving ducks and include both primarily freshwater species, such as Pochard and Tufted Duck, and sea ducks, such as eiders and scoters. All species dive from the surface. **Sub-family Merginae** are the sawbills, a group of fish-eating diving ducks with serrated bill margins. Lastly, the **sub-family Oxyurinae** are the stifftails. They are dumpy diving ducks with stiff tails, often held erect.

A flock of Brent Geese at high tide. These birds winter in large numbers around the coasts of north-west Europe, including the large estuaries of south and east Britain.

Mute Swan
Cygnus olor L 15cm W 215cm

Adults have all-white plumage and orange bill with black basal knob. Immatures have brown-patched plumage and a pinkish bill, black at the base. When swimming, neck often held in 's' shape, bill down-tilted and wings sometimes held arched high above body. In flight, neck held outstretched. Powerful wingbeats creating a high-pitched throbbing sound. Feeds on water plants, usually in shallow water. Sometimes upends in deeper water. In many places, is accustomed to man and will come readily to food. In breeding season, territorial males often aggressive to human intruders as well as rival males. Non-breeding birds seen in flocks.

Voice Hisses loudly at intruders. Occasional trumpeting calls are heard but otherwise the species is silent.

Habitat All sorts of freshwater habitats from gravel pits, rivers and lakes to boating ponds and canals. Builds large platform nest among reedbeds or other emergent vegetation. Sometimes around coast in winter.

Distribution Widespread and common throughout NW Europe including almost all of Britain.

Occurrence Present throughout year in range. Some movement during severe winter weather, particularly to the coast.

R	1–12	N 4–7

Whooper Swan
Cygnus cygnus L 155cm W 225cm

Neck generally held straight, bill level. Head and bill wedge-shaped, similar to Bewick's Swan. Upper surface of bill flat, forming continuous line with head. Yellow on bill extensive, extending beyond nostril and forming wedge shape at front. Immatures have greyish-buff plumage and pinkish bill. Told from immature Mute Swan by bill and head shape and pale base to bill. In winter, often in sizeable flocks, among which family parties can be discerned. This species is more often seen grazing on land than Mute Swan. Sometimes flies in 'v' formation. Wingbeats make a thin whistling sound.

Voice Trumpeting calls, loud and musical.

Habitat Breeds on tundra bogs and northern marshes. Outside breeding season, found on large lakes, coasts and fields.

Distribution Breeds in Iceland, where year-round resident in the south, and N Scandinavia eastwards. Moves south in winter to NW Europe where mostly coastal.

Occurrence On breeding ground from April to September. Regular in Scotland, N England and Ireland from October to March. Easy to see at Caerlaverock in Dumfries. Harsh weather drives flocks further south where they are usually found on extensive flood meadows in broad river valleys.

W	10–3	—

Bewick's Swan
Cygnus columbianus L 120cm W 190cm

Similar to Whooper Swan but smaller and with shorter, thicker neck. Yellow pattern on bill variable but always less extensive than Whooper Swan and ends bluntly, not in a point, above nostrils. Outside breeding season, seen in family parties or sizeable flocks. Immatures have similar appearance to immature Whooper Swan. These are difficult to distinguish, particularly at a distance, and best identified by association with adult birds.

Voice Bugling, musical calls, higher-pitched than Whooper Swan.

Habitat Breeds on Arctic tundra. Winters on extensive flood meadows.

Distribution Breeds in Arctic Russia. Main wintering range NW European coast, S England and Ireland.

Occurrence Present on traditional wintering grounds in NW Europe from October to March. Easy to see at Slimbridge in Gloucestershire and Welney in Cambridgeshire, usually in sizeable flocks.

W	10–3	—

Mute Swan

Mute Swan, cygnet

Bewick's Swan, adult

Whooper Swan, immature

Whooper Swan, adult

Canada Goose

Branta canadensis L 100cm W 165cm

A large goose with grey-brown body, long black neck and white cheek and throat band. Pale breast and white stern. In flight, the species has powerful wingbeats and long neck is held out-stretched.

Voice Flocks habitually call in flight. Loud, honking *honk-aa-honk*.

Habitat Breeds on large lakes or gravel pits. Flocks also feed frequently in fields and on arable land.

Distribution Introduced into Europe from N America where widespread. Now found in S Scandinavia, Denmark and adjacent Low Countries. Widespread and common in England, Wales and S Scotland. Local in N Ireland.

Occurrence Mostly a year-round resident in suitable habitats. Some winter movement in Scandinavian birds.

R	1–12	N 4–7

Brent Goose

Branta bernicla L 60cm W 115cm

A small, stocky goose, size of Mallard. Pale-bellied race *B.b.hrota* has belly markedly paler than dark-bellied *B.b.bernicla*. White stern and black neck. Adults have white half-collar on side of neck. Juveniles and first-winter birds have pale-edged wing coverts until spring and do not acquire half-collar until early winter. Note also so-called Black Brant *B.b.nigricans* which has belly and lower flanks black, upper flanks white and half-collar that meets at front. Winters in large flocks at habitual sites. In flight, has fast wingbeats. Migrates in disorderly flocks. Feeds by grazing grass or on mudflats. Swims buoyantly, sometimes upending to feed.

Voice Call a deep, cackling *krr-rrop*.

Habitat Breeds on Arctic bogs and tundra. Winters on estuaries where feeds mainly on eel-grass *Zostera*. Also visits nearby meadows to graze grass.

Distribution Pale-bellied Brent breeds Svalbard, Greenland and islands in Canadian Arctic; winters in Ireland, NE England and Denmark. Dark-bellied Brent breeds coastal Arctic Russia and winters on S and E coasts of England. The two populations seldom mix. Black Brant breeds W Arctic Canada and is rare vagrant to NW Europe.

Occurrence Breeds from May to August. Migrant flocks arrive on wintering grounds in late September and usually stay until early March, sometimes a few weeks later.

W	10–3	—

Barnacle Goose

Branta leucopsis L 65cm W 140cm

A small grey, black and white goose. Juveniles have mantle feathers tipped pale buff, not white, and white on face stippled black behind eye. In flight, shows long, pointed wings and conspicuous white underparts. Migrates in gentle curve formation rather than 'v'. In winter, invariably seen in flocks. Individual birds are usually either escapes from captivity or injured birds.

Voice Barking call, merging into loud cackle among flocks.

Habitat Nests on Arctic cliffs. Winters on coastal grasslands.

Distribution Breeds Svalbard, Novaya Zemlya and E Greenland. Winters mainly Denmark, SW Scotland and Ireland.

Occurrence Flocks arrive at traditional wintering grounds in October and stay until March. Easy to see on Solway Firth (notably Caerlaverock in Dumfries) and on Islay. Small flocks occasionally turn up elsewhere further south during severe winter weather.

W	10–3	—

Red-breasted Goose

Branta ruficollis L 55cm W 120cm

Unmistakable in good light with red, black and white plumage. In poor light, can look rather dark although white flank always conspicuous. Juveniles have duller plumage and more barring on wing coverts. In flight, shows pointed wings and dark belly.

Voice Call a sharp, nasal *kik-kwik*.

Habitat Breeds on Arctic slopes and gullies, often near nest of Peregrine or Rough-legged Buzzard for protection from other predators. Winters on wetlands, mostly out of region.

Distribution Breeds in Siberia. Small wintering populations in SE Europe. Some vagrants reach as far W as Britain.

Occurrence Individual birds occasionally join migrating flocks of other geese destined for W Europe. Has turned up in Britain among flocks of Brent and White-fronted Geese. Some sightings undoubtedly refer to escapes from captivity.

V	10–3	—

Canada Goose, adult

Brent Goose

Brent Geese, dark bellied

Barnacle Geese, flock on Islay

Barnacle Goose, adult

Red-breasted Goose, adult

Greylag Goose
Anser anser L 85cm W 170cm

Large grey-brown goose with rather uniform appearance. Pink legs and large, pinkish-orange bill in western race. Eastern race has pink bill. In flight, has noticeably pale forewing panels, pale underwing coverts and pale lower back. Outside breeding season, seen in flocks and mixes with other wildfowl. Ancestor of domestic goose.
Voice Variety of loud calls similar to domestic goose. In flight *kurang-ung-ung*.
Habitat Naturally wild populations breed on undisturbed swamps and wetlands, and islands in large lakes. Feral and semi-wild populations are found in a wide variety of other wetland habitats throughout.
Distribution Breeds locally in suitable habitats in E and N Europe including Iceland. Most of population migrates south for winter to wetlands around Mediterranean. In Britain, wild populations in the north and west. Feral and semi-wild populations in many parts of S and E England.
Occurrence On breeding grounds from April to September. Year-round resident in Britain with some movement outside breeding season. Numbers augmented by visitors from Iceland and mainland Europe.

T	1–12	N 4–8

White-fronted Goose
Anser albifrons L 75cm W 150cm

Smaller than Greylag Goose, with orange legs, irregular black bars on belly, and conspicuous white blaze on forehead, not extending to crown. Large bill is uniform colour: orange-yellow in Greenland race *flavirostris* and pink in Siberian race *albifrons*. Juvenile lacks white blaze to forehead and dark markings on belly. Bill has dark nail. In flight, White-fronted Goose has paler forewing panels than Bean Goose but less so than Greylag or Pink-footed Geese.

Voice A variety of calls including *kow yow*. Distant flocks can sometimes sound like pack of dogs.
Habitat Breeds on marshy tundra. Winters on flood meadows and fields.
Distribution Greenland race winters in Ireland and N and W Britain. Siberian race winters in S England, NW coastal mainland Europe and SE Europe.
Occurrence On wintering grounds from November to March, Greenland race usually arriving slightly earlier and leaving later. Easy to see at Wildfowl and Wetlands Trust Slimbridge in Gloucestershire in winter months.

W	11–3	—

Lesser White-fronted Goose
Anser erythropus L 60cm W 130cm

Noticeably smaller than White-fronted Goose with orange legs, small pink bill and irregular dark markings on belly. Steep forehead with white blaze extending above eye towards crown. At close range, eye has conspicuous yellow eye ring. In flight, similar to White-fronted Goose. Juvenile has pale eye-ring but lacks white blaze on forehead. Best told from juvenile White-fronted Goose by smaller size and proportionately smaller bill.

Voice Similar to White-fronted Goose but higher-pitched.
Habitat Breeds on marshy tundra. Winters on damp fields and pastures.
Distribution Breeds in N Scandinavia and E into Siberia. Winters locally in Balkan region.
Occurrence Rare in Europe both as a breeding bird and in winter. Individuals sometimes join flocks of White-fronted Geese and arrive in NW Europe. Very rare in Britain but recorded almost annually at Wildfowl and Wetlands Trust Slimbridge in Gloucestershire.

V	11–3	—

Greylag Goose

Greylag Goose

White-fronted Goose, Siberian race
Lesser White-fronted Goose, adult

White-fronted Goose
Lesser White-fronted Goose, adult

Bean Goose

Anser fabalis L 75cm W 165cm

Noticeably brown appearance with orange legs. Bill orange with black markings. Sometimes has small white patch at base of bill. Race *fabalis* has larger bill with more extensive orange than race *rossicus*. Looks longer-necked than similar Pink-footed Goose. In flight, wings look dark above and below. Juvenile similar to adult but colours duller.

Voice Cackling, nasal calls, deeper than Pink-footed Goose.

Habitat Race *fabalis* breeds on bogs in taiga forest while race *rossicus* breeds on tundra. Winters mainly on meadows, agricultural land and stubble fields.

Distribution Breeds from N Scandinavia eastwards to Siberia. Scattered winter distribution across mainland Europe, especially in central and NW.

Occurrence Breeds from May to August. Present on wintering grounds from October to March. Scarce visitor to Britain, mostly to E England. Most reliable site is at Buckenham in E Norfolk where more than 100 birds are regularly seen.

W	10–3	—

Pink-footed Goose

Anser brachyrhynchus L 70cm W 160cm

Similar to Bean Goose but smaller, with pink legs, shorter neck and greyer back. Bill is less robust than Bean Goose and dark with variable pink markings. Sometimes has small white patch at base of bill. In flight, upperwings paler than Bean Goose.

Voice Nasal calls, similar to Bean Goose but higher-pitched.

Habitat Breeds on tundra moorland. In winter, feeds on meadows, agricultural land and stubble fields but prefers to roost on lakes and estuaries.

Distribution Breeds in Iceland, Greenland and Svalbard. Winters in Britain and adjacent coastal areas of mainland Europe.

Occurrence Breeds from May to August. Present on wintering grounds from October to March.

W	10–3	—

Snow Goose

Anser caerulescens L 70cm W 150cm

Pure white plumage except for black wingtips (swans never have black wingtips). Legs and bill reddish-pink. In flight, shows prominent black primaries. Also occurs as so-called 'Blue Goose' where plumage bluish-grey except for white head and upper neck and black wingtips. A popular species in captivity.

Voice Loud cackling calls.

Habitat Breeds on Arctic tundra. Winters in meadows and agricultural land.

Distribution Breeds in Arctic N America. Winters in southern states of USA.

Occurrence Most sightings in region refer to escapes from captivity. Genuinely wild birds do occur, usually among flocks of White-fronted Geese. Rare but regular in Ireland but records from England less reliable.

V	10–3	—

Bar-headed Goose

Anser indicus L75cm W 150cm

Grey plumage, dark stripes on neck and white head with 2 dark transverse bars on crown. Legs orange and bill yellow. Juvenile lacks bars on crown. Popular species in captivity.

Voice Honking calls in flight.

Habitat Marshes and wetlands.

Distribution Breeds in central Asia and winters in India.

Occurrence All sightings undoubtedly refer to captive escapes. Feral population in Norway.

Bean Goose, adult

Bean Goose, adult

Pink-footed Goose, adult

Pink-footed Goose, adult
Bar-headed Goose, adult

Snow Goose, adult

Mallard

Anas platyrhynchos L 58cm W 90cm

Male in full plumage has head with green sheen, white collar, chestnut breast and grey-brown plumage. Bill uniform yellow. Female has mottled brown plumage with bill orange mottled with irregular dark markings, sometimes almost completely grey. Male in eclipse similar to female but retains uniformly coloured bill and has rusty breast. In flight, shows fast wingbeats, blue speculum edged with white, and white in tail. In pairs during late winter and early spring. Males form flocks for summer moult.

Voice Female has typical quacking call. Male's call is a quiet *quepp*.

Habitat All types of freshwater habitat. Nests among waterside vegetation. Sometimes feeds on agricultural land. Also found on coast in winter, in north of region.

Distribution Common and widespread throughout the region.

Occurrence Present throughout the year in most parts. Birds from far north and east of range move south in winter.

T	1–12	N 5–7

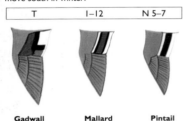

Gadwall   **Mallard**   **Pintail**

Black Duck

Anas rubripes L 55cm W90cm

Similar to female Mallard but has darker plumage with noticeably paler head and neck. Bill uniform greenish-yellow. In flight, shows purple speculum which lacks white edges of Mallard's, and no white in tail. Hybridizes with Mallard.

Voice Similar to Mallard.

Habitat Breeds on freshwater marshes. Outside breeding season, more inclined to favour coastal habitats than Mallard.

Black Duck, male

Distribution Occurs throughout eastern half of N America. Has declined markedly in recent years.

Occurrence Very rare vagrant to NW Europe, mostly in autumn and winter, and has occurred in Britain and Ireland. Individuals often stay for extended periods.

V	—	—

Gadwall

Anas strepera L 53cm W 90cm

Male has grey plumage with dark stern, most noticeable when swimming. At close range, has beautiful fine markings on breast. Female similar to female Mallard and white belly not visible on water. Note smaller bill with distinct orange sides. Both sexes show prominent black-bordered white speculum in flight.

Voice Female's call similar to female Mallard's but softer. Call of male a nasal *errp*.

Habitat Breeds on shallow, well-vegetated lakes with open water. Winters on lakes, gravel pits and reservoirs. Seldom on salt water.

Distribution Scattered distribution across much of Europe. Absent from north and east of range in winter.

Occurrence Breeds from April to July. Year-round resident in England and many sites in W Europe. Winter visitor to W Britain, Ireland and S Europe.

T	1–12	N 4–7

Pintail

Anas acuta L male 70cm female 55cm W 90cm

Male distinctive with long central tail feathers, chocolate head and nape, long white neck and greyish plumage. Females mottled brown but with characteristic long neck and elongated stern. In flight, shows green speculum with bronze sheen and white trailing edge, narrow wings and pale underparts. Flight fast and direct. Stretches neck up when alarmed. Sometimes upends to feed. Often seen in pairs. Joins other wildfowl in winter.

Voice Female has Mallard-like quack. Male utters Teal-like *kree* in spring.

Habitat Breeds on moorland and tundra pools. Winters on lakes, marshes and large estuaries.

Distribution Breeds in N mainland Europe and Iceland. Scattered breeding records in Britain and mainland Europe. Winters throughout S and central Europe including Britain.

Occurrence On breeding grounds from April to August. Widespread but local in wintering range for rest of year.

T	1–12	N 4–7

Mallard, female (left) and male

Gadwall, female

Gadwall, male

Pintail, female

Pintail, male

Wigeon
Anas penelope L 47cm W 80cm

Short neck and rounded head. In full plumage, male has reddish-brown head with yellow forecrown, reddish breast and greyish body. Underparts white with black stern. Female greyish-brown with dark smudge through eye and reddish flanks. Male in eclipse plumage (seen in newly arrived migrants in early autumn) has reddish-brown plumage and lacks black stern. In flight, male shows conspicuous white panel on forewing and green speculum. Female lacks bold markings on wing but, like male, has sharply defined white belly and grey axillaries. In winter, invariably found in flocks. Often associates with other wildfowl, especially Teal, as well as waders.

Voice Male has characteristic whistle *whee-ooo*. Female has barking call.

Habitat Breeds on moorland and tundra lakes and bogs. In winter, mainly on estuaries and mudflats but also on flooded grassland.

Distribution Breeds in N Europe, from Scandinavia eastwards and in Iceland. Breeds N Britain but there local. Outside breeding season, scattered, mainly coastal, distribution in W and S Europe. Widespread in Britain and Ireland.

Occurrence Breeds from May to August. At other times, found on wintering grounds. Locally common winter visitor to British and Irish estuaries as well as to flood meadows, usually near the coast.

T	1–12	N 5–8

American Wigeon
Anas americana L 50cm W 80cm

Similar size and shape to Wigeon. In full plumage, male has pinkish body and stippled buff head with white forecrown and broad, green streak running from behind eye. Underparts white with black stern. Female and male in eclipse have reddish-brown breast and flanks contrasting with greyish head, and no black stern. In flight, wing pattern similar to Wigeon but note the conspicuous white axillaries.

Voice Call of male similar to Wigeon but more drawn out.

Habitat Similar to Wigeon.

Distribution Widespread in N America.

Occurrence Rare but regular vagrant to NW

Europe including Britain. Hayle estuary in Cornwall has had several records in September and October.

V	9–10	—

Teal
Anas crecca L 36cm W 61cm

Smallest duck of the region. Full-plumage male has chestnut head with pale-bordered green stripe and prominent yellow patch on stern. At a distance, white horizontal stripe above flanks is prominent. Female is mottled brown, similar to female Garganey. However, streak at base of tail is pale and base of bill sometimes orange. Eclipse male similar to female. In flight, shows green speculum with white margins at front (broad) and rear (narrower). Flight rapid and swerving when in flocks on wintering grounds. N American subspecies *A.c.carolinensis* (Green-winged Teal) is similar but male lacks white horizontal stripe on scapulars, having instead vertical white stripe on side of body. Female identical to female Teal of European race *A.c.crecca*.

Voice Male has far-carrying bell-like call. Female utters quacks.

Habitat Breeds in upland wetlands. Winters on estuaries, mudflats and lakes.

Distribution Breeds throughout most of N Europe and local but widespread breeder in N Britain and Ireland. Wintering range includes most of W and S Europe.

Occurrence Present throughout year in wetlands of NW Europe including Britain and Ireland. Numbers augmented outside breeding season from September to April and then common on estuaries. Green-winged Teal is a rare vagrant from N America. Usually seen among flocks of Teal.

T	1–12	N 4–7

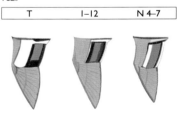

Wigeon, male   **Wigeon,** female   **Teal,** male

Wigeon, female

Wigeon, male

American Wigeon, male

Teal, male

Teal, female

Green-winged Teal, male

Blue-winged Teal
Anas discors L 38cm W 65cm

Male in full plumage distinctive with mottled brown body, deep-blue head with conspicuous white crescent in front of eye and white patch on rear flanks. Female similar to female Teal but lacks pale side to base of tail. Has pale patch at base of bill, similar to female Garganey, but lacks well-defined facial markings. In flight, both sexes have wing patterns similar to Garganey but lack trailing white edge to speculum.

Voice Mostly silent.

Habitat Freshwater marshes and lakes.

Distribution Breeds across N America. Winters mainly central and northern S America.

Occurrence Rare autumn vagrant to NW Europe including Britain.

V	10–3	—

Baikal Teal
Anas formosa L 38cm W 65cm

Slightly larger than Teal. Male in full plumage has distinctive head pattern of yellow, green and white markings. Vertical white stripes on flanks and stern. Female similar to female Teal but has well-defined white spot at base of bill, with margin of darker feathers. Pale supercilium is broken above eye. In flight, wing pattern similar to Teal but margin in front of speculum is noticeably orange-buff.

Voice Male utters *wot-wot* call.

Habitat Freshwater marshes.

Distribution Breeds N Siberia and winters SE Asia and S Japan.

Occurrence Widely kept in captivity. Records in W Europe often considered as escapes.

V?	—	—

Falcated Teal
Anas falcata L 50cm W 80cm

Male in full plumage has reddish-brown head with green gloss and maned feathers on nape. Black and white collar and black and yellow on flanks. Female resembles female Gadwall except bill black. In flight, both sexes have green speculum with white front and trailing margins.

Voice Mostly silent.

Habitat Wetlands and lakes with abundant vegetation.

Distribution E Asia.

Occurrence Popular in captivity; few records in Europe considered genuine rather than escapes.

V?	—	—

Marbled Teal
Marmaronetta angustirostris
L 40cm W 65cm

Body covered with pale-buff spots but looks uniform pale brown at a distance. Dark mask through eyes and dark bill. Head looks large and rounded and tail elongated. Sexes similar. In flight, looks uniform and unmarked, with long wings. Shy and unobtrusive. Often hidden by emergent vegetation.

Voice Mostly silent but soft squeaking calls are sometimes uttered.

Habitat Shallow freshwater and brackish lakes with good vegetation cover.

Distribution Rare and local. Breeds S Spain, NW Africa and W Asia. Some movement south in winter.

Occurrence Rare and difficult to see in Europe. Best opportunities in Coto Doñana in S Spain in spring.

Blue-winged Teal, male

Falcated Teal, male

Baikal Teal, male

Marbled Teal, male

Garganey

Anas querquedula L 37cm W 62cm

Similar size to Teal. In full plumage, male is distinctive with broad, white supercilium, brown head, neck and breast and grey flanks. Female similar to female Teal but has pale stripe below dark eye stripe, broadening at base of bill. Lacks pale side to base of tail. In flight, male has pale-blue forewing and green speculum bordered with white. Female has similar wing pattern but dull forewing pattern. White margin in front of speculum narrower than trailing margin. Usually shy and unobtrusive when breeding. Sometimes in small flocks on migration but in winter, in large flocks.

Voice Male has dry, rattling call. Female utters soft quacking call.

Habitat Marshes and shallow, freshwater lakes. Sometimes in coastal waters on migration.

Distribution Scattered breeding range from S France north to S Britain and from Greece north to S Scandinavia. Widespread but never abundant. Winters in Africa.

Occurrence On breeding grounds from April to August. Seen in freshwater habitats outside breeding range on migration, mainly March and April. Regular in S Britain, especially Kent and E Anglia.

S	4–8	N 4–7

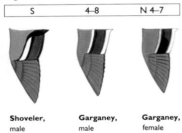

Shoveler, male

Garganey, male

Garganey, female

Shoveler

Anas clypeata L 51cm W 80cm

Both sexes have unmistakable large, flattened bill. Male in full plumage has orange-red flanks, white breast and stern and green head and neck. Female is mottled brown. Eclipse male similar to female.

In flight, bill looks long. Wings show pale-blue forewing panel and green speculum. Usually seen in small groups, dabbling in shallow water. Rather nervous.

Voice Mainly silent. In spring, male utters *tunk-tunk* call.

Habitat Shallow freshwater lakes and marshes. Nests in waterside vegetation.

Distribution Breeds from central Europe northwards to S Scandinavia. Winters throughout NW and S Europe. Widespread in Britain both as breeding species and winter visitor.

Occurrence Breeds from April to July. Most easily seen in Britain during winter months.

T	1–12	N 4–7

Wood Duck

Aix sponsa L 45cm W 70cm

Male has green head with white stripes, chestnut breast and buff flanks bordered at front by vertical white stripe. Female greyish-brown with 'spectacled' appearance. Very similar to female Mandarin but lacks pale nail on bill tip.

Voice Mostly silent.

Habitat Wooded lakes.

Distribution A N American species. No genuinely wild birds recorded in region.

Occurrence Widely kept in wildfowl collections and occasionally escapes.

Mandarin

Aix galericulata L 45cm W 72cm

Male unmistakable with large orange head and conspicuous orange fan-shaped wing feathers. Females grey-brown with mottled breast and flanks and 'spectacled' appearance. Pale nail on tip of bill. Often seen in pairs.

Voice Mostly silent. Male has whistling display calls.

Habitat Wooded lakes. Nests in holes in trees.

Distribution Natural range is E Asia. Feral populations in Britain, mostly S England.

Occurrence Feral populations are year-round residents. Well established at Virginia Water in Berkshire. Also seen as escapes from captivity.

R	1–12	N 4–7

Garganey, female

Garganey, male

Shoveler, female

Wood Duck, male

Shoveler, male

Mandarin, male

Shelduck
Tadorna tadorna L 65cm W 125cm

Distinctive duck with white, chestnut and black plumage, the latter with a green sheen. Pink legs and bright-red bill. Male has red knob at base of bill. In flight, white forewing conspicuous. Juvenile has washed-out adult plumage but lacks chestnut breast band and has white throat and pink bill. In summer months, sometimes congregates in certain areas e.g. Bridgwater Bay in Somerset, to moult in safety.

Voice Mostly silent but the male utters high-pitched whistling call in spring. The female has a cackling call.

Habitat Mostly on estuaries and mudflats but sometimes on coastal lakes. Nests in burrows, often in sand dunes.

Distribution Widespread breeding species and resident around coasts of NW Europe. Some movement south in winter. Very local breeding species in Mediterranean but more widespread in winter.

Occurrence Locally common in NW Europe and easy to see on most estuaries in Britain and Ireland throughout the year.

| R | 1–12 | N 5–7 |

Ruddy Shelduck
Tadorna ferruginea L 65cm W 135cm

Size and shape of Shelduck but distinctive orange-buff plumage. Head paler than rest of body and male has narrow black band separating the two colours. In flight shows conspicuous white forewing panel.

Voice Goose-like calls in flight.

Habitat Freshwater lakes and broad rivers with sandbanks.

Distribution Natural range includes SE Europe (mainly N Greece and W Turkey) and N Africa. In winter, some movement occurs and then very local in S Spain.

Occurrence Year-round resident in SE Europe with some local movement in winter. Widely kept in captivity, and records elsewhere in Europe probably escapes.

Egyptian Goose
Alopochen aegyptiacus L 70cm W 145cm

Distinctive with buffish-brown plumage and pale neck and head with dark patch through eye. Sexes similar. Bill pink and legs reddish. Has a rather upright stance. Usually seen in pairs or small groups.

Voice Mostly silent.

Habitat Rivers and lakes. In Britain, mostly on arable land and meadows. Sometimes nests in trees.

Distribution Natural range includes most of Africa as far north as Egypt.

Occurrence Possibly genuine vagrants in E Mediterranean. Feral British population in E Anglia, easiest to see along N Norfolk coast. Elsewhere records probably refer to escapes from captivity.

| R | 1–12 | N 5–7 |

Red-crested Pochard
Netta rufina L 55cm W 85cm

In full plumage, distinctive: male has large, orange head, black breast and vent, white flanks and buff-brown back. Feathers on head can be raised. Legs and bill red. Female has brown plumage with darker crown and nape and white cheeks and throat. Bill dark with pink tip. Male in eclipse is similar to female but retains red bill. In flight shows broad white wing bar. Feeds by dabbling in shallow margins but also dives well despite buoyant body.

Voice Mostly silent but male has wheezing call in spring.

Habitat Prefers shallow lakes, both freshwater and brackish, usually with well-vegetated margins.

Distribution Main range in Europe from S and E coasts of Spain to S France and W Turkey. Local breeding species in central Europe as far north as Netherlands but moving south in winter mostly to SE Europe.

Occurrence Local and nowhere common. Most easily seen on lagoons on E coast of Spain. Commonly kept in captivity and escapes undoubtedly account for many of the British sightings.

| V | — | — |

Shelduck, adult

Shelduck, juvenile

Ruddy Shelduck

Red-crested Pochard, female

Red-crested Pochard, male

Egyptian Goose

Greater Scaup

Aythya marila L 45cm W 75cm

Male in full plumage superficially similar to Tufted Duck but has grey back, larger bill and head rounded and without tuft. Green gloss to head difficult to see. Female has brownish plumage with distinct large white patch surrounding base of bill. Sometimes shows white 'ear' patch. Head shape characteristically rounded. Eclipse plumage of male similar to breeding female but browner. In flight, dark wings show white wing bar covering both secondaries and inner primaries. Seen in flocks outside breeding season, sometimes mixing with Tufted Ducks.

Voice Mostly silent.

Habitat Breeds on northern lakes. Winters around sheltered coasts and occasionally inland.

Distribution Breeds in Iceland and Scandinavia eastwards. Rare breeding species in N Britain. Winters mainly around coasts of NW Europe. Also locally in SE Europe and on inland lakes in central Europe.

Occurrence Rather scarce breeding species in Europe. Seen more easily as a winter visitor to NW Europe including Britain. Mostly coastal but sometimes found inland on gravel pits and reservoirs.

T	1–12	N 5–7

Lesser Scaup

Aythya affinis L 42cm W 70cm

Both sexes very similar to Greater Scaup and best told by head shape recalling female Tufted Duck. Bump on rear of crown, caused by tuft, gives irregular, not rounded, appearance. Crown sometimes looks peaked. Bill size smaller than Greater Scaup and male in full plumage has darker vermiculations on back and purple gloss to head (difficult to see). In flight, white on wing bar only covers secondaries. Beware hybrids between other *Aythya* species.

Voice Mostly silent.

Habitat Breeds on tundra pools and lakes. Winters on sheltered coasts.

Distribution Usual range covers western N America.

Occurrence Recently recorded in Britain.

V	—	—

Tufted Duck

Aythya fuligula L 45cm W 70cm

Male in full plumage is black with distinct white belly and white flanks seen when swimming. Drooping crest. Female has brown plumage. Steep forehead, flat crown and small nape tuft. Often shows small white patch at base of bill and sometimes has white under tail. Male in eclipse has much duller version of breeding plumage and lacks crest. Both sexes have yellow eye and grey bill tipped black. In flight, shows white wing bar. Dives well. Outside breeding season, often seen in flocks and sometimes becomes tame in urban settings.

Voice Mostly silent but male has whistling display call.

Habitat Freshwater lakes, gravel pits, etc., with vegetated margins. More occasionally on sheltered coasts in winter.

Distribution Year-round resident in NW Europe. Breeding species in N Europe, moving south in winter as far as the Mediterranean coast.

Occurrence Common throughout much of Europe.

T	1–12	N 5–7

Ring-necked Duck

Aythya collaris L 44cm W 65cm

Male in full plumage superficially similar to male Tufted Duck. However, has grey flanks with white stripe at front (most obvious in dull light). Lacks crest, giving head peaked appearance. Bill grey with white bands at base and behind black tip. Female similar to female Tufted Duck but has white 'spectacles' and grey bill with distinct white band behind black tip. Eclipse male plumage is browner version of breeding plumage. In flight, wing bar grey not white.

Voice Mostly silent.

Habitat Freshwater lakes.

Distribution Widespread species in N America.

Occurrence Rare vagrant to NW Europe. In Britain, recorded mostly autumn and winter, with reservoirs in Devon and Cornwall being particularly favoured.

V	11–3	—

Greater Scaup, male

Lesser Scaup, male

Greater Scaup, female

Ring-necked Duck, female

Ring-necked Duck, male

Tufted Duck, male

Tufted Duck, female

Pochard

Aythya ferina L 45cm W 78cm

Male in full plumage has orange head, whitish body with fine, grey vermiculations, and black breast and stern. Female has variable brownish plumage with grey vermiculations on body. Face has 'spectacled' appearance and hint of darker cheek patch. In both sexes, bill has bands of light and dark grey with black tip. In flight, shows broad, grey wing bar. Dives well. Usually seen in flocks containing more males than females.

Voice Male utters soft *phee-phee-phee* in display. Female's call is harsh *krraa-krraa*.

Habitat Breeds on shallow, well-vegetated lakes. In winter, also seen on gravel pits and reservoirs.

Distribution Breeds across much of central and N Europe as far north as S Scandinavia. Widespread in Britain and Ireland. NW European birds present throughout year. Elsewhere, birds move south in winter and are seen as far as Mediterranean region.

Occurrence Widespread and locally common in NW Europe. The British population is augmented in winter by visitors from mainland Europe.

T	I–12	N 4–7

Ferruginous Duck

Aythya nyroca L 40cm W 65cm

Superficially similar to female Tufted Duck but male in full plumage is chestnut with white undertail and white eye. White belly hidden when swimming. Female similar to male but duller brown plumage and brown eye. Male's eclipse plumage duller version of breeding plumage but retains white eye. Both sexes show rather peaked crown and rounded head outline, lacking bump on rear of crown of female Tufted Duck (which occasionally also has white undertail). In flight, shows conspicuous white wing bar.

Voice Mostly silent but utters *kerr-kerr* call.

Habitat Well-vegetated freshwater lakes and ponds.

Distribution Widespread breeding species in E Europe and much more locally in SW Europe. In winter, occurs mainly around the Mediterranean region.

Occurrence Locally common in E Europe but much less so elsewhere in the region. In winter sometimes west and north from usual range and is rare but regular in Britain, mostly S England

V	—	—

Ruddy Duck

Oxyura jamaicensis L 38cm W 58cm

In full plumage, male has chestnut body, blue bill and black head and neck with conspicuous white cheek. Undertail coverts white. Female has mottled brown plumage and dark bill. Cheek pale with dark stripe. Eclipse male similar to female but retains bright, white cheek. In both sexes, long tail is sometimes held stiffly erect. Sociable where common.

Voice Mostly silent. During display, however, male inflates throat and vibrates bill against it, producing fast clicking sounds and a froth of bubbles.

Habitat Naturalized populations favour the margins of gravel pits.

Distribution Widespread in N America and in western S America. Feral populations established in England.

Occurrence Colonies found mainly in central England but birds occasionally turns up elsewhere.

R	I–12	N 4–7

White-headed Duck

Oxyura leucocephala L 45cm W 65cm

Similar to Ruddy Duck but male in full plumage is distinctive with paler brown plumage and white head, except for black cap. Bill is blue and extremely swollen at base. Immature males have more black on head. Female is similar to female Ruddy Duck but has bolder markings on face and obviously swollen base to bill. Seldom seen in flight. Swims buoyantly, often with tail held stiffly erect.

Voice Mostly silent.

Habitat Found on fresh, and sometimes brackish, lakes and lagoons invariably with well-vegetated margins.

Distribution Very local around the Mediterranean region, mainly S Iberia and SE Europe.

Occurrence Has declined markedly in Europe in recent years and is now rare. Can be seen at Coto Doñana in Spain.

Pochard, female

Pochard, male

Ferruginous Duck

Ruddy Duck, female

Ruddy Duck, male

White-headed Duck

Goldeneye
Bucephala clangula L 45cm W 75cm
Male in full plumage has distinctive black and white markings. Large, rounded triangular-shaped head is black with green sheen. Conspicuous round, white patch at base of bill. Female has grey-brown plumage and chestnut-brown head. Both sexes have bright, yellow eyes. Eclipse and immature males similar to female but show hint of white loral patch. In flight, shows white wing panels and a dark underwing. Wing panel of the female is divided by two narrow bands; that of male is undivided.

Voice Mostly silent but displaying male throws back the head on to the back and utters a grating, whistling call. In flight, the wings make a whistling sound.

Habitat Breeds on northern forested lakes. Nests in holes in trees and readily takes to nest-boxes. Winters on lakes, reservoirs and sheltered coasts.

Distribution Breeds throughout Scandinavia and at similar latitudes eastwards. Also locally in N central Europe and in Scotland. Winters in Britain, coastal NW Europe and locally in S and SE Europe.

Occurrence Common throughout its northern breeding range. Scarce but increasing breeding species in Scotland. More widespread and easy to see in winter.

T	1–12	N 4–7

Barrow's Goldeneye
Bucephala islandica L 50cm W 80cm
Similar to Goldeneye but male in full plumage has crescent-shaped white patch on face and purple sheen to head. Female very similar to female Goldeneye but both sexes have characteristic head shape with very steep forehead. Eclipse and immature males have similar plumage to female but show hint of white facial crescent. In flight, shows white wing panels and dark underwing. Wing panels of both sexes are divided by a single dark band.

Voice Mostly silent but male utters grunting display calls. Wings whistle in flight.

Habitat Breeds beside northern lakes and rivers. Winters on sheltered coasts.

Distribution Common breeder in Iceland but main range is Pacific NW of N America.

Occurrence Common in Iceland and easy to see at Lake Myvatn. Very rare vagrant to NW Europe, including Britain, although some records may refer to escapes from captivity.

V	—	—

Bufflehead
Bucephala albeola L 35cm W 55cm
Distinctive male has white body with black back and black head with green sheen and large white patch from rear of head to eye. Female has grey-ish-brown body and brown head with broad, white stripe on cheek. In flight, wing patterns in both sexes similar to those of Goldeneye.

Voice Mostly silent.

Habitat Ponds and lakes in breeding season. Coasts and lakes in winter.

Distribution Widespread in N America.

Occurrence Very rare vagrant to NW Europe including Britain.

V	—	—

Harlequin Duck
Histrionicus histrionicus L 40cm W 65cm
Male in full plumage is unmistakable with bluish plumage, red flanks and white stripes, spots and patches. In poor light, however, looks dark with white markings. Female is brown with three white patches on head, the front two often merging. Beware confusion with some plumage stages of female Long-tailed Duck. Eclipse male is similar to female but retains a hint of the flank stripe and other white markings. In flight, has noticeably fast wingbeats.

Voice Mostly silent except for high-pitched whistle.

Habitat Breeds on rivers and streams that are fast-flowing. Winters around rocky coasts.

Distribution In Europe breeds fairly commonly in Iceland, but main range includes N America, E Asia and S Greenland.

Occurrence Widespread but local in Iceland. On breeding rivers from April to August. Otherwise found around coast. Very rare winter vagrant to other parts of NW Europe including Britain.

V	10–2	—

Goldeneye, female

Goldeneye, male

Barrow's Goldeneye, female
Barrow's Goldeneye, male

Harlequin, male
Bufflehead, male

Harlequin, female

Long-tailed Duck

Clangula hyemalis L male 60cm female 40cm W 75cm

Male has long tail, sometimes held erect. In breeding plumage, brown and black plumage with white flanks and cheek patch. In winter, mostly grey, white and black with buff cheeks. Female in breeding plumage is mostly brown. In winter, has pale head and neck with dark cheek patch. In flight, shows dark wings and pale underparts. In winter, found in flocks, often far from shore. Oblivious to rough seas. Dives well for molluscs and crustaceans.

Voice Displaying male calls *ow-ow-ow-lee*. Groups sometimes call in synchrony.

Habitat Breeds on tundra pools and lakes. Winters at sea.

Distribution Breeding range from N Scandinavia eastwards. Also Iceland, Arctic N America and Greenland. Winters at sea in NW Europe, mainly Baltic but also North Sea.

Occurrence Common winter visitor within range from October to March. Less numerous in inshore waters. In Britain, easier to see the further north you travel on E coast. Exposed bays in NE Scotland offer best opportunities. Occurs inland rarely on reservoirs and gravel pits.

W	10–3	—

Common Scoter

Melanitta nigra L 50cm W 85cm

Male looks all-dark with yellow patch on dark-grey bill. In flight, flight feathers look paler than rest of body. Female is dark brown with buff cheek and side of neck. Immature male has brown plumage but lacks pale area on head and neck of female. Usually seen in flocks at sea. Dives well for marine invertebrates. Flies low over the water, usually in lines but in tighter bunches on migration.

Voice Mostly silent but males have whistling call.

Habitat Breeds on tundra and northern lakes. Winters at sea.

Distribution Common breeding species in Scandinavia eastwards. Also in Iceland and rare breeder in N Scotland and Ireland. Winters off W coast of Europe from S Scandinavia southwards to S Spain but most in North Sea and Baltic.

Occurrence Breeds from May to August. Otherwise found at sea. Migrating flocks seen off British and Irish coasts in October and April. Usually close to shore only during onshore winds.

T	1–12	N 5–8

Velvet Scoter

Melanitta fusca L 55cm W 90cm

Male has mostly black plumage with yellow patch on bill and white crescent under the white eye. White wing patch on secondaries most noticeable in flight and generally hidden when swimming. However, can be glimpsed occasionally by prolonged observation. Female has brown plumage with 2 white patches on face and white wing patch. Immature male similar to female. In winter, seen in small flocks, sometimes mixing with Common Scoters. Dives well.

Voice Mostly silent but male has whistling display call.

Habitat Breeds on northern lakes. Winters at sea.

Distribution Breeding range from Scandinavia eastwards. Winters off coasts of NW Europe from S Scandinavia south to N Spain.

Occurrence Found on breeding grounds from May to August. Otherwise at sea. Often seen among feeding or flying flocks of Common Scoters but invariably much less frequent.

W	10–3	—

Surf Scoter

Melanitta perspicillata L 50cm W 80cm

Male has all-black plumage but with prominent white patches on nape and forecrown. Bill is large and wedge-shaped with orange-red, white and black markings. Female similar to female Velvet Scoter but lacks white on wing. Both sexes have different head shape from other scoters with flattened crown and small forehead.

Voice Mostly silent.

Habitat Breeds on Arctic lakes. Winters at sea.

Distribution Breeds Arctic N America and winters on E and W coasts.

Occurrence Rare but regular winter visitor to NW Europe including Britain where invariably found among flocks of Common and Velvet Scoters.

V	10–3	—

Surf Scoter, male

ong-tailed Duck, female

Long-tailed Duck, male

Common Scoter, female

Common Scoter, male

Velvet Scoter, female

Velvet Scoter, male

Eider

Somateria mollissima L 65cm W 100cm

Male in full plumage is striking, mainly black below and white above. Breast tinged with pinkish-buff and lime-green patches on nape. Shows white forewing in flight. Female is mottled brown and shows faint white wing bar in flight. Male in eclipse is blackish-brown. Dives well for marine invertebrates, mainly mussels. Nest lined with down plucked from breast and incubating females sit tight. Young families gather in creches. Outside breeding season, seen in flocks.

Voice Displaying male utters characteristic *ah-OOooo* call. Female has chuckling call.

Habitat Coastal, mainly on sheltered rocky shores.

Distribution Breeds around coasts of N Britain, Iceland and Scandinavia with isolated colonies further south. Winter range extends south to Brittany.

Occurrence Adult birds are mostly sedentary while juveniles may disperse. Common breeding bird in much of its northerly range. In Britain, common in N England and Scotland and easy to see on Farne Islands.

T	1–12	N 4–7

King Eider

Somateria spectabilis L 60cm W 95cm

Male in full plumage has mainly black body with white breast and greyish head. Bill red with enlarged orange shield. Conspicuous white wing panels in flight. Female similar to female Eider but has smaller bill and appearance of smiling gape. Thin white wing bar in flight. Male in eclipse has mainly dark plumage but retains slightly enlarged bill shield.

Voice Calls similar to Eider.

Habitat Breeds beside tundra pools. Winters around coasts.

Distribution Breeds in Arctic and rarely in Iceland. Winter range N Scandinavia and Iceland.

Occurrence Individuals occasionally recorded S of normal range in winter. Rare but regular visitor to Britain, recorded among flocks of Eiders. Coasts of NE Scotland and Shetland Islands are particularly favoured.

V	11–2	—

Spectacled Eider

Somateria fisheri L 55cm W 90cm

Superficially similar to Eider but male in full plumage has diagnostic spectacle markings and white patch around eye and black breast. Female similar to female Eider but has pale patch around eye and hint of spectacle. Eclipse male similar to female.

Voice Mainly silent.

Habitat Breeds beside tundra pools and winters at sea.

Distribution Breeds in high Arctic of W Alaska and E Siberia. Winters in Bering Sea.

Occurrence Very rare winter vagrant to northern latitudes.

Steller's Eider

Polysticta stelleri L 45cm W 75cm

Male in full plumage is unmistakable with white and black body, pinkish-orange tint to underparts and white head with green tufts. White wing panels seen in flight but concealed when at rest. Female has dark, rusty-brown plumage with long tertials, tipped with white. Note also the squarish head shape and comparatively small bill for an eider. Eclipse males are similar to females but show more mottled plumage.

Voice Mostly silent.

Habitat Breeds on tundra in E Siberia and rarely N Norway. Some winter off N Norway.

Distribution Breeds in high Arctic. Small numbers winter in far N of Europe.

Occurrence Scarce visitor to N Norway and very rare vagrant to NW Europe including Britain.

V	—	—

Steller's Eider, male

Eider, female   **Eider,** male

King Eider, female   **King Eider,** male

Spectacled Eider, female   **Spectacled Eider,** male

Red-breasted Merganser

Mergus serrator L 55cm W 85cm

Thin, red bill in both sexes with serrated edges. Male in full plumage has green-glossed head with shaggy crest, reddish-brown breast and black, grey and white body. Female has grey-brown plumage with orange-brown head and shaggy crest. In flight, male shows white forewing panel and speculum. Female has white speculum divided by dark stripe. Eclipse male similar to female but retains male wing pattern. Swims and dives well for fish. Seen in flocks in winter when males perform display involving arching head and wings.
Voice Mostly silent but female utters soft barking call in flight.
Habitat Breeds beside northern lakes and rivers. Winters around coasts.
Distribution Breeds in N Britain and Ireland, Iceland and Scandinavia eastwards. Winters around coasts of NW Europe as far south as Spain. Also locally in Mediterranean but less numerous.
Occurrence Reasonably common breeding species within range. Widespread and locally common around coasts in winter. In Britain, easiest to see along S and E coasts of England.

T	1–12	N 4–7

Goosander

Mergus merganser L 65cm W 95cm

Both sexes share characteristic sawbill of Red-breasted Merganser. Male in full plumage has green-glossed head which looks puffed-up, and mostly white body with pink tinge and black back. Female similar to female Red-breasted Merganser but clearer demarcation between orange-brown head and white throat. Conspicuous white throat and substantial, drooping crest. In flight, male shows forewing and speculum forming continuous white patch. Female has undivided white speculum. Eclipse male similar to female but retains male wing pattern. In winter, often seen in flocks. Swims and dives well for fish and sometimes feeds cooperatively, forming lines to drive fish.
Voice Mostly silent but in spring displaying male has ringing call.
Habitat Breeds on northern lakes and rivers and nests in tree holes. Winters on fish-rich lakes and reservoirs.
Distribution Breeds N Britain, Iceland and eastwards from Denmark and Scandinavia. Also breeds locally in Wales and in Alps. Winters across much of NW Europe in suitable habitats.

Occurrence Locally common breeding species becoming less so in south of range. Locally common in winter on suitable lakes. In Britain, most easily seen on large, inland reservoirs in England. Sometimes driven south by severe winter weather.

T	1–12	N 4–7

Smew

Mergus albellus L 40cm W 65cm

Male in full plumage is distinctive looking, mostly white with black markings including stripes on flanks, black back and patch around eye. At close range, flanks have subtle grey markings. Female has grey-brown plumage with orange-brown head and white cheeks and throat. Eclipse male similar to female but more white on wing. Does not acquire full plumage until early winter. Immature male similar to female but has more white on head. Acquires full plumage in second winter. In flight, both sexes show white wing patches. Swims and dives well and usually seen in small groups in winter.
Voice Mostly silent.
Habitat Breeds beside northern lakes, nesting in tree holes. In winter, on lakes and reservoirs, and also sheltered coasts.
Distribution Breeding range from N Scandinavia eastwards. In winter, has scattered range from NW to SE Europe.
Occurrence Seen mostly in the region as a winter visitor from October to March where most numerous in coastal regions from Netherlands to Poland. Regular but usually scarce winter visitor to Britain, mostly SE England. Influxes sometimes occur during severe winters.

W	10–3	—

Hooded Merganser

Lophodytes cucullatus L 45cm W 68cm

Male in full plumage has orange flank, black and white flank stripes and flattened, fan-shaped crest showing conspicuous white patch. Female has greyish-brown plumage with bushy, orange crest. Eclipse male similar to female but retains yellow eye (that of female is brown).
Voice Mostly silent.
Habitat Ponds and lakes.
Distribution Widespread in N America.
Occurrence Very rare vagrant to NW Europe including Britain, mostly in winter.

V	—	—

Red-breasted Merganser, female

Red-breasted Merganser, male

Goosander, male

Goosander, female

Smew, male

Smew, female

Hooded Merganser, male

BIRDS OF PREY
ORDERS ACCIPITRIFORMES AND FALCONIFORMES

This varied group comprises diurnal predators with powerful feet and talons, and hooked beaks for tearing flesh. Most catch live prey but some, such as the vultures, scavenge. Females are often larger than males. All species are excellent fliers, in one way or another and most species often soar. Plumages are sometimes variable in some species.

Family Accipitridae
This family includes buzzards, Honey Buzzard, eagles, kites, harriers, hawks and vultures. Most species are large with broad wings designed for prolonged soaring on thermals and upcurrents of air. Hawks have relatively short, rounded wings and long tails, and catch their prey in dashing, horizontal flight. Harriers have long, narrow wings and long tails; their flight is relatively slow and leisurely, and they locate their prey by quartering the ground. Vultures are somewhat atypical of the group as a whole. Although they soar effortlessly on broad wings, they feed exclusively by scavenging at carcasses and kills.

Family Pandionidae
This family comprises the Osprey, a large eagle-like bird that is an exclusively fish-eating species. It dives dramatically into surface water for its food, plucking the fish from the water with its talons.

Family Falconidae
In this family are the well-known falcons, such as the Kestrel and Peregrine, with relatively narrow, pointed wings. Most fly at great speed and catch their prey on the wing.

A Lammergeier soars effortlessly against an arid, Spanish landscape. This species is one of the spectacular raptors of the region.

Egyptian Vulture

Neophron percnopterus L 65cm W 145cm

Adult distinctive with white body and black flight feathers. Yellow facial skin. Wedge-shaped tail seen in flight. Soars effortlessly on flat wings. Juvenile birds have brownish plumage and similar flight silhouette to adult. Take several years to acquire full plumage. Scavenges carrion and waste, sometimes visiting rubbish tips. Also takes small, live prey. Migrates in small flocks.

Voice Mostly silent.

Habitat Mountainous areas, gorges and ravines. Nests on cliff ledges and crevices.

Distribution Widespread summer visitor to S Europe. Winters in Africa.

Occurrence Occurs in breeding range from April to September. Locally common, particularly in central Iberian peninsula and SE Europe.

Griffon Vulture

Gyps fulvus L 100cm W 255cm

Distinctive flight appearance. Broad wings with rounded trailing edge narrowing towards tip. Comparatively short tail and compact-looking head and neck. In flight, finger-like primaries splayed upwards. Soars with wings angled slightly upwards. Hunched-up appearance when perched. Head and neck covered with white down. Neck collar of white feathers. Juvenile similar to adult but neck collar brownish and under-wing coverts paler brown. Seen soaring on thermals, often in sizeable flocks. Feeds on carrion. Sometimes roosts communally on cliffs.

Voice Comparatively silent but sometimes utters grunting and hissing calls.

Habitat Mountainous terrain, ravines and gorges. Nests on cliff ledges, usually in colonies.

Distribution Iberian peninsula, SE Europe and larger Mediterranean islands. Very local in S Alps.

Occurrence Year-round resident in most of range but summer only in Alps. Locally common in central Spain where easiest to see.

Black Vulture

Aegypius monachus L 105cm W 260cm

Largest bird of prey in the region. In flight, silhouette superficially similar to White-tailed Eagle, with which unlikely to be seen. Broad, parallel wings with splayed fingertips and short tail slightly wedge-shaped. Soars on flat wings and generally looks all dark in flight. When seen perched at close range, plumage looks dark brown with black neck collar and greyish head and neck. Feeds on carrion and takes precedence over other vultures at kills.

Voice Generally silent.

Habitat Mountainous regions with wooded slopes. Nests in trees.

Distribution Extremely local in Iberian peninsula, Majorca and SE Europe.

Occurrence One of Europe's most endangered birds but still comparatively easy to see in mountainous regions in central Spain, such as the Sierra de Guadarrama range, and in N Majorca.

Lammergeier or Bearded Vulture

Gypaetus barbatus L 110cm W 265cm

Characteristic flight appearance with long, narrow and pointed wings and long, wedge-shaped tail. Wings dark but underparts orange in adult. At close range, note whitish head with black through eye and black whiskers. Immature similar silhouette to adult but underparts greyish-brown and head and neck dark. Takes several years to acquire adult plumage. Generally solitary and prefers fresh kills. Drops bones from a great height to break them.

Voice Mostly silent, but whistling calls near nest site.

Habitat Mountainous regions. Nests in inaccessible cliff caves.

Distribution Extremely local in Europe with populations in Pyrenees, Corsica and SE Europe.

Occurrence Very rare throughout the region but comparatively easy to see at Ordesa National Park in Spanish Pyrenees.

Egyptian Vulture, adult

Griffon Vulture, adult

Black Vulture, adult

Egyptian Vulture, adult

Griffon Vulture, adult

Black Vulture, adult
Lammergeier, adult

White-tailed Eagle
Haliaeetus albicilla L 90cm W 240cm
Recognized by immense size and broad, parallel-sided wings and wedge-shaped tail. Adults have white tail and head slightly paler than body. At close range, note huge yellow bill and yellow claws. Juvenile appears mostly dark at a distance including tail. At close range, note pale axillaries and pale centres to tail feathers. Takes several years to acquire full adult plumage. Soars on flat wings and flies with shallow, slow wingbeats. Often perches for extended periods on favourite lookout. Feeds on fish, birds and carrion. Frequently mobbed by corvids and gulls.
Voice Loud *kyee kyee kyee kyee*.

White-tailed Eagle, adult

Habitat Mostly around coasts but also on lakes and larger rivers. Nests on cliff ledges or in trees.
Distribution Widespread breeding species in coastal N Europe and throughout E Europe. Also locally in SE Europe and NW Iceland. Reintroduced and established on Rhum in Scotland and now spreading slowly. In winter, some birds move south and west of breeding range.
Occurrence Generally uncommon throughout range. In winter, however, congregates in good feeding sites, such as Lac d'Orient and Lac du Der Chantercoq in NE France. Mainland European birds occur as very rare winter vagrants to Britain.

| R+V | — | — |

Golden Eagle
Aquila chrysaetos L 85cm W 220cm
A large eagle with golden-buff nape feathers. Soars with wings held in shallow 'v'. In flight, adults may look all-dark but immatures have variable amounts of white in wings and on base of tail. Gradually acquire full adult plumage over several years. Generally seen soaring high or perched on elevated lookout such as rocky crag or bare tree. Performs steep dives to catch prey such as hares and grouse in low-level flight. Also takes carrion.
Voice Mostly silent, but occasional yelping calls.
Habitat Mountainous and upland regions. Nests on cliff ledges or in trees, in same nest each year.
Distribution Found in most mountainous areas of Europe. In Britain, mainly in Scottish Highlands.

Generally resident but some movement by immature birds in winter.
Occurrence Widespread but never common. Perhaps most easily seen in the Alps or mountains of central Spain.

| R | 1–12 | N 4–7 |

Imperial Eagle
Aquila heliaca L 80cm W 210cm
Superficially similar to Golden Eagle. Adults have buffish nape feathers and grey inner tail. Spanish race *adalberti* has white on scapular and on forewing while eastern race *heliaca* has white only on scapulars. Juvenile has pale brown body, streaked below in eastern race, and darker flight feathers. Perches for extended periods and flies with wings held flat. Feeds on small to medium-sized mammals and birds, and also on carrion.
Voice Mostly silent, but barking calls near nest.
Habitat Open plains and hills. Nests in trees.
Distribution Spanish race *adalberti* found in S Iberian peninsula; eastern race *heliaca* occurs in SE Europe. Mostly resident.
Occurrence Rare and threatened species throughout range. Spanish race can be seen at Coto Doñana National Park.

Imperial Eagle

Steppe Eagle
Aquila nipalensis L 75cm W 215cm
Dark-brown eagle with longish tail and long wings. In flight, adult looks mostly dark but with slightly paler flight feathers with dark bars seen from underneath. Pale base to primary feathers sometimes visible. Juvenile is more distinctive. Larger underwing coverts white producing broad, white wing bar. Seen from above, shows wing bar, pale base to primaries and pale band on uppertail coverts. Pale trailing edge to wings and tail visible from above and below. Soars on flattish wings.
Voice Mostly silent.
Habitat Open, steppe country.
Distribution Breeds from E Europe and winters in E Africa. Breeding ranges extends eastwards into Asia; also in N Africa.
Occurrence Rare breeding species in E Europe. Immatures occasionally wander.

White-tailed Eagle

Golden Eagle

Golden Eagle

Steppe Eagle

Steppe Eagle

Spotted Eagle
Aquila clanga L 70cm W 175cm

Medium-sized eagle. Adult appears uniform dark brown when perched. In flight, flight feathers appear greyish from beneath and lighter than underwing coverts. Looks uniform brown from above, sometimes with indistinct pale bases to primaries. Juvenile also shows contrast between dark underwing coverts and paler flight feathers from beneath. From above, looks dark with conspicuous white spots on secondary coverts, white rump and trailing white edge to wing and tail. Often holds wings bowed downwards slightly in flight.

Voice Generally silent.

Habitat Forested country, with marshes or lakes nearby.

Distribution Breeds from NE Europe eastwards. Moves south in winter, some remain in SE Europe.

Occurrence Rare breeding species in Europe and scarce in winter.

Spotted Eagle

Lesser Spotted Eagle
Aquila pomarina L 65cm W 155cm

Similar to Spotted Eagle but marginally smaller. Adult usually has pale-brown plumage contrasting in flight with darker flight feathers seen from above and below. Seen from above, inner primaries show distinct white bases and tail coverts have pale tips. Juvenile also shows contrast between dark flight feathers and pale wing coverts. From above, has white spots on secondary coverts, pale tail coverts and pale bases to inner primaries.

Voice As Spotted Eagle.

Habitat Breeds in forests with adjoining marshes.

Distribution Breeds in E Europe. Winters in E Africa.

Occurrence Rare breeding species in Europe. Present May to August. Seen on migration across Bosphorus.

Lesser Spotted Eagle

Bonelli's Eagle
Hieraaetus fasciatus L 72cm W 165cm

Medium-sized eagle. Distinctive when seen from below with pale body and coverts on forewing; remaining wing coverts dark brown. Flight feathers greyish with darker barring and pale bases to pr maries. Tail relatively long with dark terminal ban Looks dark from above but with pale patch o upper back. Juvenile has pinkish-buff plumag replacing pale body and forewing coverts of adult greyish flight feathers and tail lacking terminal band Usually soars with flattened wings.

Voice Mostly silent.

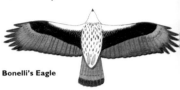

Bonelli's Eagle

Habitat Mountainous regions.

Distribution Scattered range in S Europe from Spain, Majorca and S France to SE Europe.

Occurrence Scarce year-round resident.

Booted Eagle
Hieraaetus pennatus L 50cm W 125cm

Buzzard-sized eagle with long tail and long wings with splayed 'fingers'. Two colour phases. Pale phase seen from below has pale body and underwing coverts contrasting with dark flight feathers. Dark phase is dark brown with blackish flight feathers and paler-brown tail. Can be confused with Black Kite. Soars but also hangs on updraughts against hillside. Plunges with closed wings in pursuit of small mammals, birds and lizards.

Voice Shrill calls in display flight and at nest.

Distribution Breeds in Spain, S France and SE Europe. Most winter south of region.

Occurrence Scarce breeding species, present from April to August.

Short-toed Eagle
Circaetus gallicus L 65cm W 155cm

Distinctive eagle when seen in flight. From below, shows pale body and wings with variable amount of barring and no carpal patch. Dark head and upper breast and long, pale tail showing 3 darker bands. From above, looks rather uniform greyish-brown. Frequently hovers or hangs motionless scanning the ground below. Specialist feeder on reptiles, especially snakes.

Voice Mostly silent.

Habitat Hilly country with open slopes.

Distribution Breeds locally in S Europe. Winters south of region.

Occurrence Widespread but scarce breeding species, present from March to August.

Booted Eagle, dark phase, at nest with young

Booted Eagle, light phase

Short-toed Eagle

Short-toed Eagle, at nest with young

Buzzard

Buteo buteo L 55cm W 125cm

Medium-sized raptor with variable plumage. Generally dark brown with pale breast band usually apparent. Very pale forms also occur but are rare in Britain. In flight, flight feathers appear paler than rest of body with dark terminal band, also present on tail. Soars and circles on broad wings, held in shallow 'v'. Seldom hovers. Often perches for long periods on posts or other lookouts scanning for prey including earthworms. Also takes carrion. **Voice** Call, often given in flight, a mewing *pee-ooo*. **Habitat** Occurs where scattered woodland for nesting exists close to open country for feeding. Common on farmland where not persecuted. **Distribution** Widespread resident across most of Europe except Ireland, Iceland and N Scandinavia. Northern birds move south in winter. **Occurrence** The commonest medium-sized raptor in much of Europe. In Britain, common in W and N but almost absent from S and E England.

R	1–12	N 4–6

Rough-legged Buzzard

Buteo lagopus L 55cm W 140cm

Similar to Buzzard but generally paler and distinctive in flight. Seen from below, note pale underwing with dark carpal patches and wingtips and white tail with dark terminal band (in fact comprising 2-4 narrower bands). Pale band on breast contrasts with usually darker throat and dark lower breast and undertail. From above, shows dark wings and back, white tail with dark terminal band and pale head. Frequently hovers and often flies lower over ground than Buzzard, showing kink in wings.

Occurrence

Fairly common breeding species i NE Europe. Widespread but seldom commc winter visitor further south. Scarce winter visitc to Britain, mostly S and E England.

W	10–3	—

Long-legged Buzzard

Buteo rufinus L 60cm W 145cm

Distinctive buffish-red appearance when seer perched. In flight, looks longer-winged than Buzzard. Shows pale rufous head, upper breast an wing coverts, contrasting with darker lower breast. Dark carpal patches and paler flight feathers with dark trailing edge. Tail looks pale and unmarked but barred in juveniles. From above, shows pale tail, head and leading edge to wing **Voice** Similar to Buzzard.

Habitat Breeds in mountainous and steppe regions. Winters in open country. **Distribution** Breeds and winters in SE Europe and N Africa. **Occurrence** Locally common in SE Europe. Fairly easy to see in rocky regions in N Greece.

Honey Buzzard

Pernis apivorus L 55cm W 145cm

Mostly seen in flight. Superficially similar to Buzzard but has long, narrow head and neck, like Cuckoo's, greyish wings with dark carpal patches, barring on wing coverts and trailing edge to wing. Underparts heavily barred and tail with dark terminal band. Wings held slightly depressed when soaring and shows angled carpals and straight trailing edge to wing when gliding. Bright yellow eye at close range. Generally rather secretive. Feeds almost exclusively on larvae and pupae of wasps and bees. Dugout nests sometimes found in woodland rides.

Voice Call a rather mournful *pee-luu*.
Habitat Forests and extensive woodlands.
Distribution Breeds across much of mainland central Europe as far north as S Scandinavia and as far south as N Spain. Winters in Africa.

Buzzard   **Rough-legged Buzzard**   **Long-legged Buzzard**   **Honey Buzzard**

Voice Mostly silent.
Habitat Breeds on Arctic tundra and winters in open country.
Distribution Breeds from N Scandinavia eastwards. Moves in winter, main range extending from Low Countries to SE Europe.

Occurrence Fairly common across most of breeding range, particularly central France and Germany. In Britain, very rare breeder in S England and also seen on passage, mostly in spring.

S	5–8	N 6–8

Buzzard

Buzzard

Rough-legged Buzzard

Rough-legged Buzzard, at nest

Honey Buzzard

Honey Buzzard

Goshawk

Accipiter gentilis L male 50cm female 60cm
W male 100cm female 120cm

Larger and heavier than Sparrowhawk with grey-brown upperparts and pale, barred underparts. Juvenile has boldly streaked underparts. Male is smaller than female but still larger than female Sparrowhawk from which told by flight silhouette and heavier wingbeats. Soars on broad wings which look pale and barred. Tail looks proportionately shorter and rounder than Sparrowhawk's. White, bushy undertail coverts are conspicuous in flight and often fluffed out. Seen soaring over woodland and, in early spring, male engages in display flight with slow wingbeats. Dives from a great height in pursuit of prey such as pigeon-sized birds, rabbits, etc. Also has low-level attack flight and is adept at flying through comparatively dense woodland. Often mobbed by corvids, when large size is soon apparent.

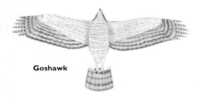

Goshawk

Voice Alarm call a loud *kyee-kyee*.

Habitat Extensive forests, mainly coniferous.

Distribution Widespread across most of Europe except Ireland and Iceland.

Occurrence Scarce resident breeding species made more so by persecution. Seldom seen away from extensive areas of forest. Rare breeding species in Britain but seen more regularly in recent years. Some winter movement south by birds in north of range. Regularly seen at raptor-watching spot at Haldon Forest in Devon.

R	1–12	N 3–6

Sparrowhawk

Accipiter nisus L male 30cm female 38cm W male 60cm female 80cm

Male much smaller than female with blue-grey upperparts and orange-red barring on underparts and underwing coverts. Yellow eye visible at close range. Flight feathers and tail pale greyish with darker barring. Larger female has grey-brown upperparts and dark-brown barring on underparts and underwing. Distinct barring on tail. Female could be confused with male Goshawk but generally slimmer appearance with proportionately longer tail and lighter wingbeats. Juvenile has brown upperparts with paler feather margins and underparts looking rather streaked or spotted. Seen soaring over woodland or flying low through woodland or along rides with fast wingbeats interspersed with short glides. Also seen flying beside hedgerows, suddenly skimming from one side to the other after prey. Occasionally makes surprise attacks on garden bird feeders in urban areas. Catches small birds on the wing and uses regular plucking-posts.

Voice Persistent alarm call *kyee-kyee* heard near nest.

Habitat Nests in dense woodland but often in small copses surrounded by farmland.

Distribution Widespread across most of Europe except Iceland and N Scandinavia.

Occurrence Fairly common resident species in much of Europe. Despite persecution, found in most sizeable areas of woodland in Britain and sometimes in surprisingly urban locations.

R	1–12	N 3–6

Levant Sparrowhawk

Accipiter brevipes L male 35cm female 38cm
W male 65cm female 80cm

Similar to Sparrowhawk. In flight, shows pale underparts and wings contrasting with dark wingtips. Upperparts are blue-grey in male with unbarred central tail feathers but browner in female. At close range, red eye visible and grey cheeks (reddish in Sparrowhawk). Juvenile has brown plumage with spotted underparts. Catches mainly ground-dwelling prey such as lizards and some small mammals.

Voice Call a loud *keewik keewik*.

Habitat Dry, open terrain.

Distribution Breeds in SE Europe and winters in E Africa.

Occurrence Fairly common breeding species in SE Europe, present from May until August. Seen on migration in sizeable flocks through the Bosphorus, in September and April.

Sparrowhawk, male

Sparrowhawk, female

Goshawk, female

Levant Sparrowhawk

Levant Sparrowhawk, adult male

Red Kite

Milvus milvus L 65cm W 160cm

Distinctive, buzzard-sized raptor with reddish plumage, grey, streaked head and long, deeply forked tail. In flight, underside shows reddish belly and wing coverts, grey, barred tail with dark tips to outer feathers and white patches on primaries contrasting with black wingtips. From above, tail is reddish and wings show pale bar. Juveniles similar but with more streaked plumage. Flight graceful and buoyant with wings held slightly arched and tail continually flexed for manoeuvring. Feeds on carrion but also takes birds and small mammals.

Voice A weak, buzzard-like whistle.

Habitat Nests in trees and feeds over open country. Usually associated with hilly terrain dotted with small copses.

Distribution Widespread but local in central and S Europe with main areas of distribution in Iberian peninsula and S France. In Britain, last stronghold is in central Wales.

Occurrence Most birds are resident although juveniles occasionally wander in winter. Soaring birds fairly easy to see over wooded hillsides in central Wales. Reintroduction programmes elsewhere in Britain suffer badly from persecution.

R	1–12	N 3–6

Black Kite

Milvus migrans L 55cm W 140cm

Similar to Red Kite but distinguished in flight by smaller size, shorter, less forked tail and proportionately broader wings. Tail can look straight-ended, rather than forked, when fully spread. Plumage mostly brown and can appear all-dark when seen from below in flight. From above, can be confused with female Marsh Harrier but pale wing markings on wing coverts not fore-edge of wing. Black Kite soars on flat wings and flexes tail. Feeds on carrion but also takes fish from surface of water as well as small mammals, amphibians, etc.

Voice Call a high-pitched, whinnying mew.

Habitat Nests in trees and found in areas of patchy woodland, surrounded by farmland or open country, and usually in the vicinity of water.

Distribution Breeding range includes much of S and central Europe as far north as Baltic coast and occasionally further north. Winters in Africa and Asia. Extremely widespread in the Old World.

Occurrence Present within breeding range from April to August. Seen in large numbers at migration spots in S Europe in spring and autumn. Very rare spring and early summer vagrant to Britain, sightings usually of transient individuals.

V	5–7	—

Black-winged Kite

Elanus caeruleus L 33cm W 80cm

Small and compact raptor with distinctive appearance and plumage essentially grey, black and white. Perches regularly on posts and trees and shows grey upperparts, white underparts, black shoulders and black over eye giving owl-like face. In flight, wings look pale grey with black wingtips from below and black patch on forewing above. Wings broad but pointed and tail is short and rounded when fully spread. Juvenile similar but has brownish upperparts and brown streaks on breast. Flight buoyant. Glides on wings held in 'v', hovers frequently and in direct flight, looks owl-like. Feeds on lizards, insects and small mammals and birds.

Voice Call a plaintive whistle.

Habitat Dry, open country with scattered trees.

Distribution Only found in SW Iberian peninsula. More widespread distribution in Africa.

Occurrence Rare and local and seldom seen outside breeding range.

Red Kite

Red Kite

Black Kite

Black Kite

Black-winged Kite

Hen Harrier

Circus cyaneus L 45–50cm W 105–120cm

Elegant and distinctive in flight. Male has pale-grey plumage, generally darker above than below, with black wingtips and pure white rump. Female has brown plumage, streaked below and with pure white rump. Barring on tail and markings on face give owl-like appearance. Juvenile similar to female. Legs, iris and base of bill yellow. Generally seen flying low over ground and often quarters fields, scanning for prey. Wings look proportionately broader than those of Montagu's or Pallid Harriers with more rounded wingtip formed by primaries 2–5. Flies with slow wingbeats, interspersed with glides where wings held in a 'v' and often slightly swept back. In spring, males fly high in display flight. Solitary when feeding but sometimes roosts communally in winter in deep heather on moorland or in dense reedbeds. **Voice** Alarm call an insistent *chek-chek-chek*.

Hen Harrier, male

Pallid Harrier, male

Habitat Nests on open moorland and bogs. Sometimes uses conifer plantations in their first few years. Winters mostly in open lowland terrain such as heathland, downland, farmland and coastal marshes.

Distribution Breeds across much of N Europe. Generally local, especially so in Scotland, N Wales and Ireland. Birds from NE Europe move south in winter, range then covering most of Europe.

Occurrence Nests from May to August and resident in many parts of south of breeding range including N Britain. Winter visitor to S Britain with influx of birds from mainland N Europe.

T	1–12	N 5–7

Montagu's Harrier

Circus pygargus
L 43–48cm W 100–115cm

Graceful appearance in flight with slimmer body and proportionately longer, narrower wings than Hen Harrier. Wingtips, formed by primaries 2–4, look long and pointed. In flight, adult male has grey upperparts, darker than on male Hen or Pallid Harriers, with a single black wing bar across secondaries and black wingtips. Faint barring on outer tail feathers and no white on rump. From below, shows 2 black wing bars on secondaries and reddish-brown streaking on belly and underwing

coverts. Female has streaked brown plumage with barred tail and white rump. Superficially similar to female Hen Harrier but less white on rump and very different flight proportions, especially narrower, more pointed wings. Extremely similar to female Pallid Harrier; faint wing bar on secondaries can sometimes be seen from above. From below, shows well-defined barring on wing with hind pale bar on secondaries broader than Pallid and dark bar on trailing edge paler than inner bars and of uniform width. Generally shows more white behind eye than female Pallid and distinct dark patch on ear coverts. Juvenile has rusty-brown plumage with dark facial markings extending from ear coverts almost to base of bill. Usually lacks distinct pale collar which defines these markings in juvenile Pallid Harrier.

Voice A sharp yicking call.

Habitat Nests on heaths, grasslands and in cornfields. Feeds over open country.

Distribution Widespread breeding species across much of lowland Europe as far north as Baltic coast. Rare and irregular breeder in S England. Winters in Africa.

Occurrence In breeding range April to August. In Britain, mostly seen on migration or lone birds in potential breeding habitat.

S	4–9	—

Pallid Harrier

Circus macrourus L 40–45cm W 95–115cm

Male like a washed-out version of male Hen Harrier but with proportions and flight silhouette of Montagu's. Very pale grey plumage with narrow-pointed wings appearing more so because of short second and fourth primaries and narrow, wedge-shaped black wingtips. Female similar to female Montagu's but underwing shows the bar on trailing edge of secondaries darker than rather indistinct inner bars and becoming broader towards base of wing. Juvenile has rusty-brown plumage similar to juvenile Montagu's but usually shows distinct white collar behind, and defining, dark facial markings.

Voice Mostly silent but call similar to Montagu's.

Habitat Steppe country and grassy terrain.

Distribution Breeds from E Europe eastwards and winters in Africa.

Occurrence Seen on migration through E Mediterranean region in spring and autumn. Extremely rare elsewhere in Europe.

V	—	—

Hen Harrier, female

Montagu's Harrier, female

Montagu's Harrier, male

Montagu's Harrier, male

Pallid Harrier, female

Marsh Harrier
Circus aeruginosus L 48–55cm
W 115–125cm

Identified as a harrier by flight silhouette, with long wings and tail, and buoyant, low-level flight. Adult male has pale bluish-grey on wings and tail, reddish-brown belly, back and wing coverts, and paler head. Adult female has brown plumage with pale buff on forewing and on crown and throat, giving skull-like appearance. Immatures are similar to female but plumage generally darker. Most frequently sighted flying low over reedbeds when flight appears light and comprises slow flaps alternating with glides on wings held in 'v'. Often hangs motionless on wind as it scans for prey before dropping into reeds. Patrols up and down, quartering reedbeds in search of small mammals, young birds, amphibians, etc. In the spring, males perform display flights high in sky.

Voice Male utters Lapwing-like call in display flight. Otherwise mostly silent.

Habitat Invariably associated with large reedbeds although sometimes seen feeding over neighbouring farmland. Nests among dense areas of reed.

Distribution Widespread in Europe as far north as S Scandinavia. Extremely local because of habitat requirements and seldom common. Extremely local in Britain, mostly in E Anglia and SE England.

Occurrence Present in breeding range from April to September. Most migrate south in winter although some are resident. In Britain, comparatively easy to see at reserves such as Minsmere in Suffolk and N Norfolk reserves with extensive reedbeds. Scarce on migration along S and E coasts of England.

S	3–9	N 5–7

Osprey
Pandion haliaetus L 55–65cm W 45–160cm

Distinctive raptor with dark-brown upperparts, white underparts and white head with dark eye band. In flight, white underwing coverts contrast with darker secondaries and wingtips and prominent dark carpal patches. Dark feathers of juvenile have pale margins. In active flight, silhouette can look gull-like with rather tapering, and slightly bowed, wings. However, sometimes dangles feet, when talons visible, and also hovers when feeding. Feeds by plunge-diving exclusively for fish, often becoming completely immersed.

Voice Male utters a mournful yelping display call. Alarm call *pew-pew-pew*.

Habitat Because of diet of fish, invariably seen near water. Breeds near northern lakes, building huge stick nests in trees which are used year after year. Also seen on rocky coasts in Mediterranean, and there nests on cliffs.

Distribution Widespread in Scandinavia and at similar latitudes eastwards. Very local in Scottish Highlands beside large lochs and has staged something of a comeback in recent years. Most birds winter in Africa. Very local in W Mediterranean where resident.

Occurrence Present in breeding range from May to August. Easy to see at RSPB's Loch Garten reserve in Scotland. Regularly visits nearby fish farms. Seen on migration elsewhere and juveniles sometimes stop off at fish-stocked reservoirs in S England for a few days.

S	4–9	N 5–7

Marsh Harrier, male

Marsh Harrier, male

Osprey

Osprey

Gyrfalcon

Falco rusticolus L 55–60cm W 125–130cm

Large falcon with variable coloration. Generally greyish upperparts with paler underparts with darker bars and streaks. Some individuals are pure white with only a few black spots. Other individuals are much darker but still never as dark on upperparts as Peregrine. Juvenile brownish-grey with more streaking on underparts. In flight, proportionately longer tail and broader wings than Peregrine can lead to confusion with Goshawk. Feeds mainly on grouse and Ptarmigan but also takes small mammals and carrion.

Voice Alarm call a series of deep, harsh screams.

Habitat Typically on tundra and coasts in the Arctic, breeding on cliffs and mountain ledges.

Distribution Breeds in N Scandinavia and at similar latitudes eastwards. Also breeds in Iceland. General movement southwards in winter.

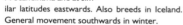

Gyrfalcon

Occurrence Rather scarce within breeding range but comparatively easy to see in Iceland. Very rare winter or spring vagrant to Britain, mostly N Scotland.

V	11–3	—

Peregrine

Falco peregrinus L 40–50cm W 95–110cm

Medium-sized falcon, the male of which is considerably smaller than the female. Adult has dark, bluish-grey upperparts, black and white markings on the head and white underparts with dark spots and bars. Juveniles are dark brown with heavily marked underparts. Powerful and impressive flight. Sometimes seen 'stooping' from a great height to hit small to medium-sized birds in flight. Also pursues quarry in swift, level flight.

Voice Alarm call a loud *kek-kek-kek.*

Habitat Breeds on cliff ledges. In winter, often seen on estuaries and in other coastal areas.

Distribution Widespread across Europe but rare and local in many parts.

Occurrence Has suffered badly from pesticide poisoning and persecution by egg collectors and falconers. Has recovered, however, in many areas, especially Britain. Comparatively easy to see on many W coast cliff areas and over English estuaries in winter.

R	1–12	N 3–7

Lanner Falcon

Falco biarmicus L 45–50cm W 95–115cm

Similar to Peregrine but has proportionately longer tail and broader wings, more rounded at tips. Upperparts brownish-grey, underparts white with dark spots and streaks, and head with pale-chestnut to buff crown and nape and black moustachial markings and through eye. Juvenile has browner plumage and has heavily marked underparts. Feeds on small birds and, more occasionally, small mammals.

Voice Similar to Peregrine but higher-pitched in tone.

Habitat Dry, rocky terrain with plains for feeding and cliffs for nesting.

Distribution Widespread in N Africa but also locally in S Europe, mainly S Italy, Sicily, Greece, Yugoslavia and Turkey.

Occurrence Resident and rare in Europe.

Saker

Falco cherrug L 48–55cm L 110–125cm

Large falcon with brownish upperparts, pale head and pale underparts with darker streaks in adult. In flight, shows barred outer tail feathers from above and underwing coverts darker than flight feathers. Juvenile is generally darker brown with heavier markings on head and underparts. Powerful level flight and often soars on broad wings. Feeds mainly on small mammals.

Saker

Voice Mostly silent, but alarm call similar to Peregrine but deeper.

Habitat Open steppe country. Nests in trees.

Distribution Breeding range includes SE Europe. Some birds winter further south and east along Mediterranean coast of SE Europe.

Occurrence Rare and local. Occasionally seen wintering in E Mediterranean from October to March.

Gyrfalcon

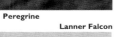

Peregrine

Lanner Falcon

Peregrine

Lanner Falcon

Hobby
Falco subbuteo L 30–35cm W 70–80cm
Adult has dark-grey upperparts, white underparts heavily streaked with black, red undertail coverts and thighs, and black and white markings on head revealing prominent white cheeks. Juvenile has brown feathers with pale margins. In flight, often resembles large swift with scythe-like swept-back wings and relatively short tail. Superbly aerobatic, sometimes catching Swifts, Swallows or even bats in flight. Also catches insects, especially dragon-flies, on the wing and seen hawking over gravel pits and lakes, especially in spring and early summer. Dismembers and eats insect prey in flight.
Voice Largely silent, but alarm call *kee-kee-kee* near nest.
Habitat Open, lowland country such as heath-land and farmland, with scattered clumps of trees for nesting. Nests in abandoned crow's nests.
Distribution Widespread breeding range across much of Europe as far north as S Scandi-navia. In Britain, confined mainly to S England. Winters in Africa.
Occurrence Rather scarce throughout range and present from May to September. In Britain, most easily seen over southern heathlands in spring.

S	5–9	N 6–8

Eleonora's Falcon
Falco eleonorae L 36–40cm W 90–100cm
Elegant falcon with distinctive flight silhouette. Longer wings and tail than Peregrine or Hobby. Colour very variable but with two extremes. Pale phase has dark-grey upperparts, black cap and moustachial stripe, white cheeks and throat, and underparts tinged with orange-buff and heavily streaked. Dark phase is all sooty-brown. Incredi-bly aerobatic, riding updraughts off sea cliffs in seemingly effortless flight. Plunges at great speed after prey, which comprises mainly birds. Special-izes in catching migrant birds and breeding timed to coincide with autumn migration in August and September. In spring, often seen feeding at dusk over coastal marshes around Mediterranean, catching dragonflies.
Voice Call a rasping *kyee-kyee-kyee*.
Habitat Mediterranean sea cliffs and small rocky islands.

Distribution Breeds very locally throughout Mediterranean. Most winter in Madagascar but a few remain in E Mediterranean.
Occurrence Present within breeding range from late April to October. Relatively easy to see on Majorca's Formentor peninsula.

Merlin
Falco columbarius L 25–30cm W 60–65cm
Europe's smallest raptor, male smaller than fe-male. Male has blue-grey upperparts with under-parts washed with orange-brown and streaked. Female has dark-brown upperparts and pale underparts streaked and marked with reddish-brown. In flight, has broad-based but pointed wings and relatively long tail. Seen flying low over ground chasing small birds which it pursues vigorously.
Voice Alarm call a rapid *kee-kee-kee*.
Habitat Breeds on moorland and open upland country. Nests in old Crows' nests or sometimes on the ground. Winters on lowland heaths and in coastal areas.
Distribution Breeds in N Europe from Scandi-navia eastwards at similar latitudes. Also in Ice-land, Ireland and N Britain. Winters in much of central and S Europe including S Britain.
Occurrence Rather scarce breeding species, especially in Britain. Regular but scarce winter visitor to many estuaries in S Britain.

R	1–12	N 4–7

Eleanora's Falcon,
pale phase   dark phase

Hobby

Merlin, male (right)

Hobby

Merlin, female

Red-footed Falcon

Falco vespertinus L 28–33cm W 65–70cm

Adult male slate-grey with pale flight feathers and red legs, 'trousers' and undertail coverts. Base of bill and eye-ring also red. Female is grey on back with buffish-orange underparts which are largely unmarked. Head also buffish-orange with dark patch through eye and limited moustachial stripe. Juvenile similar to female but has brown back, the feathers with buff margins, pale underparts which are heavily streaked and a pale forehead. Flight behaviour with elements of Kestrel and Hobby. Regularly hovers but also catches dragonflies in low-level flight using talons. Sometimes feeds in flocks at dusk. Perches on posts and telegraph wires.

Voice Mostly silent when solitary. Hobby-like calls in flocks.

Habitat Open terrain including heaths, farmland and steppe, with scattered clumps of trees. Nests colonially, generally in Rook's nest.

Distribution Breeding range from SE Europe eastwards. Winters in Africa.

Occurrence Locally common in breeding range from May to September. Rare but regular overshooting spring visitor to W Europe, including Britain.

V	5–9	—

Kestrel

Falco tinnunculus L 33–36cm W 70–75cm

Europe's most common and widespread falcon. Male has reddish-brown back with dark spots, pale underparts, grey head with dark moustachial stripe, and grey tail with a dark terminal band. In flight, looks pale from beneath except for buffish wash on breast and dark tail band. From above, reddish-brown mantle and wing coverts contrast with dark flight feathers. Female and juvenile are brown and heavily marked with barred tail. A familiar roadside bird, often seen hovering or perched on road signs or posts. Feeds on small mammals, especially voles, and insects.

Voice Call near nest is shrill *keekeekeekeekee*.

Habitat Found in a wide variety of open country. In Britain, commonly seen on grassy motorway and roadside verges. Nests in tree holes and Crows' nests but also on man-made structures e.g. wide office-block window ledges.

Distribution Found throughout Europe including most of Scandinavia but not in Iceland.

Occurrence Common resident and general easy to see.

R	1–12	N 4–7

Lesser Kestrel

Falco naumanni L 28–32cm W 60–70cm

Similar to Kestrel but slightly smaller and with proportionately shorter tail. Adult male differs in having unmarked reddish-brown back and lesser wing coverts with blue-grey greater wing coverts, most noticeable in flight. No moustachial stripe and underwing paler and less marked than male Kestrel. Female very similar to Kestrel. Distinguished by shorter tail and, at close range, white claws, not black as in Kestrel. Nests colonially and generally gregarious, flocks often hunting insects in flight. Hovers less frequently than Kestrel.

Voice Call a chattering *keekeekee*.

Habitat Feeds in open country and nests on cliffs and buildings such as churches.

Distribution Breeding range includes central and S Iberian peninsula, and locally in S France and S Italy to SE Europe. Winters in Africa.

Occurrence Present within range from April to September. Locally common in Spain but generally scarce elsewhere.

American Kestrel

Falco sparverius L 27cm W 58cm

Adult male is boldy marked with reddish-brown tail and back, blue-grey wing coverts, white cheeks with 2 black, vertical stripes and a blue-grey crown with a central reddish-brown spot and black spot on nape. Female similar to female Kestrel but has white cheek with 2 black, vertical stripes and a reddish-brown crown. Perches on telegraph wires and hovers.

Voice Generally silent but alarm call *kyee-kyee-kyee*.

Habitat Open country.

Distribution Widespread in N America.

Occurrence Very rare vagrant to W Europe including Britain.

V	—	—

d-footed Falcon, immature
ale

Kestrel, female

Kestrel, male

Kestrel, male

esser Kestrel, male

American Kestrel, male

GAMEBIRDS
ORDER GALLIFORMES

Mainly ground-dwelling with powerful feet and stubby bills. Can run fast. Flight brief, usually with bursts of rapid wingbeats interspersed with long glides. Sexes dissimilar. Males often perform ritualized courtship displays.

Willow Grouse
Lagopus lagopus L 40cm W 55cm
Plumage variable and changes throughout year. Spring male is white below with chestnut-brown head, neck and upper breast. Reddish-brown more extensive on back and breast in summer but wings and belly always white. Summer female has orange-brown plumage with white on wings. In winter, both sexes are all white except for black tail but male retains red wattle over eye. Fast and low flight comprises bursts of rapid wingbeats interspersed with long glides on bowed wings. Feeds on buds, shoots, berries and insects.
Voice Best known call *goback-goback-goback* but also gives a strange laughing call. Female's call a quiet *vek*.
Habitat Moorland and upland regions, usually associated with willow and birch scrub.
Distribution Scandinavia and similar latitudes eastwards.
Occurrence Generally common resident in suitable habitats within range.

Red Grouse
Lagopus lagopus scoticus L 40cm W 60cm
British and Irish equivalent of Willow Grouse. Male has chestnut-brown plumage throughout the year with dark wings and a conspicuous red wattle above eye. Female is similar but plumage is paler buff and more mottled in appearance. Behaviour and appearance in flight same as Willow Grouse.
Voice Same as Willow Grouse.
Habitat Invariably associated with heather moorland where habitat maintained to encourage birds for shooting. Nests inconspicuously amongst heather. Seen in flocks in winter.

Distribution Found only in Britain and Ireland but distribution dictated by habitat preference. In Britain, found on heather moorland from Peak District northwards. Also in Wales and isolated populations on Dartmoor and Exmoor.
Occurrence Generally common in suitable habitats. Typical *goback-goback-goback* call often heard and carries well. Often seen by hill walkers but can also be seen from moorland roads of North York Moors National Park, central Scotland and other suitable areas.

R	1–12	N 4–6

Ptarmigan
Lagopus mutus L 35cm W 55cm
Similar to Willow Grouse at some times of the year. Plumage changes throughout year, providing camouflage among lichen-covered ground or snowfields. In winter, both sexes are pure white except for black tail. Male, however, has black loral stripe. In spring, male acquires mottled dark grey on head and neck, becoming more extensively greyish-brown as summer progresses. Wings and underparts remain white. In all seasons, except winter, plumage is distinctly greyer and more lichen-like than Willow Grouse. Female in summer has greyish-buff plumage with irregular dark markings, affording it excellent camouflage when on nest. White wings most noticeable in flight. Generally rather tame and seen creeping unobtrusively among boulders. Flies at speed downhill when disturbed, when white wings attract attention.
Voice Male has rattling call *kurr-kurr-kurr*.
Habitat Upland and northern habitats above the treeline. Usually on lichen-covered ground strewn with boulders and with comparatively little vegetation.
Distribution Found from N Scandinavia eastwards, Iceland, the Alps and Pyrenees and in N Scotland.
Occurrence Fairly common resident in suitable habitats but numbers vary from year to year. In Britain, usually comparatively easy to see in Cairngorm Mountains.

R	1–12	N 5–7

Willow Grouse

Red Grouse, female
Red Grouse, male

Ptarmigan, female
Ptarmigan, male summer

Ptarmigan, incomplete
winter plumage (below)

Capercaillie

Tetrao urogallus L male 85cm female 65cm
W male 120cm female 90cm

Largest gamebird in the region, male considerably bigger than female. Male identified by huge size and plumage appearing generally dark. Long tail is fanned out during courtship display. Female has mottled brown plumage with orange-brown patch on breast. When disturbed on forest floor, bursts noisily into flight. Wings held stiffly during flight comprising rapid wingbeats interspersed with glides. Sometimes lands in trees. Despite size, can be rather difficult to locate. Tell-tale signs of presence include dust baths on paths and piles of cylindrical droppings. Males hold courtship display around dawn from March to May. Feeds mainly on pine needles but also on shoots and berries. Occasionally seen collecting grit for digestion from roadside.
Voice Typical dawn display call by male comprises clicking sounds ending in cork-popping and saw-whetting sounds.
Habitat Mature pine forests.
Distribution Found throughout Scandinavia and at similar latitudes eastwards. Also in forests on central European mountains and in N Spain. Re-established in Scotland.
Occurrence Resident and generally rather local. In Britain, stronghold is Cairngorms area but by no means easy to see there.

R	1–12	N 4–6

Black Grouse

Tetrao tetrix L male 55cm female 40cm
W male 80cm female 65cm

Male has mostly dark plumage with long, lyre-shaped tail seen in flight or display. Prominent white wing bars and white under tail. Prominent red wattle above eye. Female is mottled greyish-brown and shows thin white wing bar in flight. Males have dawn display at traditional leks where they adopt crouched posture with tail and under-tail raised and fanned. Males face each other and sometimes jump into the air or fight. After dawn

display males disperse but may continue display from tree top. Feeds on buds, shoots and berries.
Voice Display call mostly cooing sounds with occasional loud hissing *shoo-eesh*.
Habitat Coniferous or mixed woodland with large clearings or adjacent moorland.
Distribution Widespread in N Europe and upland areas of central Europe. In Britain, from mid-Wales and central England northwards.
Occurrence Resident species. Widespread but nowhere common and declining in Britain.

R	1–12	N 4–6

Hazelhen

Bonasa bonasia L 35cm W 50cm

Plumage of male is an intricate pattern of bluish-grey, brown, black and white. Conspicuous black throat bordered with white and slight tuft on crown. Female similar but colours and markings less bold. In flight, lower back and tail are bluish-grey, the tail with black sub-terminal and white terminal bands. Perches in trees when flushed Unobtrusive but not shy.
Voice High-pitched whistle, like a Goldcrest.
Habitat Typical habitat is dense, mixed forest, often close to stream or damp gully. Also found in other types of forest.
Distribution Mainly in E and N Europe from Scandinavia eastwards, but also more locally in upland forests in central Europe.
Occurrence A local resident species, rather scarce in much of its range.

Hazelhen

Capercaillie, female

Capercaillie, male

Black Grouse, female

Black Grouse, male

Red-legged Partridge
Alectoris rufa L 33cm
Boldly marked, dumpy gamebird. Conspicuous white throat with broad black border extending to black patches and spots on lower margin. Back greyish-brown and has vertical black stripes on flanks and bright-red bill and legs. Sexes similar. Orange-red tail visible in flight which is low, with long glides. Generally prefers to run from danger. Perches on posts and fences.
Voice Call a repeated *kerchekchek kerchekchek*.
Habitat Arable farmland and other open country.
Distribution Widespread in W Europe from Iberian peninsula north to Britain where commonest in the south.
Occurrence Generally common resident although numbers affected by changes in farming practices in some areas.

R	I–12	N 4–7

Rock Partridge
Alectoris graeca L 33cm
Similar to Red-legged Partridge but pure white throat border edged by narrow black border lacking spots. Lower edge of black is distinct and does not spread into patches and spots. Black stripe through eye continues down base of bill to lower mandible. Sexes similar. Behaviour similar to Red-legged Partridge.
Voice Call a repeated *cher-tsivitt-chee*.
Habitat Hills and mountain slopes.
Distribution S Europe from S France east to N Greece. Also in S Italy.
Occurrence Scarce resident within range.

Chukar
Alectoris chukar L 33cm
Very similar to Rock Partridge from which distinguished by creamy throat and black stripe through eye not extending down base of bill. Behaviour similar to Red-legged Partridge.
Voice Call a loud *chuk chuk chukar*.
Habitat Hill and mountain slopes.
Distribution Normal range from Turkey eastwards but also just into SE Europe. Range extended by man.
Occurrence Locally common resident. Also seen in W Europe in areas where gamebirds released for shooting.

Barbary Partridge
Alectoris barbara L 33cm
Body markings similar to Red-legged Partridge. Blue-grey throat bordered by chestnut band speckled with white on lower throat. Crown and nape brown and buff stripe through eye. Rather secretive.
Voice Call a repeated *kechek kechek*.
Habitat Dry, Mediterranean-type habitat both cultivated and semi-natural.
Distribution Widespread along N African coast but also on Corsica and Gibraltar.
Occurrence Locally common resident.

Chukar   Rock   Barbary
            Partridge   Partridge

Grey Partridge
Perdix perdix L 30cm
Delicately marked with intricate, grey vermiculations on underparts, brownish upperparts and vertical, chestnut bars on flanks. Orange-red on face extending to supercilium in male. Supercilium is buffish-grey in female. Dark-brown patch on belly, considerably larger in male than female. Seen in coveys for most of year although pairs in spring. Generally crouches or runs from any danger but when disturbed, whole covey takes to the wing together. Feeds on seeds, leaves and insects.
Voice A creaking *kierr-ik kierr-ik*.
Habitat Open, arable farmland.
Distribution Widespread in most of mainland Europe. Only in north of Iberian peninsula and in south of Scandinavia. Widespread in Britain and Ireland.
Occurrence Generally common resident, although has declined in some areas owing to changes in agricultural practices. Most successful where traditional farming methods and mature hedgerows exist.

R	I–12	N 4–7

Red-legged Partridge

Grey Partridge, male

Grey Partridge, female

Black Francolin

Francolinus francolinus L 34cm

Distinctive male has black underparts with white spots, chestnut collar and black face with white cheeks. Female is greyish-brown with scaly appearance and chestnut patch on nape. In flight, both sexes show dark outer tail feathers and brown wings. Retiring and can be difficult to see. Best located first of all by loud call.

Voice Call is high-pitched, rhythmic, 7-syllable *kek-keek-kek-kek-kaa-kek-keek*.

Habitat Areas of low scrub or cultivated land.

Distribution Main range from Turkey south-eastwards. Also on Cyprus.

Occurrence Rather local resident. Difficult to see but presence announced by call.

Quail

Coturnix coturnix L 18cm

Tiny and secretive gamebird, far more often heard than seen. Has brown plumage streaked with paler feathering. Male has black throat and black-bordered white neck band. Female has pale throat and brown facial markings. Seldom leaves the cover of vegetation, preferring to run from danger. If flushed, however, flies low with fast, shallow wingbeats.

Voice Characteristic call *whit, whit-whit*, sometimes written 'wet-my-lips'. Uttered day or night from dense cover.

Habitat Fields of arable crops, grasslands and meadows.

Distribution Breeding range includes most of Europe as far north as Baltic coast. Winters in southern Africa.

Occurrence Present in Europe from May to August. Once common in Britain but now a rare spring visitor, mostly to S England.

S	5–8	N 5–7

Pheasant

Phasianus colchicus L male 85cm
female 65cm

Male unmistakable with chestnut to orange plumage, long tail and large red facial wattle contrasting with blue-green, sheeny head. Presence of white neck ring depends on geographical origin of stock. Female has pale-brown plumage, the feathers with a scaly appearance, and also has a long tail. Explodes noisily into flight when disturbed showing short, rounded wings. Soon drops into cover again. Roosts in trees. Feeds on seeds, grain, and berries. Often comes to food and may become tame.

Voice Displaying male utters loud, 2-note crowing call. This is followed by loud and rapid wing beats, during which the male seems almost to fall over backwards. A soft clucking sound is sometimes heard from feeding birds at close range.

Habitat Wooded farmland, hedgerows and more open country.

Distribution Originally comes from Asia but long introduced and now thoroughly established across most of mainland Europe as far north as S Scandinavia, as well as Britain and Ireland.

Occurrence Common resident bird in most of Europe. Numbers augmented by the annual release of young birds for shooting.

R	1–12	N 4–7

Lady Amherst's Pheasant

Chrysolophus amherstiae L male 95cm
female 65cm

Distinctive male a gaudy mixture of white, green, yellow, blue and red. Long, white tail has distinct barring. Female similar to female pheasant but broad tail has blacker barring.

Voice High-pitched rasping version of Pheasant call.

Habitat Woodland with dense undergrowth.

Distribution Originally from China. Introduced into England.

Occurrence Established locally in S England e.g. around Woburn.

R	1–12	N 5–7

Golden Pheasant

Chrysolophus pictus L male 95cm
female 65cm

Male is mostly orange-red with blue on wings, green and buff on nape and a yellow crown. Female is similar to female pheasant but with more barred appearance on body and tail.

Voice Similar to Lady Amherst's Pheasant.

Habitat Woodland with dense undergrowth and young conifer plantations.

Distribution Originally comes from China. Introduced to Britain.

Occurrence Established in E Anglia and Galloway in Scotland. Escapes from captivity seen elsewhere.

R	1–12	N 5–7

Black Francolin

Quail

Pheasant, female

Pheasant, male

Lady Amherst's Pheasant, male

Golden Pheasant, male

CRANES AND ALLIED BIRDS
ORDER GRUIFORMES

A group of mostly wetland birds comprising cranes, bustards and rails. Cranes (family Gruidae) are large birds with long legs and necks, held outstretched in flight. Migrate and winter in flocks. Bustards (family Otididae) are medium to large birds with thick necks, robust legs and broad wings. Rails, moorhens and coots (family Rallidae) are small with relatively long legs and toes and weak flight. Associated with marshes and swamps.

Andalusian Hemipode
Turnix sylvatica L 16cm
Related to cranes although very similar to Quail. Has orange wash on breast and dark spots on flanks. Very shy and difficult to see or flush.
Voice Song like a distant cow mooing, heard at night.
Habitat Dense ground cover such as grassland with scrub thickets.
Distribution In Europe, restricted to a few sites in Andalusia. Also in N Africa.
Occurrence Now very rare and seldom seen.

Andalusian Hemipode

Crane
Grus grus L 125cm W 220cm
Tall, stately bird with upright stance, bushy tail-end and slow and deliberate gait. Adult plumage mostly grey with mottled brown on back. Long, dark legs with black and white on head and neck and red on nape. Juvenile mostly greyish-brown. Flies with head and neck extended and trailing legs, showing dark flight feathers. Migrates in 'v'

formation or long line. Usually very wary and especially so when breeding. At nest, pairs perform a display dance, often jumping into the air. Feeds on seeds, fruits, insects and even small mammals.
Voice Loud trumpeting calls heard by duetting pairs and also in flight on migration.
Habitat Breeds on extensive bogs and marshes. In winter and on migration, feeds in arable fields and roosts in marshes.
Distribution Breeds NE Europe from Scandinavia and N Poland eastwards at similar latitudes. Winters mainly S Iberian peninsula, N Africa and Turkey.
Occurrence Breeding pairs are widely scattered. Easier to see in numbers in winter, especially in the vicinity of large lakes in central Spain. Good numbers also winter around large lakes in NE France. In Britain, rare migrant mainly early spring and late autumn. A few individuals have stayed for extended periods, and have bred.

V	3–5, 9–11	—

Sandhill Crane *Grus canadensis* is uniform grey with red forecrown as adult and grey mottled with rufous, especially on head and neck, in juvenile. Very rare vagrant to NW Europe, including Britain, from N America.

Demoiselle Crane
Anthropoides virgo L 85cm W 175cm
Similar to Crane but smaller and with uniform grey plumage. Long white ear-tufts and long black breast plumes are characteristic. Very similar to Crane in flight and mixes where ranges overlap. Behaviour generally similar to Crane.
Voice Similar to Crane but higher-pitched.
Habitat Breeds on grassy plateaux and winters on fields and marshes.
Distribution Breeds from E Turkey eastwards. Isolated and threatened populations in N Africa.
Occurrence Very rare in Europe but occasionally seen on migration in E Mediterranean region, especially Cyprus, early spring and late summer.
Siberian Crane *Grus leucogeranus* is pure white with black wingtips and red face in adult. Juvenile is rufous, mottled with white. Very rare vagrant to Europe from Asia.

...ane, on breeding ground

...ane

Demoiselle Crane

Great Bustard

Otis tarda L male 100cm female 80cm
W male 240cm female 180cm

Huge bird, males being the heaviest in Europe at around 17kg. Upright stance and slow, deliberate gait. Male has brown back, white underparts, grey neck and long white 'whiskers'. Female similar but smaller and lacking 'whiskers'. In flight, shows large white wing patches and black primaries and outer secondaries. Usually seen in flocks, especially in winter. Very alert and wary. In spring, male performs spectacular display where throat is inflated, head and neck held over back and tail expanded and raised forward and white undertail feathers fluffed up. Feeds on plant material, insects and small mammals.

Voice Mostly silent.

Habitat Open plains and arable land.

Distribution Local breeding species in Iberian peninsula and E Europe.

Occurrence Has declined markedly owing to changes in agricultural practices. However, still found in reasonable numbers in central Spain and best looked for in winter and early spring. Mostly resident but some movement westward from E Europe during severe winter weather when occasionally reaches SE England.

V	11–3	—

Little Bustard

Tetrax tetrax L 44cm W 95cm

Much smaller than Great Bustard. Male in breeding season has striking black-and-white markings on head and neck but otherwise finely marked brown upperparts and white underparts. In winter, resembles female with mostly brown plumage but white underparts. Very striking in flight with black wingtips but most of wing appearing white. Flight similar to a gamebird with rapid wingbeats. In spring, males display by inflating necks and jumping in the air. Alert and generally rather wary of man. In winter, seen in large flocks. Feeds on plant material, seeds, insects and small animals.

Voice Display call a rasping *prerrr*.

Habitat Open plains and large arable fields.

Distribution Local in W Europe from France to S Iberian peninsula. More so in SE Europe and Sardinia.

Occurrence Population in N France moves south in winter, otherwise resident. Locally common only in SW Europe and easiest to see in central Spain.

V	—	—

Houbara Bustard

Chlamydotis undulata L 65cm W 160cm

Much larger than Little Bustard. Adult has buffish brown upperparts, pale underparts and a greyish neck with conspicuous, shaggy black stripe on side. In flight, shows extensive black trailing edge to wing with white patch on primaries. Wary of man. Feeds on plant material, including seeds and leaves, and insects.

Voice Mostly silent.

Habitat Bird of the steppes, but may be found in agricultural country and semi-deserts near cultivation.

Distribution Asia, N Africa and Canary Isles.

Occurrence Very rare vagrant to Europe. Threatened and difficult to see in most of range, with best opportunities in Canary Isles.

Houbara Bustard

Great Bustard, male

Great Bustards

Little Bustard, male

Little Bustards

Little Bustard, female

Water Rail

Rallus aquaticus L 26cm

A rather retiring bird, heard more often than it is seen. Adult has warm-brown upperparts, blue-grey face, throat and breast and black-and-white stripes on flanks and belly. Undertail coverts white. Bill long and red and legs pinkish. Juvenile similar but colours much duller. Generally rather skulking but occasionally shows itself at edge of reeds. More inclined to feed in the open during severe winter weather when easiest to observe. When disturbed, flies with fluttering wings and dangling legs. Feeds on a range of plant material as well as aquatic invertebrates. Will also take carrion and occasionally tackles and kills injured small birds and mammals.

Voice Most characteristic call a loud and piercing pig-like squeal. Also utters a range of other grunting calls.

Habitat Reedbeds and areas of dense marshy vegetation, often where inundated alders and willows occur.

Distribution Found throughout most of Europe including Britain, Ireland and Iceland. Mostly resident but northern and eastern birds move south and west in autumn, many arriving in Britain.

Occurrence Common in suitable habitats throughout range.

T	1–12	N 5–7

Spotted Crake

Porzana porzana L 23cm

Rather dumpy waterbird with secretive habits similar to Water Rail. Brownish upperparts and greyish underparts. At close range, white spots visible on most of body. Buff undertail coverts, yellow and orange bill and greenish legs. Juvenile similar to adult with spots on head and body, but underparts brown and bill dull. Very difficult to see except sometimes on migration. Feeds on water plants and invertebrates.

Voice Song a rhythmically repeated *whitt whitt whitt*, sung at night. Recalls sound of whiplash or dripping tap.

Habitat Lives in areas of dense, aquatic vegetation in marshes and margins of lakes and rivers.

Distribution Very local across most of Europe as far north as S Scandinavia during summer. Winters in Africa.

Occurrence Rather scarce breeding species in Europe but very rare in Britain and seen more regularly during autumn migration.

M	9–10	—

Sora Rail

Porzana carolina L 23cm

Similar to Spotted Crake but adult has all-yellow bill, black face mask and white undertail coverts. Juvenile lacks face mask and has dull-yellow bill. Crown and breast orange-brown without white spots, face gradually darkens. Habits similar to Spotted Crake.

Voice Mostly silent in region.

Habitat As with Spotted Crake.

Distribution Widespread in N America.

Occurrence Very rare vagrant to W Europe including Britain, mostly in autumn.

V	—	—

Baillon's Crake

Porzana pusilla L 18cm

Resembles miniature, short-beaked Water Rail with brown upperparts, blue-grey face, neck and breast and barred flanks and belly. Irregular white spots on wing coverts, bill stubby and greenish-yellow and legs pinkish. Undertail coverts barred. Juvenile similar but underparts brownish not blue-grey. Usually secretive and retiring. Clambers over aquatic vegetation using long toes. Feeds on small invertebrates.

Voice Song is a frog-like rattle.

Habitat Wetlands of all sorts with dense waterside vegetation and overgrown reedbeds.

Distribution Very local breeding species, mostly in S Europe. Winters mostly in Africa.

Occurrence Scarce in S Europe from April to September. Very rare vagrant to Britain.

V	—	—

Little Crake

Porzana parva L 19cm

Rather similar to Baillon's Crake. Male, however, has red spot at base of bill, less extensive barring on flanks and greenish legs. Female similar but has buffish underparts and white throat. Juvenile similar to juvenile Baillon's Crake but spots arranged regularly in rows. Habits similar to Baillon's Crake.

Voice Male's song is a series of croaking barks, ending in an accelerated trill.

Habitat Same as Baillon's Crake.

Distribution Main breeding range in E and SE Europe but also in S France. Winters mainly in south of region, mostly Africa.

Occurrence Local breeding species, present from April to September. Seen outside breeding range on migration and rare vagrant as far north as Britain.

V	—	—

Spotted Crake

Sora Rail, autumn adult

Water Rail

Baillon's Crake, spring male

Little Crake, winter

Corncrake
Crex crex L 28cm

Heard far more frequently than seen. Partridge-sized bird with mostly chestnut-brown and black plumage and bluish-grey on throat and above eye. Usually extremely difficult to see, even when vegetation is no taller than bird itself. However, persistent scanning of location of calling bird is often rewarded. When moving around, creeps along with body almost horizontal. When calling, male adopts more upright posture. In flight, shows chestnut wings and dangling legs. Feeds on a variety of plant and animal matter.

Voice Call an unmistakable *crek-crek* or *errrp-errrp* repeated for minutes or even hours on end. Heard mostly at night but also more occasionally during daytime.

Habitat Damp hay meadows and marshes. In Outer Hebrides, often associated with large stands of Yellow Iris. Nests on ground and hence vulnerable to destruction if hay meadows rolled or cut early.

Distribution Breeds throughout most of central and N Europe from S France to S Scandinavia. In Britain, confined mainly to NW Scotland including many Scottish islands. Also in Ireland. Winters in Africa.

Occurrence Present in Europe from April to September. Conrcrakes have suffered greatly in Europe from mechanization in farming and have declined markedly this century. Once widespread and common in Britain, their range is now extremely restricted and even within it they are scarce. Best opportunities for observation in Britain are in Outer Hebrides, notably at RSPB's Balranald reserve on North Uist.

S	5–9	N 5–7

Purple Gallinule
Porphyrio porphyrio L 47cm

Unmistakable chicken-sized bird with glossy blue-purple plumage, long red legs and feet and a massive red bill. Undertail coverts white, best seen when tail is nervously flicked. Juvenile is greyish-brown with dull bill and leg colour. Bill size still massive. In flight, shows trailing legs. Mostly keeps to cover of dense vegetation but occasionally ventures out. Feeds on a variety of plant material including Reedmace pith.

Voice Calls a variety of clucking and hooting sounds.

Habitat Marshes and reedbeds.

Distribution Very local in Europe and restricted to S Iberian peninsula, Sardinia and S Turkey.

Occurrence Resident species but local and scarce. Can be seen at Coto Doñana National Park in Spain.

American Purple Gallinule
Porphyrula martinica L 35cm

Size and shape of Moorhen but with glossy blue-purple plumage and glossy-green back. Bill red tipped with yellow and with pale-blue frontal shield. Long, yellow legs and feet and all-white undertail coverts. Juvenile has greyish-brown plumage and dull-coloured bill. Swims and dives well and walks with tail-flicking action.

Voice Coarse, Moorhen-like calls.

Habitat Wetlands.

Distribution South-eastern states of USA

Occurrence Very rare vagrant to W Europe including Britain.

V	—	—

Moorhen
Gallinula chloropus L 33cm

Adult is distinctive with mostly sooty-black plumage, brown back, yellow-tipped red bill extending to frontal shield and undertail coverts white with black central line. White stripe visible along flanks and legs greenish-yellow. Juvenile mostly brownish but shares adult's undertail markings and white stripe on flank. Swims and walks with tail characteristically flicked or jerked and neck lowered. Feeds on a range of plant and animal matter.

Voice Calls a variety of croaking, grunting sounds, mainly *kurr-ekk*.

Habitat All sorts of freshwater habitats, even town ponds. Builds quite large nest among emergent vegetation.

Distribution Found throughout most of Europe as far north as S Scandinavia. Not in Iceland. Widespread in Britain and Ireland.

Occurrence Common and widespread resident.

R	1–12	N 3–8

Purple Gallinule, display

American Purple Gallinule

Corncrake

Moorhen, adult

Moorhen, juvenile

Coot
Fulica atra L 38cm

Easily identified with sooty-black plumage and white bill and frontal shield. Juvenile is greyish with pale markings on face and throat. Has typical Coot profile and lacks white undertail of juvenile Moorhen. Swims and dives well for water plants and small aquatic invertebrates. Also seen grazing in fields. Gait rather deliberate because of huge, lobed toes. Young chicks have almost featherless heads with reddish-blue, bruised appearance. Very aggressive and territorial in spring but often seen in large flocks in autumn and winter. In flight, legs trail behind and shows white trailing edge to secondaries. Take off from water's surface involves extended running along surface. Often becomes rather tame on urban lakes and where fed.

Voice Typical calls include a loud *kowk kowk* and a high-pitched *pitts*.

Habitat All sorts of freshwater habitats with abundant growth of aquatic vegetation. Builds often huge platform nest of water plants.

Distribution Occurs throughout most of Europe as far north as S Scandinavia.

Occurrence Common resident in much of W Europe including Britain and Ireland, winter population being boosted by birds from E Europe.

R	1–12	N 4–7

Crested Coot
Fulica cristata L 40cm

Similar to Coot and mixes freely where ranges overlap. Has sooty-black plumage and white bill and frontal shield like Coot. In breeding season, however, has two conspicuous red knobs on forehead. These are much duller and reduced in size at other times of year. Shape of bill base and frontal shield differ from Coot. A smooth, curved edge runs from the gape around the frontal shield in Crested Coot, making the two seem smoothly continuous. In Coot, dark feathering creates a sharp angle between the upper mandible and the frontal shield. In flight, shows all-dark wings. Behaviour similar to Coot but generally rather shy.

Voice Calls rather Coot-like.

Habitat Freshwater lakes with reedbeds and good growths of aquatic vegetation.

Distribution Small populations in S Spain and N Morocco. Main range is E and S Africa.

Occurrence Rare and extremely local resident. Can be seen at Coto Doñana National Park in Spain.

American Coot
Fulica americana L 40cm

Similar to Coot with sooty-black plumage. White bill has dark band near tip, like Pied-billed Grebe, and white frontal shield has reddish-brown patch on forehead. Undertail coverts white with dark central band. Juvenile similar to adult but markings and colours of bill and frontal shield are dull. Beware rare hybrids between Moorhen and Coot. Behaviour and habits similar to Coot.

Voice Similar to Coot.

Habitat Same as Coot.

Distribution Central and S USA.

Occurrence Very rare vagrant to W Europe, recorded in Iceland and Ireland.

Coot

Coot, and young

Crested Coot

American Coot

WADERS OR SHOREBIRDS PART OF ORDER CHARADRIIFORMES

A large and diverse group of birds, most of which are associated with water at some point in their lives. Except for pratincoles and some of the plovers, most are long-legged and many have long or specialized bills for probing deep into mud, sand or soil for their invertebrate food. Almost all are ground-nesting species, and many form large, or sometimes enormous flocks, on the coast outside the breeding season, hence the alternative name for the group. In the region, the waders are represented by six families.

Family Haematopodidae
This family includes the Oystercatcher, which is a striking black-and-white bird with a stout bill for feeding on intertidal animals of the rocky shore, such as mussels.

Family Charadriidae
This includes the plovers: relatively dumpy waders with short bills and rather long, pointed wings.

Family Scolopacidae
Most of the typical waders of the region are included in this family. Sandpipers and stints are characteristic. They have excellent powers of flight, and many migrate long distances between their summer breeding grounds and their wintering range.

Family Recurvirostridae
Stilts and avocets, distinctive and atypical of the group as a whole, are found in this family. Legs and bills are long in both, the bill being upturned in the case of avocets.

Family Burhinidae
Comprises stone-curlews of which only one species is found in Europe. Partly nocturnal in habits, they have large eyes and are rather secretive and difficult to see.

Family Glareolidae
This family includes both the pratincoles – swallow-like waders that feed partly on the wing – and coursers, of which one species is found rarely in Europe.

A flock of Knot flying in tight formation.

Oystercatcher
Haematopus ostralegus L 44cm

Unmistakable with black upperparts, neck and head and white underparts. Striking orange-red bill and eye and pink legs. Juveniles and winter plumage adult have white collar on throat. In flight, shows black wings with conspicuous white wing bar. Tail white with black tip. Nestlings are mottled grey-brown and show superb camouflage on lichen-covered rocks. Extremely noisy birds and will persistently mob intruders near nest. Displaying males seen running in groups with neck and head held forward and bill open and pointing downwards. Coastal Oystercatchers feed on marine invertebrates such as mussels. Inland birds feed on earthworms and freshwater invertebrates.
Voice Call a loud *kabeek, kabeek*. Alarm call a shrill *bik, bik*.
Habitat Seashore and, mainly in N Britain and S Scandinavia, inland beside lakes and rivers. Nests in scrape on ground.
Distribution Widespread breeding species around coasts of N Europe including Britain, Ireland and Iceland. Excluded from many suitable nesting areas, especially S England, by human disturbance. Winters along coasts of W Europe and more locally in Mediterranean.
Occurrence Common within range. In Britain, can be seen on most stretches of rocky coast in W and N during breeding season and, in winter, on estuaries everywhere.

T	1–12	N 4–7

Spur-winged Plover
Holopterus spinosus L 28cm

A striking bird with sandy-brown back, white neck and black cap, throat stripe and underparts. Legs long and dark. In flight, shows white underwing coverts with black flight feathers and sandy-brown upperwing coverts separated from black flight feathers by white band. Juvenile similar to adult but pale-edged feathers on back give scaly appearance. Feeds on small animals picked from surface of soil or mud.
Voice Alarm call a shrill and repeated *chip*.
Habitat Marshes, lake margins and, occasionally, ploughed fields.
Distribution Breeds in N Greece and Turkey. Winters in Africa where also a common resident.
Occurrence Very local breeding species in SE Europe where a recent colonist. Very rare vagrant elsewhere in Europe.

Lapwing
Vanellus vanellus L 30cm

Characteristic pied plumage with conspicuous thin crest. At close range, dark feathers on back have green, blue or purple sheen. Female has duller plumage and shorter crest than male and has pale feathers around base of bill and on throat. Adult in winter has white chin and throat and buff margins to covert feathers. Juvenile has very short crest, buff margins to most upperpart feathers, and white throat. In flight, all ages show extremely rounded wings with white underwing coverts and black flight feathers except for white windows on primaries. Very aerobatic display flight, male sometimes appearing to loop-the-loop, accompanied by humming sound from wings. Readily mobs and dive-bombs intruders near nest site. When feeding, characteristically runs a short distance, leans forward to pick up a small animal from soil surface, and then stands upright and motionless for a few seconds.
Voice Alarm call an almost choking *peeoo-wit*.
Habitat Meadows, marshes, arable fields and moorland. In winter, can also be found around coast.
Distribution Breeds throughout most of Europe, N Scandinavia and Mediterranean coast. In winter, northern birds move south and are then found throughout central and S Europe.
Occurrence A common bird and in Britain very much a farmland species.

T	1–12	N 3–7

Sociable Plover
Chettusia gregaria L 30cm

In breeding plumage, has grey-brown plumage, black and chestnut on belly and black stripe through eye, white supercilium and black cap. In winter, belly becomes pale. Juvenile is buffish-brown with scaly upperparts, streaked breast and pale-buff supercilium with dark crown. In flight, all ages show upperwing markings similar to juvenile Sabine's Gull with white secondaries, black primaries and brown upperwing coverts. Tail white with black subterminal band. Legs long and dark.
Voice Alarm call a sharp *chek*.
Habitat Steppes, fields and marshes.
Distribution Breeds in central Asia and winters further south.
Occurrence Rare vagrant to Europe including Britain. Usually mixes with Lapwing flocks.

V	—	—

Oystercatcher, winter   **Lapwing**   **Spur-winged Plover**

Oystercatcher

Lapwing, winter   **Sociable Plover**

White-tailed Plover
Chettusia leucura L 28cm

Adult has buffish-brown plumage merging to greyish on the breast and white on belly. Extremely long, yellow legs. In flight, upperparts superficially similar to Sociable Plover but tail all-white and white on wings more extensive on forewing. Juvenile similar but has more scaly brown feathers on upperparts.

Voice Recalls Lapwing but more subdued.

Habitat Marshes and lake margins.

Distribution Breeds central Asia and winters further south.

Occurrence Very rare vagrant to Europe.

V	—	—

Caspian Plover
Charadrius asiaticus L 20cm

Long legs and long wings. In summer plumage, male is distinctive with broad, reddish breast band with narrow black lower border. Face largely white except for sandy-brown crown and nape and stripe behind eye. Upperparts sandy-brown and underparts white. Summer female similar to male but reddish breast band almost entirely replaced by brown. Juvenile similar to female but back appears scaly. In winter, retains grey-brown breast band. In flight, shows uniformly brown tail, grey underwings and faint wing bar.

Voice Call a sharp *quip*.

Habitat Nests on steppes and plains but in Europe seen on short turf.

Distribution Breeds in central Asia and winters in E Africa.

Occurrence Very rare vagrant to Europe, mainly in the spring, and has been recorded in Britain.

V	—	—

Greater Sand Plover
Charadrius leschenaultii L 23cm

Rather long, dull olive legs and, by plover standards, a long, heavy bill. Head looks disproportionately large. In all plumages upperparts mostly sandy-brown and underparts white. In summer, male has broad, reddish chest band which extends around white throat and black eye stripe to forecrown. Female plumage a much duller version of male. In winter, plumage sandy-brown and

white, with chest band broadest on side, often appearing incomplete and recalling Kentish Plover. Juvenile similar to winter adult but has scaly upperparts. In flight, all ages show conspicuous white wing bar and white underwings.

Voice Call *prrup*.

Habitat During breeding season, on plains and steppe. On migration and in winter, on estuaries and mudflats.

Distribution Breeds from Turkey eastwards into Asia. Winters in Africa.

Occurrence Rare visitor to Europe including Britain. Rare but regular spring migrant on Cyprus.

V	—	—

Lesser Sand Plover
Charadrius mongolus L 20cm

Similar to Greater Sand Plover but smaller, with shorter, dark legs and shorter, smaller bill. In summer, male similar to Greater Sand Plover but white throat edge with thin, black line. Female is a duller version of the male. In winter, very similar to Greater Sand Plover with breast band often incomplete. Best told by smaller bill size and shorter legs. Recalls also winter Kentish Plover. Juvenile similar to winter plumage but with scaly upperparts.

Voice Call *kirrit*.

Habitat Similar to Greater Sand Plover.

Distribution Breeds in Asia and winters in Africa, the Far East and Australia.

Occurrence Very rare vagrant to Europe.

Killdeer
Charadrius vociferus L 25cm

Like a larger, longer Ringed Plover with two conspicuous black bands on white breast. Black and white markings on face and pale buff supercilium. In flight, shows white underwing, white wing bar and reddish-brown rump and tail.

Voice Call a loud *kill-dee*.

Habitat Fields and short turf.

Distribution Widespread in N America.

Occurrence Rare and irregular autumn and late-winter vagrant to W Europe including Britain.

V	—	—

White-tailed Plover

Greater Sand Plover

Caspian Plover

Lesser Sand Plover

Killdeer

Ringed Plover
Charadrius hiaticula L 19cm

Dumpy little wader with stubby bill. Upperparts buffish-brown and underparts white. Characteristic black and white markings on head with black collar (less extensive on female than male) and black on forehead and through eye. In summer, legs and base of bill bright orange. In winter, legs dull, bill dark and dark head-markings less striking. Juvenile has pale feather margins giving scaly appearance, dark bill, dull orange legs and white above and behind eye. In flight, all ages show rather long wings with conspicuous white wingbar. Feeds on small invertebrates picked from surface. Characteristically runs fast on whirring legs, then stops still and bends forward to feed. Seldom seen in large flocks and often mixes with other small waders, e.g. Dunlin. Stiff-winged display flight in spring is rather bat-like.

Voice Call is a muted, di-syllabic *too-ip*.

Habitat Mainly coastal, favouring sandy and shingle beaches for nesting and beaches and estuaries for feeding. Less frequently on similar freshwater habitats.

Distribution Breeds around coast of NW Europe from Brittany northwards. Northern breeders move south in winter, range extending to Mediterranean coasts.

Occurrence Common breeding species in NW Europe in areas where not excluded by human disturbance. Mostly resident in Britain and Ireland with influx of birds from mainland Europe in winter.

T	1–12	N 4–7

Semipalmated Plover
Charadrius semipalmatus L 19cm

Almost identical to Ringed Plover and best distinguished by call. Slight webbing between toes only visible at close range. White above eye usually less extensive than on Ringed Plover in summer and bill is even more stubby.

Voice Call a sharp, upslurred whistle *chu-wit*. A good identification feature if familiar with Ringed Plover's call.

Habitat Same as Ringed Plover.

Distribution Coastal N America.

Occurrence Very rare autumn vagrant to Britain.

V	—	—

Little Ringed Plover
Charadrius dubius L 16cm

Slimmer and less robust than Ringed Plover. Adult has dark bill and conspicuous yellow eyering. Female markings duller than male. Legs dull yellowish. Juvenile has pale-brown, scaly upperparts and washed-out adult markings on head. Best told from juvenile Ringed Plover by slimmer proportions and lack of white above and behind eye. All ages show no wing bar in flight.

Voice Call a loud *pew*. Display call *kree-kree-kree*.

Habitat Nests on shingle and gravel beside broad rivers, lakes and in gravel pits. On passage, seen beside freshwater and on coast.

Distribution Nests locally throughout most of Europe as far north as S Scandinavia. Not in Iceland. In Britain, confined mainly to S England. Winters in Africa.

Occurrence Rather local and generally scarce breeding species, present from April to August. In Britain, more or less restricted to abandoned gravel pits in S England, especially Thames valley. More widespread on migration but always near water.

S	4–8	N 5–7

Kentish Plover
Charadrius alexandrinus L 16cm

Pale-looking plover with dark legs and bill. Summer male has chestnut crown and black on forecrown and through eye. Incomplete black breast band forming shoulder patches. Female has black markings of male replaced by uniform pale brown. Juvenile similar to female but scaly appearance to upperparts. In flight, shows white wing bar. Shows typical small plover gait and feeding behaviour.

Voice Call a sharp *kwip*.

Habitat Sandy shores, lagoons and salt pans.

Distribution Almost entirely coastal, main breeding range covering most of Mediterranean. Occurs much more locally on coasts of W and NW Europe as far as Denmark. Winters mainly in S Mediterranean.

Occurrence Resident in Mediterranean but summer visitor, between April and September, to NW Europe. In Britain, is seen only as a scarce passage migrant, mainly to the S coast of England.

M	4–5, 8–9	—

Ringed Plover, juvenile

Ringed Plover, adult

Semipalmated Plover

Little Ringed Plover, on nest

Kentish Plover, male

Kentish Plover, female

Grey Plover
Pluvialis squatarola L 29cm

A dumpy plover which usually adopts a rather hunch-necked appearance making head look disproportionately large. In summer plumage, has spangled black and white upperparts, black running from the face and neck to the belly and a thick white border to the black. The male is boldly marked, the female having more mottled underparts. In winter, has greyish plumage which is paler underneath. Juvenile is similar to winter adult but has yellowish-buff wash. In flight, shows pale underwing with striking, black axillaries. This feature is most noticeable in winter plumage when underparts are pale. Also shows strong white wing bar and white rump. Usually solitary when seen in winter although sometimes roosts in flocks and migrates in small parties. Feeds in a characteristic plover manner by running rapidly, then standing motionless and finally bending forward to pick food from surface of mud. Feeds on small invertebrate animals.

Voice Characteristic call is a 3-syllable *peeoo-eee*, which often sounds like a human whistle.

Habitat Breeds on high Arctic tundra. In winter, invariably found around coasts, usually on estuaries and mudflats.

Distribution Breeds in Arctic Siberia and N America. Winters around the coasts of NW and W Europe, and the Mediterranean.

Occurrence A common winter visitor to Europe including Britain. Although mostly seen in winter plumage, new arrivals in early autumn and late departing birds in spring occasionally have full summer plumage.

W	9–5	—

Golden Plover
Pluvialis apricaria L 27cm

In all plumages has upperparts spangled with yellow-golden, separating it from Grey Plover. In summer plumage, male has black from face and neck to belly, with a broad white border. Black on breast is much less extensive in southern forms than in northern breeding birds and often more mottled in appearance. Female plumage similar to male but black on face and neck particularly is often mottled with paler feathers and may be absent altogether. In winter plumage, both sexes lose black underparts, all parts having golden-yellow wash except for paler belly, chin and indistinct supercilium. Juvenile similar to winter adult but golden wash more extensive on belly. In flight, all ages show white underwing with tail and rump concolorous with upperparts. The underwing colour is the most clear-cut feature for separating this species from American and Pacific Golden Plovers (see next page). In winter and on migration seen in flocks in fields, often mixing with Lapwings. Sometimes migrates in 'v' formation. At nest, has display flight with slow wingbeats. Feeds on small invertebrate animals picked from surface of soil.

Voice Flight call a melancholy *peeuh*. Display song a mournful and evocative *plerr-eee-err*.

Habitat Nests on moorland, bogs and tundra. Winters mainly on arable land, wet meadows and short-turf fields. More rarely coastal.

Distribution Breeds in Scandinavia and northwards and eastwards but mainly coastal. Also nests in N Britain and Iceland. Winters in S and W Europe as far north as S England and S Ireland. Seen on migration throughout Europe.

T	1–12	N 5–7

Pacific Golden Plover
Pluvialis fulva L 24cm

Very similar to Golden Plover from which told by longer legs, slimmer body and grey underwing seen in flight. Very similar also to American Golden Plover (see next page) from which told in winter and juvenile plumage by more extensive golden wash, especially in juvenile. Usually shows pale supercilium and dark ear patch. Breeding male has black underparts not extending to undertail and bordered white even along flanks. Behaviour and habits as Golden Plover.

Voice Call *chu-wip*, similar to Spotted Redshank.

Habitat Breeds on tundra. In winter, same as Golden Plover.

Distribution Breeds in Arctic Asia and W Alaska. Winters in Far East, Australia and N Pacific Basin.

Occurrence Very rare vagrant to Europe including Britain, generally in summer.

V	—	—

Grey Plover, winter

Grey Plover, summer
Golden Plover, summer

Grey Plover, winter
Golden Plover, winter

American Golden Plover
Pluvialis dominica L 26cm

Very similar to Golden Plover but differs in having less dumpy proportions, longer legs and grey, not white, underwing visible in flight. At rest, wings extend well beyond tail. Winter plumage and juvenile appear more greyish than Golden Plover with reduced golden spangling on mantle and wings. Summer plumage has extensive black underparts extending to undertail coverts. White border confined to face and neck. Behaviour and habits same as Golden Plover.

Voice Call a whistling *kluu-eeh*.

Habitat Breeds on tundra. In winter, as Golden Plover.

Distribution Breeds Arctic N America and winters in S America.

Occurrence Very rare but regular vagrant to W Europe including Britain. Mainly in autumn.

V	—	—

Golden Plover   **American Golden Plover**

Dotterel
Charadrius morinellus L 22cm

Adult is very distinctive with dumpy appearance, greyish-brown plumage, chestnut and black lower breast and belly and white crescent on upper breast. White on face includes prominent supercilium. Legs yellowish and bill dark. Female colouring more intense than male. Juvenile has buffish-brown plumage and scaly appearance on back. Outline of belly patch and crescent on upper breast usually visible. Winter adult resembles juvenile. In flight, shows greyish underwing and no wing bar. Often indifferent to man and appears tame, especially when breeding. Female

courts male and he incubates the eggs. Feeds on insects and other invertebrates picked from surface of ground.

Voice Rather silent but utters a soft *kwip, kwip* call.

Habitat Breeds on lichen- and moss-covered mountain plateaux. On migration and in winter, uses short turf, arable fields and heaths.

Distribution Very local breeding species from Scandinavia and Scotland. Extremely local in a few mountain ranges in SE Europe. Also breeds, strangely, in arable fields at sea-level in Dutch polders. Winters in N Africa.

Occurrence Present on breeding grounds from May to July. Can be seen, in Britain, in Cairngorm Mountains. Small parties ('trips') stop off on spring migration at traditional sites in S Britain, usually during first 2 weeks of May. These are usually bare fields or short turf sites, usually elevated above surrounding countryside.

S	5–9	N 5–7

Turnstone
Arenaria interpres L 23cm

A stocky wader with variegated reddish-brown, black and white plumage, short, red legs and short, triangular bill. Summer male has extensive black on chest and black and white on face. Summer female, winter plumage and juvenile are more subdued. In flight, all ages show variegated pattern. Small parties seen feeding unobtrusively on shoreline, often at edge of waves. Characteristically turns over stones and lifts up seaweed in search of small invertebrates.

Voice Call a loud *kuk*. At close range, feeding birds utter quieter calls to each other.

Habitat Breeds on northern coastal tundra and winters around coasts, mainly rocky shores.

Distribution Breeds around Scandinavian coast and winters on coasts of NW and W Europe.

Occurrence Present on breeding grounds from May to August. Otherwise found on shoreline and seen around British coast from August to April. A few immature birds spend summers on shores in wintering range.

W	8–4	—

American Golden Plover

Dotterel, juvenile

Dotterel, adult

Turnstone, winter   Turnstone, summer

Snipe
Gallinago gallinago L 25cm
Distinctive with very long bill and bold brown, black and white markings on head and body. Chevron markings and barring on underparts not extensive and so belly white. In flight, shows white trailing edge to wing and limited amount of white in outer tail feathers. When flushed, rises almost vertically and then flight pattern rapid and initially zigzag. When alarmed, often crouches. On breeding territory, will stand on guard on fence posts. Male performs aerial display ('drumming') during which he dives steeply, the outer tail feathers being spread to produce a humming sound. Feeds by probing soft mud with long bill in jerky fashion for invertebrates.
Voice Calls *tick-a tick-a* from fence posts and utters sharp *ketch* when flushed.
Habitat Marshes, bogs and muddy lake margins.
Distribution Breeds throughout most of N and central Europe including Britain, Ireland and Iceland. In winter, birds from north of range move south, range extending to S Europe.
Occurrence Common resident in W and central Europe including Britain and Ireland. Numbers boosted in autumn by influx of northern birds. Present in S Europe from October to March.

T	1–12	N 5–7

Great Snipe
Gallinago media L 28cm
Similar to Snipe but slightly larger and more dumpy appearance and relatively shorter bill and legs. Has much more extensive and bolder barring on underparts including belly. In flight, shows much more extensive white on outer tail than Snipe. Wings have thin but distinct white wing bar but lack white trailing edge to wing seen in Snipe. Flight pattern not zigzag but usually straight. More reluctant to flush than Snipe and then often silent. In spring, males gather in groups and display by standing very upright with bill wide open, breast puffed-up, tail splayed and calling. Food and feeding behaviour as Snipe.
Voice Display calls a variety of clicking and buzzing sounds. Sometimes utters subdued *etch-etch* when flushed.
Habitat Breeds on northern bogs and mountain slopes. On drier habitats on migration.
Distribution Breeds locally in NW Scandinavia and from NE Europe eastwards. Winters south and east of Europe.
Occurrence Very local breeding species in Europe. Rare on migration in SE Europe. Very rare vagrant to W Europe including Britain.

V	—	—

Jack Snipe
Lymnocryptes minimus L 18cm
Similar to Snipe but much smaller and with relatively smaller bill. Lacks pale crown stripe of Snipe but shows conspicuous pale stripes on back. Usually very difficult to flush, and sits tight until almost trodden on. On rising, tail looks pointed and head and neck are held extended and upright. Drops back into cover after short distance. Has undulating display flight. Generally rather secretive and seldom seen far from water except occasionally during severe winter weather.
Voice Mostly silent but soft call sometimes heard when flushed. Displaying bird sounds like distant galloping horse.
Habitat Breeds on extensive northern bogs. In winter, on marshes and in wet fields.
Distribution Breeds from Lapland eastward and winters in S, SW and W Europe as far north as Britain and Ireland.
Occurrence Local but reasonably common breeding species. Widespread but never common in wintering range including Britain but probably greatly overlooked.

W	10–3	—

Woodcock
Scolopax rusticola L 36cm
Much larger and dumpier than Snipe with short legs and large eyes. Plumage is a mixture of brown, black and white and provides excellent camouflage against background of fallen leaves on woodland floor. Feeds in damp woodland soils probing for invertebrates. Seldom seen flying but if flushed, zigzags away showing reddish-brown upperparts. In spring and summer, male performs display flight ('roding') at dusk by flying over tree tops with slow wingbeats, bill pointing down and uttering characteristic calls.
Voice Roding calls comprise duck-like grunt followed by a high-pitched squeak.
Habitat Damp woodland, usually broadleaved with open rides. Nests among leaf-litter.
Distribution Resident in most of NW Europe. Breeding birds from N and E Europe move south and west in autumn. Wintering range extends to S and SW Europe.
Occurrence Common but easily overlooked in breeding range throughout year.

T	1–12	N 3–7

ipe

Woodcock

ck Snipe

Great Snipe

Curlew

Numenius arquata L 55cm

Large, long-legged wader with long, downcurved bill. Mottled and streaked greybrown plumage with indistinct eye-stripe and no crown stripe. Plumage similar throughout year although, in spring, has buffish wash. In flight, shows long pointed wings and white wedge on rump. Female larger and longer-billed than male. Probes for worms and other invertebrates with long bill. Sometimes seen in flocks in winter.

Voice Characteristic call a loud *cuur-lee*. Display song a series of fluty whistles, rising in pitch and ending in a bubbling trill.

Habitat Breeds in meadows, moorlands and extensive bogs. Winters on estuaries, coastal fields and meadows.

Distribution Breeds throughout N and NW Europe. Northern and eastern populations move south and west in autumn. Winter range extends throughout S Europe in suitable habitats.

Occurrence Locally common breeding species within range. Widespread and common around coasts of W and NW Europe in winter and easy to see around Britain.

T	1–12	N 4–7

Whimbrel

Numenius phaeopus L 40cm

Similar to Curlew but is noticeably smaller with relatively shorter bill. Plumage grey-brown but with darker eye stripe and dark crown with pale central stripe. In flight looks similar to Curlew but has faster wingbeats.

Voice Characteristic whinnying call comprises a series of sharp whistles, descending in pitch and usually 7 in number. Occasionally gives a Curlew-like call and display call is also Curlew-like.

Habitat Breeds on northern moorland, bogs and tundra. Winters on coasts.

Distribution Breeds from Scandinavia eastwards, in Iceland and, in Britain, on Orkney and Shetland Islands. Winters mainly coast of Africa.

Occurrence Common in north of breeding range. Less so in Orkney and Shetland but still easy to see there from April to August. Rather uncommon coastal migrant in W Europe March–April and September–October.

S	4–10	—

Slender-billed Curlew

Numenius tenuirostris L 40cm

Similar size and shape to Whimbrel but lacks distinct head markings. Best adult distinguishing features are whitish underparts with heart-shaped dots. Underwing paler than Curlew or Whimbrel and white wedge on rump extends further down tail. Bill distinctly tapering.

Voice Call Curlew-like but higher-pitched

Habitat Breeds on steppes and winters on coasts.

Distribution Breeds central Asia. Wintering range formerly included N African coast.

Occurrence Very rare and may be heading for extinction. Rarely seen except very occasional in N Greece on migration or on Moroccan coast in winter.

Little Whimbrel   **Slender-billed Curlew**

Little Whimbrel

Numenius minutus L 34cm

Tiny version of Whimbrel with relatively much smaller bill. Dark eye-stripe, pale buff supercilium and dark crown with buff central stripe. In flight rump is dark and concolorous with upperparts.

Voice Call a quiet, 3-note whistle.

Habitat Breeds on moors and bogs. In winter and on migration on short grassland.

Distribution Breeds locally in N Siberia and winters in Australia.

Occurrence Very rare vagrant to Europe including Britain.

V	—	—

Curlew, calling

Whimbrel

Black-tailed Godwit
Limosa limosa L 40cm

Long, straight bill, long legs and rather slim body. In summer, male has orange-red head and neck. Female is less coloured. In winter, both sexes have greyish plumage. Juvenile has greyish plumage, rather scaly upperparts and sometimes an orange-buff wash to neck and breast. At all ages, best distinguishing feature is white, square-shaped upper tail with broad, black terminal band, best seen in flight along with white wing bar on upperwing and white underwing. On breeding grounds, sometimes stands guard on fence posts. In winter, seen in flocks. Probes for invertebrates with long bill.
Voice A variety of creaking Lapwing-like calls given in display and at nest.
Habitat Nests in wet meadows and marshes. In winter, on estuaries and mudflats.
Distribution Breeds across central Europe but restricted by habitat choice. Also in S England and Iceland. In winter, found on coasts of W, NW and SE Europe.
Occurrence Local breeding species in most of range and rare in Britain. Most easily seen in W Europe, including Britain, as a wintering species from September to March. Estuaries of S England and E Anglia offer best opportunities.

T	1–12	N 5–7

Bar-tailed Godwit
Limosa lapponica L 38cm

Similar to Black-tailed Godwit but dumpier appearance, shorter legs and noticeably upturned bill. In summer, male has orange-red head, neck and underparts while female has buffish wash. In winter, has greyish-brown plumage. Juvenile similar to winter adult but feather markings are rather Curlew-like. In flight, wings lack wing bar and shows white wedge on upper tail extending up back and terminal barring on tail. In winter, plumage in flight recalls Curlew. Seen in flocks outside breeding season.
Voice Variety of creaking calls including *ku-woy*.
Habitat Nests on tundra bogs. Winters on estuaries and coastal mudflats.
Distribution Breeds from N Scandinavia eastwards along Siberian coast. Winters on coasts of W and NW Europe.
Occurrence On breeding grounds from May to August. Seen elsewhere in Europe from September to April and found in suitable habitats around most of British coast.

W	9–4	—

Hudsonian Godwit
Limosa haemastica L 40cm

In all plumages, very similar to Black-tailed Godwit. However, in flight shows smaller area of white on tail, reduced wing bar on upperwing and dark underwing. Habits and behaviour as Black-tailed Godwit.
Voice Mostly silent but occasionaly *tu-wit* call.
Habitat As Black-tailed Godwit.
Distribution Breeds northern N America and winters southern S America.
Occurrence Very rare vagrant to Europe including Britain.

V	—	—

Hudsonian Godwit

Bar-tailed Godwit, summer

Bar-tailed Godwit, winter

Black-tailed Godwit

Hudsonian Godwit

Black-tailed Godwits

Black-tailed Godwit

Common Sandpiper
Actitis hypoleucos L 20cm

Adult brownish upperparts and breast with contrasting white underparts. Barred outer margin to tail and white wing bar seen best in flight. Legs pinkish-olive. Juvenile similar but with barring on mantle. Frequently stands on waterside stones. Body held horizontally with rear of body and tail bobbing regularly up and down. Flight is mostly low over water with rapid wingbeats interspersed with short glides. Wings held bowed downwards.

Voice Call a thin but far-carrying *twee-wee-wee*.
Habitat Found close to upland streams, rivers and stony lake margins. Nests close to water.
Distribution Breeds throughout central and N Europe, including N and W Britain. Winters from Mediterranean coast south to Africa.
Occurrence On nesting grounds from April to July. Common on migration throughout region but always near water. A few stragglers winter around coasts of W and NW Europe.

S	3–10	N 5–7

Spotted Sandpiper
Actitis macularia L 19cm

Similar to Common Sandpiper but with shorter tail and yellowish legs and base to slightly downcurved bill. In summer plumage, has dark spots on underparts. In winter, shows more barring on wing coverts than Common Sandpiper and less on mantle. Juvenile shows strongly barred wing coverts contrasting with plainer mantle and flight feathers.

Voice Similar to Common Sandpiper but thinner.
Habitat Same as Common Sandpiper.
Distribution Breeds in N America and winters in S America.
Occurrence Rare but regular vagrant to W Europe including Britain, mainly in autumn.

V	—	—

Wood Sandpiper
Tringa glareola L 21cm

Small wader of elegant proportions with straight bill and yellowish legs, longer than those of Green or Common Sandpiper. Adult in summer has greyish-brown upperparts, with pale spots, and white underparts. Juvenile is similar but upperparts warmer brown and spotted buff and orange-brown. In flight, shows white rump with barred tip to tail and pale-brown underwings. Generally solitary, seen wading in shallows.

Voice Call *chiff-chiff-chiff*. Yodelling display call.
Habitat Breeds on northern bogs. In winter and on migration, on freshwater marshes.

Distribution Widespread breeding species Scandinavia, and similar latitudes eastwards. Ve rare breeder in N Scotland. Winters in Afric
Occurrence Common in breeding rang Widespread on migration across Europe.

M	4–5, 8–9	—

Green Sandpiper
Tringa ochropus L 23cm

Can be confused with Wood Sandpiper but h shorter, greenish legs and darker upperparts cor trasting with pure white underparts. At clos range, small white spots visible on upperparts ar prominent white supercilium in front of eye. flight, wings look broad and dark and wingbea clipped. Shows conspicuous white rump in fligh with solid dark bands to tip of tail. When feedir or walking, bobs rear end of body and tail. Rathe shy and easily disturbed.

Voice Call *tueet-wit-wit*. Yodelling display ca

| Wood | Green | Solitary |
| Sandpiper | Sandpiper | Sandpiper |

Habitat Breeds in northern forests with bo and marshes. In winter and on migration, found marshes, streams and watercress beds.
Distribution Widespread in NE Europe. Wir ters in S Europe southwards to Africa.
Occurrence Uncommon breeding species i range. In W and S Europe, seen on migration wit many remaining for the winter.

W	10–4	—

Solitary Sandpiper
Tringa solitaria L 21cm

At rest, similar to Green Sandpiper but wings pre ject beyond tail, upperparts with more prominer pale spots and pale eye-ring. In flight, shows dar wings but no white rump. Sides to tail are barre
Voice Call similar to Green Sandpiper bu higher-pitched and softer.
Habitat Same as Green Sandpiper.
Distribution Breeds in N America and winter mainly in S America.
Occurrence Very rare vagrant to W Europ including Britain, mainly in autumn.

V	—	—

Common Sandpiper

Spotted Sandpiper

Green Sandpiper

Wood Sandpiper

Solitary Sandpiper

Redshank
Tringa totanus L 28cm

Medium-sized wader with grey-brown plumage and bright orange-red legs and base to bill. In winter, plumage is largely unspotted while in summer, plumage is variably spotted and streaked. Juvenile has dull base to bill and feathers on back show pale margins. In flight, has broad, white trailing edge to wing and white wedge on lower back and upper tail. Usually very nervous and alert, aptly deserving nickname 'Watchdog of the Marshes'. In winter, seen feeding singly or in small groups but sometimes roosts in large flocks.

Voice Alarm call a loud and persistent *chip chip chip*. Flight call *teu-hu*. Song a yodelling medley of flight calls.

Habitat Breeds on moors and wet meadows. In winter, on coastal marshes and estuaries.

Distribution Widespread breeding species in E and N Europe. Also breeds in coastal W and NW Europe, including Britain and Ireland, and very locally in S Europe. In winter, widespread around coasts of W and S Europe.

Occurrence Locally common breeding species from May to July. Common wintering species in W Europe. In Britain, numbers augmented in winter by visitors from mainland Europe.

T	1–12	N 5–7

Spotted Redshank
Tringa erythropus L 30cm

Similar to Redshank but with longer legs and bill. Bill straight and narrow but with slight downcurve at tip. In summer plumage, unmistakable with sooty-black plumage and dark legs. In winter, looks greyish with faint patterning on back – always paler than Redshank – and has legs orange-red. Juvenile has similar plumage to juvenile Redshank but bill and orange-red legs always appear longer. In flight, shows white wedge on lower back and uniform wings without white trailing edge. Very active feeder, often venturing into deep water.

Voice Call a characteristic, sharp *chuwit*.

Habitat Breeds in northern forests and on tundra. Winters on coastal and freshwater marshes.

Distribution Breeds from N Scandinavia eastwards. Winters mainly in Africa but also locally on coasts of W and S Europe.

Occurrence Rather local breeding species from May to July. Widespread but never common on migration, May and August–September. In Britain, best seen on coastal wetlands in E Anglia and SE England on migration where summer plumage adults appear July onwards. A few birds overwinter on estuaries in S England.

M	4–5, 7–10	—

Greenshank
Tringa nebularia L 32cm

More robust than Redshank with long, olive-yellow legs and long grey bill with slight but distinct upturn. Legs can look bright yellow in some circumstances. In summer plumage, has grey-brown upperparts with irregularly arranged black feathers on mantle, and dark streaks and arrow-head markings on neck and breast. In winter, upperparts more uniform grey-brown and head and neck much paler. At a distance and in strong light, shows strong contrast between white underparts and dark back. Juvenile similar to winter adult but feathers on back have off-white margins. In flight, shows uniform dark wings and white wedge on rump. Feeds actively and deliberately. Mostly solitary in winter.

Voice Call a loud, 3-note whistle *chu chu chu*. Song, given in flight, a loud *tew-wu tew-wu tew-wu*.

Habitat Breeds on bogs and open moors with scattered trees. Winters on coasts but found by freshwater on migration.

Distribution Breeds in N Scandinavia and NE Europe eastwards. Rare breeding species in N Scotland. Winters mainly S Europe to Africa but also increasingly in W Europe.

Occurrence Fairly common in its breeding range from May to July. Seen on migration throughout Europe, April–May and August–September, including Britain and Ireland. Overwinters on many British and Irish estuaries in small numbers.

T	1–12	N 5–7

Redshank, winter

Redshank, summer

Greenshank

Redshank

Spotted Redshank, winter

Spotted Redshank, summer

Willet
Catoptrophorus semipalmatus L 38cm
Large, dumpy wader with grey-brown plumage, paler underneath and mottled during breeding season. Dark bill and blue-grey legs. In flight, shows striking black-and-white pattern on wings.
Voice Call a loud *will-willet*.
Habitat Coastal marshes and estuaries.
Distribution N America.
Occurrence Very rare vagrant to W Europe.

Marsh Sandpiper
Tringa stagnatilis L 23cm
Elegant small wader. Body size similar to Wood Sandpiper but with long, dull-yellowish legs and long, slender bill. White underparts with uniform grey-brown upperparts in winter. In summer, has black markings on mantle feathers, recalling miniature Greenshank, and spots and streaks on breast and flanks. In flight, shows white wedge on rump and lower back with legs projecting beyond tail.
Voice Call a sharp *kew*.
Habitat Breeds beside taiga lakes and rivers. At other times, on freshwater lakes and marshes.
Distribution Breeds from E Europe eastwards. Winters mainly in Africa.
Occurrence In Europe, seen mainly on migration in April–May and August–September. Common in E Mediterranean but rare in W Europe. Rare but regular visitor to Britain, mainly in spring.

V	—	—

Stilt Sandpiper
Micropalama himantopus L 22cm
Size and shape recalls Marsh Sandpiper but long bill has distinctly downcurved tip. Legs long and yellow. In summer, has barred underparts, chestnut ear coverts and lores, and white supercilium. In winter, shows uniform grey-brown upperparts and pale underparts. Juvenile similar to winter adult but has mantle feathers with pale margins. In flight, shows white, square-shaped rump with dark terminal band to tail.
Voice Flight call a trilling whistle.
Habitat Found beside freshwater.
Distribution Breeds northern N America and winters mainly in S America.
Occurrence Very rare vagrant to W Europe.

V	—	—

Terek Sandpiper
Xenus cinereus L 23cm
Size of Common Sandpiper. Has distinctive long, upcurved bill, rather dumpy body, exaggerated by short, yellow legs set rather far back on body. In summer, has upperparts grey-brown with black lines on scapulars and pale underparts. Winter and juvenile birds have less distinct markings. In flight, shows uniform grey-brown upperparts including rump, except for white trailing edge to wing.
Voice Call a trilling whistle.
Habitat Breeds beside northern freshwater lakes and rivers. On migration and in winter, often on coasts.
Distribution Nests in NE Europe and eastwards through Siberia. Winters around coasts of Africa, Asia and Australia.
Occurrence In Europe, seen mainly on migration April–May and August–September. Scarce in E Mediterranean and very rare but regular in W Europe including Britain.

V	—	—

Ruff
Philomachus pugnax L male 30cm
female 24cm
Unusual wader with variable plumage. Legs pinkish-red to yellow and, at all ages, head looks disproportionately small for size of body. Breeding males have ruffs and ear-tufts of variable colour but commonly black, white or chestnut. Mantle and breast variably marked with black feathers. Smaller female ('Reeve') lacks ruff and ear-tuft feathers but shows irregular black markings on upperparts. In non-breeding plumage both sexes have more uniform upperparts and pale underparts. Head and neck sometimes very pale. Juvenile much buffer than non-breeding adult and mantle and wing-covert feathers have pale margins. In flight, shows narrow white wing bar, long wings and dark central stripe to mostly white rump. Breeding males perform elaborate displays at communal lek. Behaviour includes 2 males jumping in the air with wings flapping and then standing motionless in crouching bow with ruff splayed.
Voice Mostly silent.
Habitat Breeds on meadows and marshes. In winter and on migration, beside freshwater.
Distribution Breeding range from coastal Low Countries northwards and eastwards. In Britain, rare breeding species mainly in E England. Winters mostly from Mediterranean region south to Africa but in small numbers in W Europe.
Occurrence Locally common breeding species in mainland Europe. Widespread in Europe, including Britain, on migration March–May and July–September. Small numbers winter in S England.

T	1–12	N 5–7

Willet

Marsh Sandpiper

Stilt Sandpiper

Terek Sandpiper

Reeve (female Ruff)

Ruff

Greater Yellowlegs
Tringa melanoleuca L 34cm

Size and appearance recall Greenshank but with long, yellow legs. Bill long and slightly upturned. Mantle and wing coverts brownish, the feathers with pale spots and scalloped margins, especially prominent in juvenile. Breeding adult has irregular arrangement of black feathers on mantle. In flight, shows square-shaped white rump but lacks Greenshank's white wedge on lower back. Wings lack wing bar. Uses long legs to good effect, often feeding in deep water.
Voice Similar to Greenshank.
Habitat Freshwater and brackish habitats.
Distribution Breeds northern N America and winters mainly S America.
Occurrence Very rare vagrant to W Europe including Britain.

V	—	—

Lesser Yellowlegs
Tringa flavipes L 25cm

Elegant wader, much smaller than Greater Yellowlegs. Recalls long-legged Wood Sandpiper with fine bill. Mantle and wing coverts in juvenile covered with pale spots and scalloped margins. Adult is more uniformly marked on back. In flight, shows square-shaped white rump and trailing legs. Wings lack wing bar.
Voice Call *chew* similar to Redshank.
Habitat Generally found beside freshwater.
Distribution Breeds N America and winters mainly S America.
Occurrence Rare vagrant to W Europe including Britain, mainly in autumn. More regular than Greater Yellowlegs.

V	—	—

Long-billed Dowitcher
Limnodromus scolopaceus L 30cm

Medium-sized, dumpy-looking wader with very long, straight bill and fairly long legs. In breeding plumage, entire underparts orange-red. Upperparts darker, the feathers with pale margins. In winter, has grey-brown plumage with paler underparts. Juvenile plumage largely grey-brown, but mantle feathers with contrasting brown margins. Tertial feathers usually dark with only narrow pale margin. In flight, shows white wedge on lower back, white trailing edge to wing and barred tail, the black bars as wide or wider than the white bars. These markings, together with call, are best

features for separation from Short-billed Dowitcher. Feeds by probing with sewing machine-like action of bill.
Voice Flight call an Oystercatcher-like *keep*
Habitat Found beside freshwater and brackish marshes.
Distribution Breeds mainly W Alaska and Siberia, and winters in southern states of N America.
Occurrence Rare vagrant to W Europe including Britain. Mainly in autumn but occasionally overwinters.

V	—	—

Short-billed Dowitcher
Limnodromus griseus L 29cm

Very similar to Long-billed Dowitcher. Bill length of both species vary and size ranges overlap. In summer, orange-red on underparts does not extend to belly which remains white. In winter greyish-brown very similar to Long-billed species. Juvenile is more uniformly buff-brown than Long-billed and tertials are usually more heavily marked brown. However, these markings vary and best features are call and barring on tail where white bars are at least as wide as black bars. Behaviour similar to Long-billed.
Voice Flight call a Turnstone-like rattle *chu-ru-ru*.
Habitat Same as Long-billed Dowitcher.
Distribution Breeds northern N America and winters mainly Central and northern S America.
Occurrence Although breeding range is close to Europe than Long-billed, it is much rarer in occurrence.

V	—	—

Upland Sandpiper
Bartramia longicauda L 29cm

Redshank-sized wader but recalls female Ruff with long neck, proportionately small head and thin, straight bill. Very long tail extending well beyond wings at rest. Legs yellowish.
Voice Flight call *kwip-wip-wip-wip*.
Habitat Grassland and short turf.
Distribution Breeds N America and winters S America.
Occurrence Very rare vagrant to W Europe including Britain. Mainly seen in autumn, most records from SW England.

V	—	—

Greater Yellowlegs

Lesser Yellowlegs

Short-billed Dowitcher

Upland Sandpiper

Knot
Calidris canutus L 25cm

Rather stocky wader with rather short, straight bill and olive-yellow legs. In summer, face, neck and underparts are orange-red with spots of same colour on mantle. In winter, rather uniform pale grey. Juvenile similar to winter adult but scaly appearance on mantle and wing coverts, the feathers having pale margins with subterminal dark margin. Also breast and flanks suffused buff. In flight, shows white wing bar and pale rump. In winter, seen in flocks in flight and at roost.

Voice Call a short *knut*.

Habitat Breeds on Arctic tundra and winters on estuaries and mudflats.

Distribution Breeds in high Arctic of Canada, Greenland and Siberia. Widespread global non-breeding distribution that includes NW Europe.

Occurrence Locally common winter visitor to coastal NW Europe including most sizeable estuaries around Britain and Ireland. Present from September to April.

W	9–4	—

Purple Sandpiper
Calidris maritima L 21cm

Slightly larger than Dunlin with dumpy appearance, darker plumage, yellow base to bill and yellow legs. In winter, looks mostly uniform dark grey. In summer, acquires brown, black and white markings on mantle and paler neck and face, showing darker ear coverts. In flight, shows white wing bar and dark centre to rump and tail. In winter, usually seen in small flocks on barnacle-encrusted rocks where waves are breaking. Often accompanied by Turnstones.

Voice Call thin *kewit-wit*.

Habitat Breeds on tundra and bare, lichen-rich moorland. In winter, found on rocky shores.

Distribution Breeds N Scandinavia, Iceland and, very rarely, N Scotland. Winters around coasts of NW Europe as far south as Brittany.

Occurrence Present in wintering range from September to April. Rather local around coasts of Britain and Ireland but small flocks widespread especially on W coasts.

W	9–4	—

Sanderling
Calidris alba L 18cm

Slightly larger than Dunlin with shorter, stout bill. In summer plumage, underparts white but head, neck, breast and upperparts variably reddish-brown with darker markings. Some individuals look extremely 'red-necked'. In winter, looks very pale with greyish upperparts and pure white underparts contrasting with black bill and legs, which lack hind toe. Black 'shoulder' patch sometimes visible. Juvenile similar to winter adult but has more strongly marked upperparts and darker patch on side of neck. In flight, all ages show broad, white wing bar. Behaviour is one of the best features for identification. Extremely active and invariably found running along beaches right at waves' edge. Characteristically runs as if propelled by clockwork.

Voice Call a short *krit*.

Habitat Nests on tundra but winters on sandy beaches.

Distribution Breeds high Arctic Canada, Greenland and Siberia. Non-breeding range includes coasts throughout Southern Hemisphere and many parts of Northern Hemisphere including NW and W Europe and E and W Mediterranean.

Occurrence Present in wintering range from August to April with passage birds boosting numbers in spring and autumn. Can be found on most undisturbed sandy beaches around coasts of Britain and Ireland in small flocks during winter months.

W	9–4	—

Knot, juvenile

Knot, summer

Purple Sandpiper

Sanderling, summer

Sanderling, winter

Dunlin
Calidris alpina L 19cm

Adult in summer has brown crown and back and pale underparts with black belly patch and spots on throat. In winter, plumage uniform greyish. Juveniles have pale margins to feathers on mantle and wing coverts and dark spots on flanks. Bill and legs black. Bill is slightly downcurved, particularly towards the tip. Variable body size, bill length and plumage make Dunlin easily confused with other Calidrids. Northern race *alpina* has longer bill and bolder markings than southern race *schinzii*. In flight, shows white wing bar and dark centre to tail. In winter and on passage, seen in flocks feeding actively or flying in tight groups.

Voice Typical call *kreeer*. Display song performed in flight is a medley of descending calls ending in a trill.

Habitat Breeds on grassy moorlands. Winters on estuaries and mudflats. Occasionally on freshwater but mainly coastal.

Distribution Race *schinzii* breeds locally N Britain, Ireland, Iceland and S Scandinavia and race *alpina* breeds further north and east. In winter and on passage, found in almost all suitable areas of coastal Europe from S Scandinavia southwards.

Occurrence Rather local breeding species in Europe from May to July. Numbers boosted on passage and in winter by birds from further north and east, then becoming the commonest wader found on the coast.

T	1–12	N 5–7

Curlew Sandpiper
Calidris ferruginea L 19cm

Superficially similar to Dunlin in size and shape but bill always distinctly and smoothly downcurved. Body often appears plumper than Dunlin with proportionately smaller head and, when feeding, neck can appear longer. Adult in summer is unmistakable with brick-red head, neck and underparts. In spring, red feathers often still have pale fringes and by late summer, adults have begun to acquire grey winter plumage. Winter adult is uniform pale grey-buff with white

underparts. Juvenile has white underparts and buff wash to neck and breast. Grey-brown feathers on mantle and wing coverts have pale-buff margins with inner dark border giving scaly appearance. In flight, all ages show wing bar but also white rump, the best feature for identification when flying among flock of Dunlins. On passage, often mixes with flocks of Dunlins on coast but also seen inland beside freshwater.

Voice Flight call rippling *cheerit*.

Habitat Breeds on northern tundra. In winter and on passage, found on estuaries and shallow margins of freshwater and brackish pools.

Distribution Breeds N Siberia and winters in tropical Africa, SE Asia and Australia.

Occurrence Seen as a passage migrant in Europe. Autumn migration route tends to be more westerly than in spring and so, in W Europe, best seen in August and September. Widespread around coasts of Britain in autumn but never common.

M	5, 9–10	—

Broad-billed Sandpiper
Limicola falcinellus L 17cm

Smaller than Dunlin with long, straight bill with downcurved tip. Facial markings are distinctive, particularly the supercilium which forks in front of eye. In most plumages, upperparts appear rather dark with stripes recalling those of Snipe. In winter, plumage greyish and rather washed-out. In flight, tail markings similar to Dunlin but wing bar less prominent. Stance rather horizontal.

Voice Flight call *chrreep*.

Habitat Breeds on northern bogs. In winter and on passage, mainly seen on estuaries and mudflats.

Distribution Breeds N Scandinavia and winters locally on coasts of Africa, Asia and Australia.

Occurrence Rather scarce and local breeding species in Europe. Generally scarce passage migrant in E Europe and rare passage migrant (mainly spring) in W Europe, including Britain.

V	—	—

Dunlin, summer

Dunlin, moulting to winter

Dunlin, juvenile

Curlew Sandpiper, winter

Curlew Sandpiper, summer
Broad-billed Sandpiper

Little Stint
Calidris minuta L 13cm

Tiny sandpiper with short, black bill and blackish legs. In summer plumage, shows white underparts and reddish-brown tone to head, neck and upperparts. Darkish centre to crown and pale buff 'v' on back. In winter, underparts white and upperparts greyish. Juvenile has white underparts and reddish-brown back with conspicuous white 'v'. The crown has a dark central stripe and a lateral stripe making pale supercilium look forked in front of eye. In flight, all ages show white wing bar and dark centre to rump and tail. Active feeder.

Voice Call a quiet *tik*.

Habitat Breeds on northern tundra. Otherwise on mudflats, estuaries and freshwater margins.

Distribution Breeds from N Scandinavia eastwards. Winters mainly Africa but also locally from Mediterranean region to Indian coast.

Occurrence Breeds from May to July. In Europe, seen mainly on migration in spring and autumn. In W Europe, more regular in autumn.

M	4–5, 9–10	—

Red-necked Stint *Calidris ruficollis* is similar. In summer, has reddish throat and neck. Juvenile very difficult to separate from juvenile Little Stint but usually shows pale, not dark, centres to coverts and tertials. Very rare vagrant to Britain from Siberian breeding grounds.

Temminck's Stint
Calidris temminckii L 13cm

Tiny wader, recalling miniature Common Sandpiper. Short, black bill and dull olive-yellow legs. At all times, adults have greyish-brown plumage, never warm-toned like Little Stint. In summer, shows irregular scattering of black and brown feathers on back. In winter, back has more uniform appearance. Juvenile similar to winter adult but feathers on back have scaly appearance. Unobtrusive on migration.

Voice Flight call a trilling *trrr-rr-rr*.

Habitat Nests beside margins of northern lakes and rivers. In winter and on migration, found on coasts and freshwater marshes.

Distribution Breeds from N Scandinavia eastwards. Small population in N Scotland. Winters in central Africa, India and SE Asia.

Occurrence Breeds from May to July. In Europe, seen mostly on migration in April–May and August–September, numbers having an eastern bias. In Britain, most reliably found on E Anglian coastal wetland reserves in spring.

M	4–5, 9–10	—

Least Sandpiper
Calidris minutilla L 12cm

Smallest *Calidris*, with short, black, slightly downcurved bill and yellowish legs. Pale supercilium, which meets at base of bill and is slightly forked in front of eye, and dark loral stripe. Summer adult shows dark back, dark crown with brown tinge towards rear and distinct ear coverts. In winter, plumage more uniform greyish-brown. Juvenile similar to summer adult but shows more brown on back and sometimes a white 'v'.

Voice Call a sharp *crreep*.

Habitat Estuaries and brackish pools.

Distribution Breeds in N America and winters mainly Central and S America.

Occurrence Very rare vagrant to W Europe.

V	—	—

Long-toed Stint *Calidris subminuta* is very similar but dark crown reaches base of bill unlike Least Sandpiper. Rare vagrant to Britain.

Semipalmated Sandpiper
Calidris pusilla L 15cm

Most easily confused with Little Stint but slightly more stocky. Heavier bill with blob tip and broad base is a good feature for identification. Slightly webbed toes only visible at close range. Adults rather uniform greyish-brown. Juvenile has more brown on back with dark lores and ear coverts. Pale supercilium does not fork as markedly as juvenile Little Stint and back lacks white 'v'.

Voice Flight call *chrrup*.

Habitat Estuaries and freshwater margins.

Distribution Breeds N America and winters mainly northern S America.

Occurrence Rare autumn vagrant to W Europe.

V	—	—

Western Sandpiper
Calidris mauri L 15cm

Similar to Semipalmated Sandpiper and also has slight webbing between toes. Black bill is generally longer than Semipalmated and downcurved at tip. Summer adult shows chestnut on ear coverts, sides of crown and on scapulars, and arrow-head spots on breast. Winter adult has greyish plumage. Juvenile similar to juvenile Semipalmated but has paler face and chestnut fringes to scapulars.

Voice Flight call *cheep*.

Habitat Same as Semipalmated Sandpiper.

Distribution Breeds mainly N Alaska and winters southern USA and Caribbean.

Occurrence Very rare vagrant to W Europe.

V	—	—

Little Stint, winter

Little Stint, summer

Temminck's Stint

Semipalmated Sandpiper

Least Sandpiper

Western Sandpiper

White-rumped Sandpiper
Calidris fuscicollis L 16cm

Dunlin-sized wader with short, straight bill with downcurved tip and long wings, the primaries extending well beyond tertials and tail when at rest. Bill blackish but base of lower mandible usually dull orange-tan. In flight, shows faint wing bar but conspicuous white rump. In summer plumage, shows white supercilium, upperparts grey-brown with scapulars, nape and crown warmer brown. Moulting adult appears irregularly marked with black feathers on back, while in winter plumage more uniform grey-brown. Juvenile similar to breeding adult but has brown on crown and ear coverts, grey nape and upperpart feathers with pale margins.

Voice Call a thin *tseeet*.

Habitat Freshwater and brackish pools and marshes.

Distribution Breeds northern N America and winters southern S America.

Occurrence Rare but regular autumn vagrant to W Europe including Britain.

V	9–10	—

Pectoral Sandpiper
Calidris melanotos L 21cm

Larger than Dunlin with proportionately smaller head and longer neck. Legs yellowish and bill short and slightly downcurved with dull yellow base. Upperparts brownish and streaked breast shows sharp demarcation from white belly. Juveniles have warmer brown upperparts with pale feather margins on back sometimes arranged to form white lines. In flight, shows faint white wing bar and dark centre to tail.

Voice Call *chrruup*.

Habitat Freshwater marshes and pools, and wet fields.

Distribution Breeds northern N America and N Siberia. Winters in southern S America and SE Australia.

Occurrence Rare but regular vagrant to W Europe including Britain, mainly in autumn.

V	9–10	—

Sharp-tailed Sandpiper
Calidris acuminata L 20cm

Similar to Pectoral Sandpiper but lacks clear demarcation between white belly and dark breast. Crown chestnut streaked with black, the capped effect added to by the white supercilium.

In summer, shows arrow-head markings on breast extending along flanks. In winter, plumage mainly grey-brown. Juvenile shows well-marked back and warm buff colour to breast. In flight, similar to Pectoral Sandpiper.

Voice Call *weeeip*.

Habitat Same as Pectoral Sandpiper.

Distribution Breeds NE Siberia and winters in Australia.

Occurrence Very rare vagrant to Europe including Britain.

V	—	—

Baird's Sandpiper
Calidris bairdii L 15cm

Smaller than Dunlin with short, straight bill and long wings, extending well beyond tail when at rest. Legs blackish and relatively short. In all plumages, shows quite well-defined demarcation between streaked breast and white belly. Adult has greyish-brown upperparts, in summer some feathers having dark centres. In autumn the feathers usually show pale margins but this scaly appearance is much more apparent in juveniles. In flight, shows faint wing bar and mostly dark rump and tail.

Voice Call *kruup*.

Habitat Freshwater marshes and pools but also on short turf fields.

Distribution Breeds northern N America and winters in S America.

Occurrence Rare but regular vagrant to Europe including Britain, mainly in autumn.

V	9–10	—

Buff-breasted Sandpiper
Tryngites subruficollis L 19cm

Superficially similar to juvenile Ruff. Short, straight bill, proportionately small head and yellowish legs. Feathers on back have pale margins giving scaly appearance. Streaking on cap but face, neck and breast largely uniform and unmarked buff. Pale surrounding to eye. In flight, shows no wing bar.

Voice Mostly silent, but a soft *greep* if flushed.

Habitat Usually on short grass fields, e.g. airfields or golf courses, on migration.

Distribution Breeds northern N America and winters locally in southern S America.

Occurrence Rare but regular autumn vagrant to W Europe including Britain.

V	9–10	—

White-rumped Sandpiper, autumn

Buff-breasted Sandpiper, autumn

Pectoral Sandpiper, autumn
Baird's Sandpiper

Avocet
Recurvirostra avosetta L 44cm
Unmistakable black-and-white plumage; slender, upturned bill. Legs long, blue-grey with webbed toes. In flight, shows boldly marked black-and-white pattern on wings, fast wingbeats and trailing legs. Feeds by sweeping bill from side to side in shallow water. Usually wades but also swims well.
Voice Call a repeated *klooit-klooit*.
Habitat Nests colonially, usually beside saltpans and lagoons. In winter, on estuaries and lakes.
Distribution Breeds on coasts of S and W Europe as far north as Denmark and including E England. In winter, many birds move south and are found from Iberian peninsula south to Africa. Some stay on coasts of S England and NW France.
Occurrence Local breeding species in Europe from March to August. In Britain, breeds on many coastal wetland reserves in E Anglia. In winter, seen on estuaries in SW England.

T	1–12	N 4–7

Black-winged Stilt
Himantopus himantopus L 38cm
Unmistakable, with black-and-white plumage, a long, straight bill and incredibly long red legs. Extent of black on head and neck rather variable. In female, black areas of plumage have a warmer brown tone and juvenile has feathers with pale margins. In flight, shows all-black wings and long, trailing legs.
Voice Call a repeated *kik-kik*.
Habitat Estuaries, brackish lagoons and fresh-water lakes.
Distribution Widespread breeding species in S Europe and more locally in central and NW France and SE Europe. Winters in Africa.
Occurrence Present in breeding range from March to September. Rare but regular visitor to Britain, often in spring, and has bred.

V	—	—

Stone-curlew
Burhinus oedicnemus L 40cm
Adult has pale sandy-brown plumage with darker streaking. Has proportionally large head with very large, yellow eyes and stout, yellow bill with a black tip. At rest, white wing bar visible and in flight shows two white wing bars and black-and-white on flight feathers. Usually flies low over ground with fast wingbeats. Erect posture but will crouch if alarmed. Most active at night. Very wary and skilled at concealing itself. Found in small flocks in winter and prior to migration.

Voice Calls varied and mournful, some recalling Curlew, others with an Oystercatcher-like tone.
Habitat Arable farmland, stony heaths and semi-deserts.
Distribution Widespread breeding species in S Europe but also in E Europe and W Europe as far north as S Britain. Winters in Iberian peninsula and N Africa.
Occurrence Local throughout much of its range and rare in Britain where remaining strongholds are in E Anglia and central southern counties of England. Present within breeding range from March to August.

S	3–10	N 4–7

Collared Pratincole
Glareola pratincola L 25cm
An unusual wader which feeds mainly on the wing with tern-like flight. At rest, shows short legs and stubby bill. Upperparts grey-brown, underparts pale. Throat creamy-yellow with black border and base of bill red. In flight, shows forked tail, reddish-brown underwing coverts, white rump and white trailing edge to secondaries. Often seen in flocks, catching flying insects. On the ground, runs with pattering gait.
Voice Flocks utter tern-like chattering calls.
Habitat Found beside marshes and shallow, drying lakes. Nests on sun-baked mud.
Distribution Breeds locally in S Europe and winters in Africa, south of equator.
Occurrence In breeding range from April to August. Rare vagrant to Britain, spring.

V	—	—

Oriental Pratincole *Glareola maldivarum* smaller. Shows red underwing coverts but lacks white trailing edge to wing. Very rare vagrant to Britain.

Black-winged Pratincole
Glareola nordmanni L 25cm
Very similar to Collared Pratincole. In flight, shows black underwing coverts and lacks white trailing edge to secondaries. The latter is perhaps best feature for identification since reddish underwing coverts of Collared Pratincole can appear black in harsh sunshine.
Voice Same as Collared Pratincole.
Habitat Same as Collared Pratincole.
Distribution Breeds locally in E Europe and winters locally in W and S Africa.
Occurrence Rare vagrant west of breeding range in Europe, and has occurred in Britain.

V	—	—

Black-winged Stilt

Stone-curlew

Avocet

Collared Pratincole

Collared Pratincole

Avocet

Cream-coloured Courser
Cursorius cursor L 20cm
Unmistakable with sandy-brown plumage, black and white eye-stripes and short, downcurved bill. Rather long, pale legs and upright stance. Runs extremely fast but then pauses in motionless pose. In flight, shows dark underwing and striking, black primaries when seen from above.
Voice Mostly silent.
Habitat Arid plains and semi-deserts.
Distribution N Africa and Canary Islands.
Occurrence Very rare vagrant to Europe but with records from Britain.

V	—	—

Red-necked Phalarope
Phalaropus lobatus L 17cm
Delicate wader which is invariably found swimming rather than wading. Black, needle-like bill and lobed toes. In summer plumage, has red neck, white throat and grey-brown upperparts with buffish-brown stripes on back. Female brighter than male. In winter, upperparts pale grey white longitudinal stripes, underparts white and head and neck white with dark 'panda' patch through eye. Juvenile shows dark upperparts with buffish-brown feather margins, usually arranged in longitudinal rows. Underparts pale and head and neck dirty-white with dark crown and patch through eye. In flight, all ages show conspicuous white wing bar and dark rump. Very active feeder, spinning and twisting on surface of water and stabbing at prey. Usually indifferent to the presence of man. In winter, occurs in large flocks at sea, south of region.
Voice Flight call *tirrik*.
Habitat Breeds on moorland and tundra beside small pools. In winter, found far out to sea.
Distribution Widespread breeding species in the Arctic. In Europe, nests in N Scandinavia, N Scotland and some Scottish islands, notably Shetland. Winters at sea, mostly south of region.
Occurrence Common breeding species in northern latitudes but scarce and local in Britain. Seen on passage around coasts of Britain and Ireland in small numbers in autumn and early winter, particularly after severe gales.

S (M)	5–8 (9–10)	N 5–7

Grey Phalarope
Phalaropus fulicarius L 19cm
Slightly larger and bulkier than Red-necked Phalarope with shorter, thicker bill with broad tip. In summer plumage, unmistakable with brick-red neck and underparts and black face with broad white band through eye. Male plumage duller than female. Bill with yellow base. In winter, adult has uniform grey back, extending up nape, and white underparts, head and neck with dark 'panda' patch through eye. Bill often retains yellow at base. Juvenile has pale underparts, the sides of the neck with a buff tinge, and pale head and neck showing darker crown and patch through eye. Feathers on back are dark with buff fringes. Gradually acquires irregular patterning of grey, winter-plumage feathers. In flight, all ages show white wing bar and dark rump. Habits and behaviour similar to Red-necked Phalarope and usually equally approachable.
Voice Call a sharp *kwit*.
Habitat Same as Red-necked Phalarope.
Distribution Local breeding species in the high Arctic. In Europe, breeds only in Iceland and there very local. Winters far out to sea.
Occurrence Regular but generally scarce passage migrant off coasts of W Europe, mostly in autumn and early winter. Driven close to land by severe gales.

M	9–11	—

Wilson's Phalarope
Phalaropus tricolor L 23cm
Longer bill and longer, thicker legs than other phalaropes. Summer-plumage female unmistakable with greyish-brown upperparts, with reddish stripe on back, black and reddish-chestnut stripes on neck and white underparts. Legs blackish. Male plumage duller version of female. In winter, grey upperparts and white underparts, yellow legs. Juvenile similar to winter adult but upperparts darker with buff fringes to feathers. In flight, all ages show no wing bar and a pale rump. Swims freely but also wades in shallow water for much of time.
Voice Mostly silent.

Wilson's Phalarope, winter

Habitat Freshwater pools and marshes.
Distribution Breeds in central N America and winters S America.
Occurrence Rare vagrant to W Europe mostly in autumn but occasionally in spring.

V	9–10	—

Cream-coloured Courser

Red-necked Phalarope, summer

Red-necked Phalarope, winter

Grey Phalarope, summer

Grey Phalarope, winter

Wilson's Phalarope

SKUAS, GULLS, TERNS AND AUKS
PART OF ORDER CHARADRIIFORMES

A rather diverse group of birds, distinctly different from waders that also belong to the Order Charadriiformes. Most are associated with water for at least part of their lives. Some spend their entire lives at sea apart from a few months on land during the breeding season. Nesting often occurs in loose or more regimented colonies.

Family Stercorariidae
This is the skua family. Superficially gull-like in appearance with strong flight, they obtain food to varying degrees as pirates of other seabirds. Most nest in loose colonies on coastal cliffs, but spend the rest of their lives far out to sea. Some species have elongated central tail feathers. Nest at high latitudes and winter at sea.

Family Laridae
This family comprises the gulls which are mostly coastal in habit. They are medium to large birds with stout bills and webbed feet. The wings are relatively long and pointed and the plumage of adult birds is usually largely white, but with black and grey. Full adult plumage is not achieved for several years in some species. Juveniles are usually mottled brown. Many species scavenge and some are associated with man in winter.

Family Sternidae
Terns are included in this family. They are rather elegant by comparison with the previous two families, with narrow, pointed wings and forked tail. The plumage is largely white in the genus *Sterna*. The legs are short and the bill is narrow and dagger-like. Many species dive for fish. They nest colonially.

Family Alcidae
This is the auk family of medium-sized, black-and-white seabirds with dumpy bodies. They nest on sea cliffs, but are otherwise found at sea. They fly with fast, whirring wingbeats and swim and dive well using wings for underwater propulsion. Summer and winter plumages are different. They suffer badly from marine oil pollution.

Common Terns congregating at a good feeding location. Like many other tern species, they plunge-dive for fish.

Great Skua
Catharacta skua L 60cm

Superficially similar to immature gull but has distinctive, stocky build, short tail and fierce, stout bill. Adult plumage rich brown with, at close range, a rather shaggy appearance, especially on neck. Cap normally appears distinctly darker. Wings have broad base and conspicuous white bases to primaries. Juvenile plumage similar to, but darker than, adult with white on wings less conspicuous. Flight powerful and buoyant and easily able to pursue and parasitize seabirds such as Gannets. Sometimes kills smaller seabirds, e.g. juvenile Kittiwakes, and also takes carrion and offal. Very aggressive at nest, diving and attacking intruders, including man, and sometimes drawing blood.

Voice Flight call *ah-err*.

Habitat Nests on coastal moors but otherwise found at sea.

Distribution Nests N Scotland, Scottish islands especially Shetland and Orkney, and Iceland. Winters in the Atlantic south of breeding range.

Occurrence Present on breeding grounds from May to August. Seen on passage March–April and August–October off coasts of W Europe, especially during onshore gales. In Britain, seen during autumn at regular seawatching sites such as St Ives in Cornwall.

S 5–8	M 3–4, 8–10	N 5–7

South Polar Skua
Catharacta maccormicki L 53cm

Very similar to Great Skua and often not reliably separable. Adult plumage rather grey-brown and lacking rufous tinge of Great Skua. White on wings slightly less conspicuous than Great Skua. Dark phase has golden-tipped feathers on nape while light phase has pale-grey head and neck. Underwings blackish. Habits similar to Great Skua.

Voice Mostly silent in region.

Habitat Generally found far out to sea.

Distribution Breeds in Antarctica but some spend non-breeding period (our summer) in oceans of Northern Hemisphere.

Occurrence Found in N Atlantic from May to September. Regular off E coast of N America. Recently unconfirmed reports off W coast of Britain and possibly under-recorded owing to difficulty in identification.

V	—	—

Pomarine Skua
Stercorarius pomarinus L 55cm

Told from Arctic Skua by bulkier build and long blunt tail projections that are twisted at tip. Adults occur in 2 colour phases. Dark phase uniformly sooty-brown. Pale phase has dark cap, wings and back, white face, neck and underparts with yellow tinge on cheeks. Sometimes has complete breast band. Juvenile has only short tail projection. Plumage variable shade of brown with dark barring. Underwing shows pale base to primaries and pale on primary wing coverts. Bill pale with dark tip. Feeds largely on lemmings during breeding season but otherwise parasitizes seabirds such as Kittiwakes.

Voice Seldom heard in region.

Habitat Breeds on tundra but otherwise occurs at sea.

Distribution Breeding range from Arctic Siberia to Arctic N America. Birds passing European coast on passage winter in Atlantic, south of region.

Occurrence Seen mainly on passage off coast of W Europe. In spring, numbers peak third week of April to second week of May. Autumn migration periods more extended, August–November. In Britain, spring passage seen from regular seawatching sites on English Channel, e.g. Dungeness, during strong SE winds. In autumn headlands on NE and W coast best during onshore gales.

M	4–5, 8–11	8–11

Great Skua, adult

Great Skua, adult   **Pomarine Skua,** juvenile   **Pomarine Skua,** adult

Arctic Skua
Stercorarius parasiticus L 50cm

Elegantly proportioned skua with narrow, pointed wings and elongated and pointed central tail feathers. Occurs in 2 main colour phases but with numerous intermediate stages. Dark phase (commonest in south of range) has dark sooty-brown plumage with orange-brown on cheeks and nape, and dark crown. Pale phase (commonest in north of range) has pale underparts, breast and neck, with orange wash to cheeks and nape, and dark crown. Juvenile birds have mottled and barred brown plumage, varying in shade, and central tail feathers projecting only slightly. Underwing shows pale bases to primary feathers but dark primary coverts (these are pale-based in Pomarine Skua). Seen from above, shows 3–5 outer primary shafts white. Juvenile bill looks all dark. Flight buoyant and graceful. Able to pursue and parasitize species such as Arctic Tern, forcing them to drop or disgorge food. When in active, level pursuit of prey, flight recalls bird of prey.
Voice Call a mewing *keeah*.
Habitat Breeds on northern moorland and tundra. Otherwise found at sea.
Distribution Breeds from coastal regions of Scandinavia northwards and eastwards. Also found in Iceland, N Scotland and on several Scottish islands. Winters in the Atlantic, south of the region.
Occurrence Local and rather scarce breeding species from May to August. In Britain, particularly so, but easy to see on Shetland and Orkney Islands. Also seen on passage March–April and August–October around the British and Irish coasts, especially during strong onshore winds or when lured close to land during pursuit of prey, e.g. small gulls.

S 4–10	M 3–4, 8–10	N 5–8

Long-tailed Skua
Stercorarius longicaudus L 54cm

In terms of body size, the smallest skua with slim body, long narrow wings and exceptionally long central tail feathers in summer plumage. Adult occurs as single colour phase which most resembles pale-phase Arctic Skua. Grey-brown upperparts, dark cap, pale neck and upper breast merging into darker lower breast and belly (pale breast much more extensive in pale-phase Arctic Skua). Juvenile, similar to juvenile Arctic Skua with mottled and barred plumage, is generally grey-brown without warm tones. Pale crescent usually visible on upper breast and bill noticeably two-toned with dark tip. When seen from above, only outer 2 primary shafts are white. At all ages, flight is light and buoyant and can even hover, e.g. near intruders on nest site or when searching for prey on ground. On breeding grounds, feeds mainly on lemmings but, at sea and on migration, parasitizes seabirds in manner of other skuas.
Voice Mostly silent but calls *kreeea* on breeding grounds.
Habitat Breeds on northern moors and tundra and winters at sea.
Distribution Breeds from N and NW Scandinavia eastwards and northwards. Winters in S Atlantic.
Occurrence Rather scarce breeding species whose numbers and success are greatly dependent on lemming numbers. Present from May to August. Seen on passage off coasts of W Europe in spring and autumn. In Britain, best opportunities for observation are off Outer Hebrides during northwesterly gales in mid-May and off NE and SW England during onshore gales in September–October. Juveniles in particular occasionally turn up inland after severe autumn storms.

M(S)	9–10	—

Arctic Skua

Arctic Skua, dark phase

Arctic Skua

Long-tailed Skua

Great Black-backed Gull
Larus marinus L 72cm

Large gull with dark back and upperwing. Bill massive and legs dull pink. Compared with Lesser Black-backed Gulls from W Europe, has darker back and upperwing and broader wings with more white at tip. Immature has variable mottled brown plumage. Can be told from immature Herring and Lesser Black-backed Gulls by bulk and bill size when direct comparison available. Except for size, most resembles immature Herring Gull. Tail and head paler than immature Lesser Black-backed Gull and shows contrast between dark outer primaries and paler inner primaries (primaries are uniformly dark in immature Lesser Black-backed Gull). This latter feature is less prominent than on immature Herring Gull, however. Flies with slow, powerful wingbeats. Territorial during breeding season and usually seen in well-spaced pairs. At other times, may form loose flocks for roosting. Feeds on carrion, eggs and chicks of seabirds, and, during breeding season especially, takes adult seabirds as large as Puffins.
Voice Call a deep *keeow*.
Habitat Breeds mainly on sea cliffs but rarely also beside freshwater. In winter, seen mainly around coasts but occasionally inland e.g. at rubbish tips.
Distribution Breeds around coasts of NW Europe from Brittany to N Scandinavia and Iceland. In Britain, breeds mainly in west and north but also on most Scottish islands. In winter, found along coasts from N Spain to Baltic and widespread around British and Irish coasts.
Occurrence On nesting territory from April to August. At other times, more widely distributed around coast.

T	1–12	N 4–7

Lesser Black-backed Gull
Larus fuscus L 57cm

Adult superficially similar to Great Black-backed Gull but smaller, slimmer, with smaller bill and bright yellow legs. In flight, W European ssp *graellsii* has back and upperwings slaty-grey and noticeably paler than black primaries. N European ssp *fuscus* has back and upperwing as dark as its larger relative. All adult birds show less white in wingtips than Great Black-backed Gull. Immature has mottled brown plumage typical of all the larger gulls. Shows uniformly dark primary feathers, and a generally darker tail than immature Herring and

Great Black-backed Gulls. Scavenges carrion an offal but also takes fish and eggs and chicks. I winter, visits rubbish tips.
Voice Calls include a nasal *keeow*, deeper tha Herring Gull.
Habitat Nests colonially on sea cliffs and undi turbed islands. Winters mainly around coast
Distribution Breeds around coasts of NW Europe from W and N Britain to N Scandinavi Also found on many Scottish islands and in Ice land. Ssp *fuscus* breeds in Scandinavia while ss *graellsii* breeds in Britain and W Europe. In win ter, moves south, some as far as E Africa.
Occurrence Found on breeding grounds from May to July. Scandinavian birds then migrate sout to Mediterranean and beyond. W European bird also disperse after breeding and generally mov south but with many lingering around coasts o NW Europe.

T	1–12	N 5–7

Herring Gull
Larus argentatus L 57cm

Adult has variable shade of grey on back and upperwings. Darker forms told from pale Lesse Black-backed Gull by pink legs. Distinguishe from smaller Common Gull by stout bill with re spot near tip and by yellow eye. Immature ha pale inner primaries noticeably contrasting wit darker outer ones when seen in flight. Best tol from similar immature Great Black-backed Gu by smaller size and smaller bill. Gradually acquire grey feathers of adult plumage over several year Food and habits similar to Lesser Black-backe Gull.
Voice Calls include a loud *keeow* and *gah-gah gah*.
Habitat Similar to Lesser Black-backed Gull bu also breeds in towns. In winter, commonly foun around harbours.
Distribution Breeds mainly around coasts o NW Europe from Brittany to N Scandinavia an Iceland. Widespread breeding species aroun coasts of Britain and Ireland. In winter, rang extends further south to coasts of N Spain. Als found inland in Britain and Ireland.
Occurrence Generally resident species but, i winter, disperses from breeding grounds an forms flocks at good feeding sites, e.g. estuarie or rubbish tips, and at roosts.

T	1–12	N 4–7

Great Black-backed Gull, adult

Lesser Black-backed Gull, adult

Lesser Black-backed Gull, adult **Herring Gull,** adult

Herring Gull, juvenile

Herring Gull

Yellow-legged Gull
Larus cachinnans L 57cm
Often considered a race of Herring Gull and best distinguished by yellow legs. Otherwise, very similar in all plumages but white head in winter.
Voice Same as Herring Gull.
Habitat Same as Herring Gull.
Distribution Breeds locally around Mediterranean and Black Sea. In winter, disperses around Mediterranean coast and also further northwards to inland lakes in S Europe and on Atlantic coasts of Spain and W France.
Occurrence Locally common in Mediterranean. Rather rare autumn visitor to S coast of Britain.

V	—	—

Glaucous Gull
Larus hyperboreus L 66cm
Adult is superficially similar to adult Herring Gull but distinguished by pure white wingtips and slightly larger size. Legs pink and bill heavy-looking and yellow with orange spot near tip. Winter adult has streaked and dirty-looking neck. First winter birds are pale buff, mottled with grey-brown, with buff wingtips. Dark eye and bill pink with black tip. Second winter is paler still, often with pale-grey patterning on back. Pale eye and bill is pink, dipped in black with small, pale tip. Behaviour and habits as other large gulls which it mixes in winter.
Voice Similar to Herring Gull.
Habitat Breeds on Arctic sea cliffs and winters around coasts, occasionally inland on rubbish tips.
Distribution In Europe, breeds locally in N Iceland. Main range includes coasts of Greenland and Arctic Siberia. In winter, moves south as far as coasts of NW Europe including N Britain and Ireland.

Occurrence Rather scarce breeding species in Europe. Widespread but scarce in winter. In Britain, best opportunities for observation are among winter flocks of other large gulls at fish quays, harbours and sewage outfalls in Scotland and N England.

W	11–4	—

Iceland Gull
Larus glaucoides L 55cm
Adult very similar to adult Glaucous Gull but smaller with proportionately smaller head and bill and relatively longer wings in flight. First-winter plumage resembles that of first-winter Glaucous Gull but bill is darker without sharp division. Second-winter plumage similar to that of second-winter Glaucous Gull with pale-grey feathers appearing on mantle. Bill pattern identical to that of second-winter Glaucous Gull but never so pink.
Voice Similar to Herring Gull.
Habitat Breeds on Arctic sea cliffs and winters around coasts.
Distribution Breeds in Greenland. In winter moves south, normal range including Iceland, coastal Norway and, more locally, coasts of N Britain and Ireland.
Occurrence Scarce winter visitor in variable numbers to NW European coast. Sometimes attracted to fish quays, sewage outfalls or coastal rubbish tips.

W	11–4	—

N American race, **Kumlien's Gull**, *L.g.kumlieni* is rare vagrant to NW Europe including Britain. Similar to Iceland Gull but adult has grey on primaries and darker iris

Glaucous Gull, adult

Glaucous Gull, adult

Glaucous Gull, juvenile

Yellow-legged Gull, adult

Iceland Gull, 1st winter

Common Gull
Larus canus L 40cm

Smaller than Herring Gull with an altogether more dainty appearance. Adult has unmarked yellow bill for much of year, yellow legs and dark eye. In summer, head and neck are pure white while in winter, these are streaked with dirty brown, bill is dull and sometimes acquires dark band near tip, and legs are dull. In flight, adult shows grey mantle and upperwings and black wingtips with white patches. First-winter bird has pink bill with black tip and pink legs. Mantle pure grey, upperwings patterned with black, white and brown, and a broad black band on white tail. Second winter similar to winter adult but wingtips have more black, less white. In winter, seen in flocks, often feeding in ploughed fields on earthworms etc. Mixes with other gull species.

Voice Calls include high-pitched *kee-oo* and a screaming *keeaa*.

Habitat Breeds close to coast or freshwater. In winter, found around coasts and inland on farmland.

Distribution Breeding range mainly from Baltic northwards and eastwards with isolated inland colonies further south. In Britain, breeds only in N Britain and Ireland. Winter range extends around most of coastal Europe.

Occurrence Common breeding species in north of range but rather local in Britain. Widespread and rather common in winter except inland.

T	1–12	N 5–7

Ring-billed Gull
Larus delawarensis L 47cm

Similar to Common Gull but slightly larger and with heavier bill. Adult distinctive with yellow bill bearing black band, pale yellow iris and pale grey mantle and upperwing. Legs greenish-yellow. In summer, head and neck are pure white while in winter they are streaked and spotted dirty-brown. First winter has pink bill with black tip, pink legs, dark iris, grey mantle irregularly marked with pale and dark feathers, and tail with black band. Second winter similar in plumage to winter adult with pale iris, yellow legs and dull-yellow bill with black band. However, shows remains of black tail band and patterning on secondaries. In Britain, vagrants mix freely with Herring, Common and Black-headed Gulls.

Voice Calls similar to Herring Gull but higher-pitched. Vagrants to Europe, however, generally silent.

Habitat Mainly coastal but also beside freshwater.

Distribution N America.

Occurrence Rare but regular vagrant to W Europe, including Britain. Individuals sometimes long-staying and accustomed to man.

V	—	—

Common Gull, summer

Common Gull, immature

Common Gull, winter

Ring-billed Gull

Ring-billed Gull, immature

Ring-billed Gull, 2nd winter

Audouin's Gull
Larus audouinii L 50cm
Slightly smaller than Yellow-legged Gull, the only similar-sized gull with which it regularly overlaps in its normal range. Adult has red bill, with black and yellow tip, and dark-grey legs. Bill often looks black in harsh light. In flight, shows narrow wings, pale-grey mantle and upperwing, and black wingtips with very little white. First winter has mostly dark-brown upperwings, barring on underwings and mixture of grey and brown feathers on mantle. Bill olive-brown with dark tip. In second winter, has grey mantle, pale band on secondary coverts and terminal black band on tail. Colour of bill and legs same as adult. Confident and buoyant flight, most noticeable in strong winds.
Voice Calls include subdued, harsh croaks.
Habitat Breeds on isolated, rocky islands but otherwise found at sea. Less inclined to visit harbours than most other gulls.
Distribution Breeding range confined entirely to the Mediterranean. In winter, some birds disperse within Mediterranean region, some reaching NW African coast.
Occurrence A rare gull, even within breeding range. NW Majorca offers good opportunities for observation in spring. Very rare vagrant outside Mediterranean and has even reached Britain.

V	—	—

Slender-billed Gull
Larus genei L 42cm
Superficially similar to Black-headed Gull but characteristically shows more elegant proportions, in particular a longer neck and gently sloping forehead (almost elongated) merging into long and slightly downcurved bill. Adult has dark-red bill, red legs, pale iris and pale-grey mantle and upperwings. In flight, wing pattern resembles Black-headed Gull with white leading edge and black trailing border to primaries. First winter rather similar to first-winter Black-headed Gull and best told by shape and proportions. Legs and bill pinkish-orange, the latter with dark tip.

Patterning on primaries similar to adult but wing coverts marked with pale-brown feathers. Mixes with other gulls outside breeding season.
Voice Calls similar to Black-headed Gull but deeper.
Habitat Breeds beside shallow, coastal lagoons and freshwater lakes. Winters around coasts
Distribution Very local breeding species throughout Mediterranean but predominantly in E
Occurrence Rather scarce breeding species in Mediterranean. Very rare vagrant elsewhere in Europe. Has been recorded in Britain.

V	—	—

Kittiwake
Rissa tridactyla L 40cm
Attractive gull, most similar to Common Gull but adult with black legs and pure-black wingtips Seen from above, outer wing is paler than inner wing and mantle. Summer adult has pure-white head and neck but in winter acquires grey nape and dark band behind eye. First-winter bird has black diagonal stripes on upperwings dividing the grey mantle and forewings from white on flight feathers; black bill and tip to tail, and black on ear coverts and half-collar on nape. Flight is buoyant and elegant.
Voice Characteristic call at breeding colony is *kitti-week*. Loud and far-carrying.
Habitat Nests colonially on sheer sea cliffs Otherwise found at sea – a truly marine gull.
Distribution Breeds around coast of W Europe from Brittany northwards to N Scandinavia and Iceland. In Britain, commonest at seabird colonies around N and W coasts. Winters in N Atlantic with small numbers in W Mediterranean.
Occurrence Present at breeding colonies from April to July and easy to see at noted seabird sites such as Skomer, Farne Islands and Shetland Islands. Also seen on passage during strong onshore winds and occasionally blown inland during severe gales.

S	3–9	N 4–7

Kittiwake

Kittiwake, juvenile

Kittiwake   **Audouin's Gull**   **Slender-billed Gull**

Black-headed Gull
Larus ridibundus L 38cm

Recognized in flight at all ages by white leading edge to wing, extending to white triangle formed by outer primaries, and black trailing edge to primaries. Adult in summer has chocolate-brown hood, not extending to nape, while in winter, head becomes white with dark ear coverts. Bill and legs deep red in summer, scarlet in winter. Juvenile has buffish-brown upperparts extending up crown, buffish smudges on crown and black tail band. In first winter, similar to winter adult but has brown feathering on wing coverts, flesh-coloured legs and bill, the latter black-tipped, and black tail band. Seen in flocks in winter and mixes with other gulls. Feeds on invertebrates, sometimes by 'paddling' mud with feet in shallow water. Also feeds in fields and will come to food in urban settings. Occasionally catches insects on the wing.

Voice Harsh calls including *kreaahh*.

Habitat Found in a wide variety of habitats from estuaries and mudflats to freshwater lakes and ploughed fields. Also seen on open, urban areas of grass such as school playing fields.

Distribution Widespread throughout Europe. Breeding range extends north to central Scandinavia and south to S central Europe. In winter, northern birds move south and range extends to the whole of southern Europe.

Occurrence The commonest and most widespread medium-sized gull throughout most of Europe. In Britain, can be found on almost any sheltered stretch of coast as well as inland.

T	1–12	N 4–7

Mediterranean Gull
Larus melanocephalus L 38cm

Reminiscent of Black-headed Gull in some plumages but has stockier build with more robust bill. Adult has deep-red bill with black sub-terminal band and yellow tip, and pure-white primaries. In summer, adult acquires black hood which extends down nape. In winter, the head becomes white with dark smudge through eye giving malevolent expression. Juvenile has greyish-brown plumage, the feathers on the back with pale margins. First winter similar to first-winter Common Gull with grey mantle, dark tail band and patterned wings showing pale band on secondary coverts. Bill and legs dark and face with dark smudge through eye as in winter adult. Second winter similar to winter adult but shows a few black markings on primary tips.

Voice Typical call *kow-kow-kow*.

Habitat Found mainly around coasts, visiting saline lagoons, marshes and lakes.

Distribution As name suggests, main range is around Mediterranean region, especially widespread in winter. Breeding colonies scattered and local. Has spread north and west and now breeds more or less regularly in small numbers in S England.

Occurrence Locally common, especially in Mediterranean, e.g. on saline lagoons and coastal lakes in N mainland Greece. In Britain, scarce breeder but regular in winter among flocks of Black-headed Gulls. Mainly seen along coasts of S England but also, rarely, inland at reservoirs.

T(W)	1–12 (10–3)	N 4–6

Black-headed Gull, summer

Black-headed Gull, winter

Black-headed Gull, 1st winter

Mediterranean Gull, immature

Mediterranean Gull, adult

Little Gull
Larus minutus L 28cm

Noticeably smaller than Black-headed Gull. Adult has dark underwing and grey upperwing, both showing trailing white margins. Legs red, bill black. In summer, has black hood which is replaced, in winter, by grey on nape and crown and black ear coverts. Juvenile has back and wings a mixture of brown and black. In first winter, resembles first-winter Kittiwake. Shows black diagonal stripes on upperwings, grey mantle, black tail band, and black crown and ear coverts. Flight buoyant and sometimes tern-like. Feeds mainly on insects caught on water surface and muddy pool margins. Usually feeds on the wing.
Voice Characteristic call a repeated *kek*.
Habitat Breeds around shallow, well-vegetated lakes and freshwater marshes. Winters around coasts.
Distribution Breeds NE Europe with a few isolated populations further west. Winters around coasts of W and S Europe.
Occurrence Locally common breeding species within limited European range. Seen mostly on passage and in winter. In Britain, seen mostly April–June and August–October. However, can be seen in all months and has bred.

M	4–6, 8–10	—

Little Gull, adult summer

Bonaparte's Gull
Larus philadelphia L 32cm

Resembles a miniature Black-headed Gull but told, at all ages, by white undersides to primaries (dark in Black-headed). Adult has black bill and orange legs. In summer, develops black hood which is replaced, in winter, by grey nape and black ear coverts. First winter has distinct dark diagonal band on upperwings. Flight light and buoyant, and resembling Little Gull.
Voice Chattering calls.
Habitat Nests in sparse forests and winters on coasts.

Distribution Breeds northern N America and winters southern N and Central America.
Occurrence Rare vagrant to W Europe including Britain, mainly in winter.

V	—	—

Laughing Gull
Larus atricilla L 40cm

Size of Common Gull but has slim build, long pointed wings and long, robust bill that looks slightly downcurved. Adult recognized by dark grey mantle and upperwing with black wingtips and a white trailing edge to wing. In summer, has black hood with white 'eyelids' and deep-red bill. In winter, bill duller and darker and head pale with dark-grey streaks on nape and behind eye. First winter similar to winter adult but shows grey neck, breast and flanks, brown on wing coverts and broad, black tail band. Second winter similar to adult winter but shows traces of tail band.
Voice Generally silent in region.
Habitat Mainly coastal.
Distribution Breeds N America and winters southern N America southwards.
Occurrence Very rare vagrant to W Europe including Britain, mainly in winter.

V	—	—

Franklin's Gull
Larus pipixcan L 34cm

Similar to Laughing Gull but smaller. Adult has distinctive wing pattern with dark-grey mantle and upperwings and white trailing edge which extends and separates the grey upperwing from the black wingtips. In summer, has black hood and white 'eyelids'. In winter, shows dark nape and crown again highlighting white 'eyelids'. First winter similar to winter adult but has narrow tail band and grey-brown upperwings.
Voice Generally silent in the region.
Habitat Mainly coastal.
Distribution Breeds central N America and winters off S America.
Occurrence Very rare vagrant to W Europe including Britain, mainly in winter.

V	—	—

Franklin's Gull, non-breeding adult

ittle Gull, adult non-breeding

Little Gull, immature

aughing Gull, winter

Bonaparte's Gull, winter

Laughing Gull, winter

Franklin's Gull, summer

Great Black-headed Gull
Larus ichthyaetus L 62cm

Size of Great Black-backed Gull but most resembles giant Mediterranean Gull. Adult has pale-grey wings and almost white wingtips with small black spots on primaries. Powerful bill is yellow with black band and reddish tip. Summer adult has black hood and white 'eyelids'. In winter, hood replaced with dark streaking on nape. First winter has grey mantle, grey and brown on wings and black tail band. Second winter closer to winter adult plumage but retains tail band and brown feathering on inner wing. In all winter plumages, dark streaking through eye gives menacing appearance.

Voice Loud croaking calls.

Great Black-headed Gull, adult summer

Habitat Coasts and lakes.
Distribution Breeds in central Asia and winters Africa to India.
Occurrence Rare but regular in E Mediterranean. Very rare vagrant elsewhere in Europe.

	V	—	—

Sabine's Gull
Larus sabini L 33cm

Adult in flight is distinctive with 3 triangles of different colours: outer primaries are black, inner primaries and secondaries are white and mantle and wing coverts are grey. Markedly forked tail and dark bill with yellow tip. Summer adult has dark-grey hood, replaced in winter by dark smudge on nape. Juvenile has similar patterning on wing to adult but grey on mantle and wing coverts replaced by scaly brown feathering which extends up nape to crown. Flight powerful and buoyant and swims well.

Voice Raucous call not heard in the region.
Habitat Breeds in high Arctic; winters at sea.
Distribution Breeds Arctic N America and Greenland and winters in S Atlantic.
Occurrence Seen mainly off coasts of NW Europe in autumn

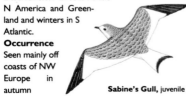

Sabine's Gull, juvenile

during periods of strong onshore winds. Regular seawatching sites such as St Ives and Porthgwarr in Cornwall and Cape Clear in Ireland can be good from late August to October.

	M	8–10	—

Ross's Gull
Rhodostethia rosea L 30cm

Size of Little Gull. Adult has relatively long pointed wings, dark underneath and pale grey above, with broad white trailing edge. Tail rather long and wedge-shaped and underparts have pale-pink flush, most noticeably during the summer months. Bill short, stubby and black and legs short and red. In summer, adult has fine black neck ring while in winter this is replaced by dark smudge on nape and behind eye. First winter shows black diagonal markings on wings and black tip to tail. Flight buoyant and tern-like.

Voice Mostly silent.
Habitat Breeds in high Arctic. Otherwise generally associated with pack-ice and high Arctic seas.

Ross's Gull

Distribution Breeding range imperfectly known but locally N Canada and E Siberia.
Occurrence Very rare visitor to NW Europe including Britain, in winter.

	V	—	—

Ivory Gull
Pagophila eburnea L 42cm

Adult is unmistakable with pure-white plumage, black legs and a yellowish bill, blue-grey at base. Feathering around base of bill sometimes matted and soiled owing to rather unsavoury diet. First winter has dirty markings on face, particularly at base of bill, and black spots on wings, mantle and tail. Flight is powerful. Feeds on carrion, offal and excrement from Polar Bears and seals, and also fish and marine invertebrates. Often rather fearless.

Voice Harsh tern-like call.
Habitat Breeds colonially in high Arctic and otherwise found near pack-ice in Polar seas.
Distribution Breeds in high Arctic including Spitzbergen, wintering range seldom extending south of Arctic Circle.
Occurrence Very rare visitor to NW Europe including Britain, mostly during winter months.

	V	—	—

Ivory Gull, adult

Sabine's Gull, adult **Ivory Gull,** adult **Ross's Gull,** 1st winter

Black Tern

Chlidonias niger L 24cm

Adult in summer unmistakable with black head, neck and breast, white undertail coverts and grey wings, upperwing being darker than underwing. Winter adult loses most of black markings except for crown and ear coverts. May begin to lose summer plumage by July. Juvenile rather similar to winter adult but has brown feathering on otherwise grey upperwing and mantle. Both winter adult and juvenile show black mark on side of breast at base of wings, a good feature for separating same-aged White-winged Black Terns. Buoyant and elegant flight. Usually seen feeding over water, catching insects, but does not dive like *Sterna* terns.

Voice Nasal calls include *kyey*.

Habitat Associated with marshes and well-vegetated lakes. Nests colonially.

Distribution Scattered breeding range across central and S Europe as far north as Baltic coast. Becomes more widespread in E Europe. Winters in Africa.

Occurrence Present in breeding range from May to July. In Britain, seen as a passage migrant April–May and July–September. Mainly coastal but occasional inland where small flocks sometimes appear at gravel pits or reservoirs, spring adults characteristically staying for very short periods of time before moving on.

M	4–5, 7–9	—

White-winged Black Tern

Chlidonias leucopterus L 24cm

Adult in summer plumage very distinctive. Seen from below, shows black head, neck, breast and underwing coverts, contrasting with white flight feathers, undertail coverts and tail. From above, shows black head, neck and mantle contrasting with white wings, rump and tail. Adult in winter similar to winter Black Tern and best distinguished by paler underwings and lack of black mark on side of breast. Juvenile also lacks the breast mark of juvenile Black Tern and shows greater contrast between dark mantle and paler wings, rump and tail. Upperwing shows dark leading edge to inner wing. Behaviour and habits similar to Black Tern.

Voice Calls include a rasping *krrech*.

Habitat Swamps, marshes and lake margins.

Distribution Breeds in E Europe and winters in Africa and Asia.

Occurrence Local breeding species in Europe and present from May to July. Rare vagrant to NW Europe including Britain, mainly May–June and August–September.

V	5–6, 8–9	—

Whiskered Tern

Chlidonias hybridus L 25cm

Plumage suggests a miniature *Sterna* tern but habits and behaviour typical of *Chlidonias* terns. Summer adult is sooty-grey from neck to belly, separated from black cap by white facial stripe, and contrasting with white undertail coverts. Underwings pale grey; mantle and upperwings pale grey. Bill and legs deep red. In winter, looks very pale with dark markings on crown. Juvenile resembles pale juvenile White-winged Black Tern but with almost uniformly pale upperwing. Behaviour and habits similar to Black Tern but also plunge-dives.

Voice Calls include a rasping *eerch*.

Habitat Marshes and well-vegetated lakes.

Distribution Scattered distribution throughout central and S Europe. Winters in Africa and Asia.

Occurrence Locally common breeding species, present from May to July. Vagrant north of breeding range and occurs regularly as rare visitor to Britain, mainly May–June and August–September.

V	5–6, 8–9	—

Black Tern, summer

Black Tern, immature
Whiskered Tern, summer

White-winged Black Tern, summer
Whiskered Tern, winter

Little Tern
Sterna albifrons L 23cm

Smallest European tern showing white forehead in all plumages. Adult has short, yellow legs and, in summer, a yellow bill with black tip. In flight, shows grey upperparts, white underparts and relatively short tail. In juvenile, cap is less distinct and upperwing and mantle have brown feathering. Bill dark and legs dull olive. Fast wingbeats but nevertheless buoyant flight. Sometimes hovers over water before plunge-diving after small fish and marine invertebrates.

Voice Shrill, trilling calls including *krrr-ik*.

Habitat Nests on shingle and sandy beaches and otherwise found around sheltered coasts and estuaries. Also occasionally inland beside wide rivers or shallow lakes.

Distribution In W Europe, mainly coastal from the Mediterranean as far north as Scotland. Distribution heavily influenced, however, by human disturbance of nest sites in many areas. In E Europe, also occurs inland. Winters south of region.

Occurrence Present in breeding range from April to August. Also occurs on passage around coasts of W Europe.

S	4–8	N 5–7

Caspian Tern
Sterna caspia L 52cm

Large tern, bigger than Common Gull. Large, dagger-like bill, bright red with black sub-terminal band in adult and orange-red in juvenile. Summer adult has plumage typical of many *Sterna* terns with black cap, pale-grey upperwings and mantle and white underparts except for dark outer primaries. Juvenile plumage similar to adult but has mottled upperparts and pale streaks on crown. Legs of adult black but pale in juvenile. Flight powerful with deep, leisurely wingbeats. Dives for fish.

Voice Call a loud and croaking *kraac-kraac*.

Habitat Nests colonially on undisturbed islands mostly around coasts but also on large lakes. Feeds on estuaries and freshwater lakes.

Distribution Very local distribution in Europe but widespread worldwide. Breeds mainly around coasts of Baltic and Black Seas. Winters in Africa with a few remaining in S Iberian peninsula and SE Europe.

Occurrence Breeds from May to August. Seen on passage around Mediterranean coasts in April–May and August–September. Rare but regular vagrant to NW Europe including Britain.

V	—	—

Sooty Tern
Sterna fuscata L 38cm

In flight, adult shows long tail streamers, white underparts except for darker flight feathers, and black upperparts extending to crown. White forehead extends back just as far as eye. Black legs and bill. Juvenile quite unlike adult with browner, speckled upperparts and head, neck and breast all dark.

Voice Mostly silent away from breeding colonies.

Habitat Nests in huge colonies on isolated, tropical islands but otherwise almost exclusively pelagic.

Distribution Tropical seas.

Occurrence Very rare vagrant to Europe including Britain.

V	—	—

Bridled Tern
Sterna anaethetus L 32cm

Superficially similar to Sooty Tern but slightly smaller. Upperparts grey-brown, contrasting with black crown and separated by pale collar. White on forehead extends back beyond eye. Black bill and legs.

Voice Mostly silent away from breeding colonies.

Habitat Breeds on remote, oceanic islands and otherwise almost exclusively pelagic.

Distribution Confined to tropical seas.

Occurrence Very rare vagrant to Europe including Britain.

V	—	—

Little Tern

Little Tern

Bridled Tern

Caspian Tern

Sooty Tern

Sandwich Tern

Sterna sandvicensis L 40cm

Medium-sized tern with slim proportions. Adult has pale-grey upperparts and white underparts. Short, black legs and bill black with yellow tip. In summer, has black cap with short, shaggy crest. In non-breeding plumage, from July onwards, fore-crown becomes white. Juvenile has all-dark bill, mostly dark crown and dark feathering on mantle and wing coverts. In flight, looks very pale but with outer primaries noticeably darker. Deep and powerful wingbeats. Dives from a considerable height.

Voice Call loud and distinctive *kee-errk*.

Habitat Almost exclusively coastal in habits, nesting on shingle and sandy beaches and feeding in estuaries and other areas of sheltered, shallow water.

Distribution Breeds mainly on coasts of NW Europe from Brittany to southern tip of Scandinavia. Widespread but local breeder around coasts of Britain and Ireland, range limited by human disturbance of potential nesting sites. European birds winter on W African coast.

Occurrence Present in breeding range from March to September. Locally common in Britain and easily seen along N Norfolk coast.

S	3–9	N 5–7

Gull-billed Tern

Gelochelidon nilotica L 37cm

Similar to Sandwich Tern but with thick, gull-like bill which is black at all ages. Legs relatively long and black. Summer adult has black cap extending down nape and without shaggy appearance of Sandwich Tern. In winter, crown is mostly white with dark streaking through eye. Juvenile similar to winter adult but with dark feathering on mantle and wing coverts. In flight, looks very pale with uniform upperwing, dark trailing edge to primaries, and relatively short and slightly forked grey tail. Generally feeds over land, on coastal marshes and fields. Hunts insects, crabs, amphibians and occasionally small mammals.

Voice Call a nasal *ku-vek*.

Habitat Breeds on coastal marshes and sandy beaches.

Distribution Very local breeding species in S Europe from S Iberian peninsula to N Greece.

Occurrence Rather scarce as a breeding species and present from May to August. Vagrant elsewhere in Europe and rare visitor to Britain.

V	—	—

Forster's Tern

Sterna forsteri L 35cm

In summer plumage resembles Common Tern but with pale primaries visible in flight. In winter, adult looks very pale except for characteristic black eye patch and black bill. Juvenile similar to winter adult but with brown feathering on crown, mantle and wing coverts.

Voice Vagrants mostly silent.

Habitat Sheltered coasts.

Distribution Breeds N America and winters southern N and Central America.

Occurrence Very rare vagrant to Europe, including Britain, in autumn and winter.

V	—	—

Lesser Crested Tern

Sterna bengalensis L 36cm

Similar to Sandwich Tern in size and appearance but has orange bill. Uniformly pale-grey upperwing, mantle, rump and tail. Summer adult has black cap. In winter, black confined to patch from rear of crown to eye. Juvenile similar to winter adult but has paler bill and patterned upperwing.

Voice Generally silent outside main range.

Habitat Essentially coastal.

Distribution Breeds locally in Red Sea and on N African coast and winters in coastal tropical Africa.

Occurrence Very rare vagrant to Europe including Britain. Individuals occasionally long-staying, and has interbred with Sandwich Tern.

V	—	—

Sandwich Tern, colony

Sandwich Tern, flock

Gull-billed Tern   **Forster's Tern**   **Lesser Crested Tern**

Common Tern
Sterna hirundo L 35cm

Typical medium-sized *Sterna* tern. Adult in summer has grey upperparts, pale underparts and a black cap. Bill orange-red with black tip and legs red. Differs from similar Arctic Tern in different bill colour, longer legs and shorter tail streamers. Wings also broader, outer primaries being streaked darker than inner ones. Winter adult acquires white forehead and darker bill. Juvenile and first winter have red legs, white forecrown, dark leading edge to upperwing and grey secondaries tipped with white. Bill of juvenile has basal half orange-red while that of first winter is mostly dark. Dives in shallow water after small fish and occasionally feeds in flocks.

Voice Calls include *kirri-kirri-kirri*.

Habitat Breeds around coasts on shingle and sandy beaches, but also beside large, inland lakes and gravel pits.

Distribution Widespread breeding species around the coasts of Europe but excluded from many areas by human disturbance of potential nest sites. Also widespread at inland lakes but local in W Europe. Winters off Africa.

Occurrence Present in breeding range from April to September. Easily seen around coasts of Britain and Ireland but breeds mostly in protected areas such as reserves on N Norfolk coast. Widespread on passage.

S	4–9	N 5–7

Arctic Tern
Sterna paradisaea L 36cm

Similar to Common Tern but adult has longer tail streamers, all blood-red bill and noticeably shorter legs. Wings narrower than Common Tern, upperwing being uniformly pale grey without contrast of dark outer primaries. Seen from below, flight feathers look translucent. Underparts usually darker than Common Tern and separated from black cap by broad white band on cheeks. Juvenile and first winter have red legs and white forecrown, but lack dark leading wing edge of similarly aged Common Terns. Also show white secondaries and mostly dark bill. Flight buoyant and vigorous. Dives well but usually prefers to take surface fish.

Voice Utters soft piping calls at nest but alarm call to human intruder *kreerr*.

Habitat Nests colonially on sand-dunes and sandy and shingle beaches. In winter, mostly oceanic.

Distribution Breeds in NW Europe from Brittany northwards to Arctic Circle. Locally common breeding species around N Britain and Ireland. Winters in Antarctic, often associated with pack-ice.

Occurrence Present in breeding range from April to September. In Britain, large colonies are easy to see on Farne Islands.

S	4–9	N 5–7

Roseate Tern
Sterna dougallii L 38cm

Compared with Common and Arctic Terns, breeding adult has paler-grey upperparts, a rosy tint to underparts (not always easily visible) and long tail streamers, these extending well beyond wings at rest. Bill mostly blackish with red base. Winter adult has long tail streamers and white forecrown. Juvenile has black bill and legs, patterned back and mostly dark forecrown.

Voice Typical call is *chu-vik*.

Habitat Nests on shingle and rocky islands, usually alongside other tern species. Winters in coastal waters.

Distribution Very local breeding range mainly around coasts of Britain and Ireland. Winters off W Africa.

Occurrence Present in breeding range from April to September. Rare and local. Small numbers found among large colonies of Common and Arctic Terns.

S	4–9	N 5–7

Common Tern, summer

Common Tern, winter

Arctic Tern, summer
Common Tern, summer

Arctic Tern, summer

Roseate Tern, summer

Razorbill
Alca torda L 38cm
Underparts white and upperparts almost jet-black with laterally flattened bill bearing vertical, white stripe. In summer, has black head and conspicuous white stripe from eye to base of culmen. In winter, throat and cheeks white. Immature similar to winter adult but with much less stout bill. In flight, shows white underwing coverts, more white on side of rump than Guillemot, and feet concealed by tail. Swims and dives well after fish.
Voice Gruff, growling calls.
Habitat Nests in loose colonies on sea cliffs, laying single egg, often among boulders or in crevices. Otherwise found far out to sea.
Distribution Breeds around rugged coasts of NW Europe from Brittany northwards to Iceland and N Scandinavia. Widespread on W and N coasts of Britain and Ireland. In winter, highly pelagic, range extending south to W Mediterranean.
Occurrence Present at colonies from March to August. In Britain, easy to see at classic seabird sites including Skomer Island in Wales and Noss in the Shetland Islands.

T		1–12		N 3–8	

Guillemot
Uria aalge L 40cm
Underparts white and upperparts chocolate-brown, becoming darker in northern races. Shows dark streaking on flanks. Neck is longer than Razorbill and bill more slender and dagger-like. In summer plumage, head and neck are all-dark. In so-called 'Bridled Guillemot' there is a white eye-ring and line extending back from eye giving spectacled effect. This form becomes increasingly common in northern birds. In winter, chin, throat and cheeks are white with black line extending back from eye. In flight, shows dull underwing coverts, less white on sides of rump than Razorbill or Brünnich's Guillemot, and projecting feet. Flies with whirring wingbeats and neck retracted.
Voice Growling call *oaarrr*. Noisy at breeding colonies but otherwise mostly silent.
Habitat Breeds locally but in huge colonies on sea cliffs, nesting side by side on inaccessible ledges. Single egg is pear-shaped. Otherwise occurs at sea.

Distribution Main breeding range from SW Britain northwards to Iceland and N Scandinavia with isolated populations on W Iberian peninsula. In Britain, found mainly on W and N coasts with huge colonies on many Scottish islands. In winter, found far out to sea.
Occurrence Present at breeding colonies from February to August, nesting actually occurring May to August. Locally common in Britain and easily seen at seabird sites such as Farne Islands, St Abb's Head in Scotland and seabird cliffs in Orkney Islands.

T		1–12		N 5–8	

Brünnich's Guillemot, winter   Guillemot, winter

Brünnich's Guillemot
Uria lomvia L 40cm
Similar to Guillemot but with shorter, thicker bill and conspicuous white streak on gape. Plumage darker than southern race of Guillemot and shows no dark streaking on flanks. In summer, head and neck all dark. In winter, white chin and throat. However, white does not extend to cheeks, and so no contrasting black stripe behind eye is visible. White gape mark still conspicuous. In flight, shows white underwing coverts, white on sides of rump and projecting feet.
Voice Grumbling calls, similar to Razorbill.
Habitat Breeds on northern sea cliffs and winters far out to sea.
Distribution In Europe, breeding confined to Iceland and N Scandinavia. Highly pelagic in winter. Range may extend south of breeding range.
Occurrence Locally common in limited breeding range but very rare outside this. In Britain, very rare vagrant to Shetland Islands and NE Scotland, and then records often of dead or unhealthy birds.

V		11–2		—	

Razorbill

Razorbill

Guillemot

Guillemot

Brünnich's Guillemot

Little Auk
Alle alle L 19cm

The smallest auk with stubby bill and compact, stocky appearance sometimes showing almost no neck. In summer, head, neck and upperparts black and underparts white except for dark underwing. In winter, chin and throat become white. Swims buoyantly, showing a lot of white on flanks. White crescent over eye in winter and summer plumages. Dives frequently for surprisingly long periods, often with only short intervals at surface. Birds returning to nests often have throats puffed out and full of food. In distant flight view could be confused with juvenile or winter Puffin but wing-beats much more whirring. Feeds on small fish and plankton.

Voice Very noisy at nest colonies with cackling and trilling calls. Otherwise generally silent.

Habitat Nests colonially on Arctic boulder slopes and cliffs. Otherwise found far out to sea.

Distribution Breeds mainly in high Arctic on Spitzbergen and Greenland. Tiny population on N Iceland. In winter, range extends south to North Sea and seas off N Scotland.

Occurrence Breeds in vast numbers, colonies often numbering millions of pairs. In winter, appears off British coast in variable numbers from October to February. Seen close to land mainly during or after severe gales when some birds may even get blown inland.

W	10–2	—

Black Guillemot
Cepphus grylle L 32cm

Very distinctive in summer with all-black plumage but for striking white wing patches. Feet and gape bright orange-red. In winter, looks much paler with white underparts, greyish back, nape and crown and dark smudge through eye. White wing panel still conspicuous against dark wings. Juvenile similar to winter adult but generally dark and with dark barring on white wing panel. Flies with fast, whirring wingbeats. Often seen on water in pairs or small groups, especially close to rocky shores or even in northern harbours. Dives well for marine invertebrates and fish, notably Butterfish.

Voice At nest, utters high-pitched whistles.

Habitat Nests under boulders in loose colonies, laying two eggs. Otherwise found in coastal waters, generally off rocky shores.

Distribution Breeds around coasts of N Europe including N Britain and Ireland, Scandinavia and Iceland.

Occurrence Widespread within range but thinly spread and seldom particularly numerous. In Britain, best seen around Scottish Islands and coast of N Scotland.

T	1–12	N 5–7

Black Guillemot, winter

Puffin
Fratercula arctica L 30cm

In summer, distinctive and unmistakable. Black upperparts and crown, white underparts and greyish-white face. Bill large and laterally flattened, grooved and brightly coloured with red, yellow and blue. Legs orange-red. In winter, face looks dirty-grey and bill loses its bright colours. Juvenile similar to winter adult but with smaller stubbier bill. Swims and dives well after fish, especially Sand Eels. In flight, shows darkish underwings but not black like Little Auk.

Voice Mostly silent but gruff calls heard at nest.

Habitat Breeds on grassy sea cliffs, nesting in burrows. Otherwise found at sea.

Distribution Breeds locally in NW Europe from Brittany and W and NW Britain and Ireland northwards to Iceland and Scandinavia. In winter ranges throughout NW Atlantic.

Occurrence Present at breeding colonies from April to July. Despite catastrophic decline in some areas, still locally abundant in some Scottish colonies such as Noss and Hermaness on Shetland and on Skomer Island in Wales. Seldom seen from shore during winter months.

T	1–12	N 4–7

Little Auk, summer

Little Auk, winter

Black Guillemot, summer

Puffin, summer

PIGEONS AND DOVES
ORDER COLUMBIFORMES,
Family Columbidae

Plump-bodied, medium-sized birds with pointed wings and relatively long tails. Sexes similar. Most are gregarious outside breeding season. Young are fed 'pigeon milk', a special crop secretion.

Rock Dove/Feral Pigeon
Columba livia L 33cm
Feral Pigeon is descended from Rock Dove. Typical ancestral Rock Dove has grey upperparts, 2 dark bars on wing, white rump and white underwing. Feral Pigeon plumage is extremely variable. Some identical to Rock Dove in appearance, others mixtures of white, reddish-brown, buff and black. Often seen in flocks. Flight is fast with rapid wingbeats. Feral Pigeons are usually accustomed to man while Rock Doves are generally wary.
Voice Cooing call *doo-roo-ooo*.
Habitat Rock Dove found on rocky coasts and, in S Europe, in mountainous regions inland. Feral Pigeon generally associated with man although some have reverted to ancestral habitats.
Distribution Rock Dove widespread in S Europe; also NW Scotland and Ireland. Feral Pigeon occurs in towns almost throughout.
Occurrence Rock Dove is common resident in S Europe but rather local in Britain and Ireland. Feral Pigeon is common throughout.

T	1–12	—

Stock Dove
Columba oenas L 33cm
Often seen with Woodpigeons, from which it differs in smaller size, more uniform grey plumage and lack of white markings. Fast wingbeats, and flight looks direct and more controlled than that of Woodpigeon. Underwing grey. Feeds in small flocks in winter.
Voice Typical call heard in spring and summer *ooo-u-oo*, sometimes described as 'Ooh-look!'.
Habitat Open farmland with scattered woods. Sometimes on cliffs and rocky terrain. Nests in holes in trees but also on cliffs.
Distribution Widespread in most of Europe N to central Scotland and S Scandinavia.

Stock Dove

Occurrence
Fairly common but rarely as numerous as Woodpigeon. Mostly resident but NE European birds move south and west in autumn

T	1–12	N 4–6

Woodpigeon
Columba palumbus L 40cm
A plump pigeon, easily recognized by white patches on side of neck and white transverse band on wing, the latter best seen in flight. Wings make loud clattering sound on take-off and landing. Widely persecuted and wary of man in most rural areas. In more urban settings, can be less wary. Seen in flocks, sometimes large, feeding in fields.
Voice Typical call a 5-syllable cooing *ooh-ooh ooh, ooh uu*.
Habitat Typically found in areas where farmland and woodland mix. Increasingly seen in gardens and urban areas.
Distribution Throughout most of Europe as far north as central Scandinavia.

Woodpigeon

Found throughout mainland Britain and Ireland.
Occurrence Common resident in much of range. E and NE European populations move south and west in autumn.

T	1–12	N 4–7

Turtle Dove
Streptopelia turtur L 27cm
Small, neatly proportioned dove. Attractive, scaly appearance on back created by dark feathers with broad, orange-brown margins. Adult has black-and-white markings on side of neck, absent in juvenile. In flight, shows pale belly and undertail and white terminal band to tail. This latter feature seen well on take-off and landing when tail often fanned. Flies with rapid and characteristically flicked wingbeats. Heavily persecuted in S Europe and consequently wary of man. Perches on overhead wires and sometimes feeds in small flocks.
Voice Call a characteristic purring *coo*.
Habitat Open agricultural land with scattered trees and hedgerows.
Distribution Widespread summer visitor to most of Europe as far north as Baltic. In Britain, occurs mainly S and E England. Winters in Africa.
Occurrence Fairly common breeding species. Seen on passage outside normal breeding range.

S	4–8	N 5–7

Stock Dove

Woodpigeon

Feral Pigeon

Turtle Dove

Collared Dove
Streptopelia decaocto L 32cm
Slim, long-tailed appearance with pinkish-buff plumage, grading to greyish-buff on belly and underwing. Adult with black collar on nape. Broad, whitish tail band seen from below, especially during display flight when tail splayed and wings held rigid. Bill delicate and dark and legs reddish. Often seen in pairs feeding on lawns or perched on roofs or aerials. Also freely associates with Feral Pigeons, Woodpigeons and garden birds.
Voice Call a trisyllabic *oo-oooo-oo*.
Habitat Generally associated with town parks and town and village gardens.
Distribution Found throughout most of Europe (except S Italy and Iberian peninsula) as far north as S Scandinavia. Occurs throughout Britain and Ireland.
Occurrence Common throughout most of range where habitat suitable. Species has undergone dramatic expansion in range. From its origins in Asia, started colonizing Europe early this century with first breeding in Britain not until 1955.

T	1–12	N 5–7

Laughing Dove
Streptopelia senegalensis L 26cm
Recalls Turtle Dove but with longer tail. Best distinguished by colouring and patterning on wing. Blue more extensive but otherwise uniform orange-brown. Lacks scaly appearance of Turtle Dove since feathers are not dark-centred. Black speckling on neck.
Voice Call a 5-syllable cooing.
Habitat Usually associated with urban environments including town gardens and roadsides.
Distribution A mainly African species that occurs in Israel and locally around Istanbul.
Occurrence Common within African range but only just creeping into European Turkey.

SANDGROUSE
ORDER PTEROCLIDIFORMES
Family Pteroclidae

Superficially pigeon-like birds with very short legs, relatively small heads and elongated tail feathers. Adapted to arid habitats, flying to drinking pools at dawn or dusk. Form flocks outside breeding season. Sexes dissimilar.

Pin-tailed Sandgrouse
Pterocles alchata L 34cm
Distinguished from other sandgrouse by white belly, pale reddish-brown breast band bordered with black, and black eye-stripe. Male has greenish-brown upperparts and black throat while female has sandy plumage and black necklace. Central tail feathers elongated. In flight, resembles Golden Plover. White belly and underwing conspicuous. Usually seen in flocks.
Voice Typical call *katar-katar*.
Habitat Found on arid steppe and semi-desert.
Distribution Widespread in central and S Iberian peninsula and very local in S France. Also in N Africa, Asia Minor and Middle East.
Occurrence Fairly common resident in Spain and scarce at La Crau S in France.

Black-bellied Sandgrouse
Pterocles orientalis L 35cm
Rather dumpy appearance enhanced by short tail. Has extensive black belly, buff band on lower breast with narrow black band on upper margin. Female has spotted upper breast and pale throat while male has unmarked upper breast and black throat. Usually seen flying in flocks to drinking pools at dusk. In flight, shows white underwing coverts and conspicuous black belly.
Voice *Churrr* call uttered in flight.
Habitat Arid plains and semi-deserts.
Distribution In Europe, only in central and S Spain. Also in E Turkey, Middle East and N Africa.

Pallas's Sandgrouse
Syrrhaptes paradoxus L 38cm
Plumage pattern recalls that of Grey Partridge with orange-brown face, grey-brown breast and dark belly patch. Also shows extremely elongated central tail feathers and slight breast band. Female

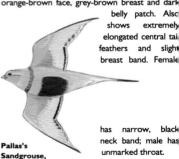

Pallas's Sandgrouse, male

has narrow, black neck band; male has unmarked throat.
Voice Variety of clucking calls.
Habitat Arid steppe country.
Distribution Central Asia.
Occurrence Very occasionally irrupts from normal range and has reached Britain.

V	—	—

Collared Dove

Laughing Dove

Pin-tailed Sandgrouse

Black-bellied Sandgrouse, male

Black-bellied Sandgrouse

CUCKOOS
ORDER CUCULIFORMES,
Family Cuculidae

Medium-sized, relatively slender birds with pointed wings and long tails. European species are nest parasites of songbirds.

Cuckoo
Cuculus canorus L 33cm

Slim and long-tailed with long, pointed wings. Adult male has slate-grey head, neck and upperparts and white belly with dark barring. Most females are similar but with brown band on breast. Some females occur as rufous-phase with reddish-brown head, neck and upperparts. At close range, both sexes have striking yellow iris. Juvenile similar to rufous-phase female but usually darker and always with pale patch on nape. Flies with straight back and quick wingbeats below body line and looks raptor-like in flight. Feeds on insects and in particular on hairy moth caterpillars. More often heard than seen. Brood parasite, laying single egg in nests of host species including Reed Warbler and Meadow Pipit. Each female produces eggs whose colour and markings match a particular host. Young Cuckoo evicts host eggs and young.
Voice Call of male is well-known *cuh-kooo*, uttered from arrival date until middle of June. Male also has chuckling call. Female has bubbling call.
Habitat All sorts of open habitats where host species are common. Avoids urban areas.
Distribution In summer found throughout Europe except Iceland. Winters in Africa.
Occurrence Fairly common from late April to September; adults depart south mid-July onwards.

S	4–8	N 5–7

Great Spotted Cuckoo
Clamator glandarius L 39cm

Adult unmistakable with slim body, slight crest and very long tail. Upperparts greyish-brown with white spots on wings, underparts white, and grey cap and cheeks. Juvenile has brown upperparts, buffish underparts and orange-brown primaries. Parasitizes Azure-winged Magpie and Magpie.
Voice Call harsh and chattering.
Habitat Open country with scattered trees and scrub, where host species common.
Distribution S and central Iberian peninsula, Turkey and very locally in S France and N Greece. Winters in Africa.
Occurrence Present in summer range from April to August. Some birds resident in S Spain.

Seen also on passage around Mediterranean and vagrant to NW Europe including Britain.

V	—	—

Yellow-billed Cuckoo
Coccyzus americanus L 30cm

Typical cuckoo shape with brown upperparts, rusty primaries, grey cap and cheeks, and white underparts. Lower mandible of bill yellow and tail is grey above and black below with broad white spots formed by pale tips to outer tail feathers.
Voice Vagrants generally silent.
Habitat Vagrants favour coastal scrub.
Distribution Breeds N and winters S America.
Occurrence Very rare vagrant to W Europe.

V	9–10	—

Black-billed Cuckoo
Coccyzus erythropthalmus L 30cm

Very similar to Yellow-billed Cuckoo but distinguished by all-dark bill, lack of rusty primaries and underside of tail grey with small white tips to outer tail feathers. Habits and behaviour similar to Yellow-billed Cuckoo.

Black-billed Cuckoo

Yellow-billed Cuckoo

Voice Vagrants generally silent.
Habitat Same as Yellow-billed Cuckoo.
Distribution Breeds N and winters S America.
Occurrence Very rare vagrant to W Europe.

V	—	—

PARROTS
ORDER PSITTACIFORMES
Family Psittacidae

Ring-necked Parakeet
Psittacula krameri L 40cm

Feral populations established in Europe. Bright-green colour, dark neck ring, red bill and long tail make it unmistakable.
Voice Typical raucous parrot calls.
Habitat Woodland. Nests in tree holes.
Distribution An Asian species, established in several parts of S England and mainland Europe.
Occurrence Resident where established.

R	1–12	N 5–7

Cuckoo, adult

Great Spotted Cuckoo, female

Cuckoo, juvenile

Great Spotted Cuckoo

Yellow-billed Cuckoo

Ring-necked Parakeet

OWLS
ORDER STRIGIFORMES

Small to large predatory birds that hunt mostly at night. Proportionally large head which can be rotated to considerable extent. Broad facial disc, large eyes and large ear holes.

Scops Owl
Otus scops L 20cm

Small and compact species with distinct ear-tufts. Plumage with delicate vermiculations. Ground colour generally either grey-brown or rufous-brown. Head shape varies according to whether ear-tufts raised (giving startled expression) or lowered. Entirely nocturnal habits. Very difficult to locate at roost during daytime among foliage, often pressed close to bark on tree trunk. Presence in an area invariably indicated initially by call. Feeds mainly on insects.

Voice Call a monotonous and far-carrying whistle, repeated every 2–3 seconds. Rather like sonar 'blip'.

Habitat Found in orchards, olive groves, gardens and parks. Often in villages and towns.

Distribution Widespread summer visitor to S Europe as far north as central France. Some winter in Mediterranean region but most migrate to Africa.

Occurrence Common within breeding range from April to August. Occasional north of range in spring and very rare vagrant to Britain.

V	—	—

Pygmy Owl
Glaucidium passerinum L 18cm

Smallest owl in Europe with very compact and rounded shape. Chocolate-brown plumage with white spots and short, white 'eyebrows'. Belly pale with brown streaks. Often active during daytime when seen perched on top of conifer or other vantage point. Flight between perches undulating. Feeds on small mammals and birds such as Blue Tits.

Voice Call a muted whistle, repeated every 2 seconds or so. Usually delivered at dawn and dusk, often from prominent perch.

Habitat Breeds in conifer forest and seen along edges of rides and clearings. In winter, sometimes moves to more open terrain within range.

Distribution Breeds S and central Scandinavia eastwards and locally in mountainous regions of SE and E Europe.

Occurrence Fairly common resident. Easier to locate than some other owls because of partly diurnal habits.

Little Owl
Athene noctua L 22cm

The most commonly seen owl of its size in much of Europe except the north. Compact body with large, rounded head and long, white 'eyebrows' continuous with pale rim to facial disc. Flies with undulating flight. Partly diurnal and very active at dusk. Often seen perched on telegraph poles, fence posts, etc., when relatively long legs noticeable. If alarmed, extends and retracts neck in series of agitated bows and stretches. Feeds mainly on insects such as beetles, but also small mammals and birds.

Voice Typical call a cat-like mewing *ki-ooo*.

Habitat Found in open country with scattered trees and stone walls, including farmland. Nests in holes in trees, stone walls and rocks.

Distribution Widespread in Europe as far north as Baltic coast. Introduced into Britain and established in Wales and England as far north as Scottish border.

Occurrence Common resident throughout much of range.

R	1–12	N 4–7

Tengmalm's Owl
Aegolius funereus L 25cm

Looks particularly large-headed, pale facial disc having dark rim. Juvenile has chocolate-brown plumage. Entirely nocturnal species. Retiring during daytime, roosting in conifer foliage. Feeds mainly on small mammals but also takes birds.

Voice Territorial call comprises a rapid series of whistles *po-po-po-po-po-po*.

Habitat Mature conifer forests.

Distribution Widespread in Scandinavia and eastwards at similar latitudes. Also locally forested upland regions of E and SE Europe.

Occurrence Fairly common resident in much of range. Occasionally moves beyond range and very rare vagrant to Britain.

Tengmalm's Owl

Scops Owl

Pygmy Owl

Little Owl

Hawk Owl
Surnia ulula L 39cm

Distinctive hawk-like appearance with long tail and compact body. Identification made even easier by often diurnal behaviour and habit of perching on high vantage point such as treetop or even telegraph pole. Feeds mainly on voles and lemmings, their presence and abundance greatly influencing abundance and distribution of the owl.

Voice Territorial call a rapid trilling.

Habitat Taiga forests of conifer and birch.

Distribution Occurs in N Scandinavia and eastwards at similar latitudes.

Occurrence Fairly common resident within range although sometimes completely absent from previously suitable areas owing to lack of small mammals. Occasionally irrupts south and west, when very rare vagrant to Britain.

Eagle Owl
Bubo bubo L 70cm

Europe's largest owl. Stocky appearance, large ear-tufts and bright-orange eyes. Plumage generally warm brown but varies considerably and usually paler in south of region. In flight, shows broad, rounded wings, thickset and pointed head and fast wingbeats. Largely nocturnal but seen hunting at dawn and dusk. Presence in an area best detected by call of male in early spring. Catches prey up to size of hares and grouse.

Voice Call of male a deep and booming *hoo-o*, repeated at 8-second intervals and heard mainly at dawn and dusk.

Habitat All sorts of rugged terrain, from wooded slopes to semi-deserts, but invariably where cliffs or ravines provide nest sites.

Distribution Widespread but extremely local in S, E and NE Europe. Absent from Britain, Ireland, Iceland and lowland mainland NW Europe.

Occurrence Rare resident throughout range.

Snowy Owl
Nyctea scandiaca L 60cm

Huge size and mostly white plumage make this species unmistakable. Males have small numbers of dark spots while females and juveniles are more heavily marked. In flight, shows broad wings and powerful wingbeats. Despite size and colour, and open nature of preferred terrain, often takes full advantage of rocky outcrops or other irregularities in landscape for camouflage. Can be surprisingly difficult to locate. Feeds mainly on

lemmings and other small rodents. Precise distribution, numbers and nesting success highly dependent on abundance of prey.

Voice Call of male is a subdued *gawh*.

Habitat Tundra and northern moors.

Distribution N Scandinavia eastwards at similar latitudes and central Iceland. Has bred on Shetland and one or more birds not infrequently summer there.

Occurrence Rather uncommon throughout range. Has a more coastal distribution during winter months, some birds moving south. Occasional and rare winter vagrant to N Scotland.

V	11–3	—

Great Grey Owl
Strix nebulosa L 65cm

A very large owl. Slimmer than Eagle Owl with grey-brown plumage and proportionately large head, the face with dark, concentric rings and yellow irises. In flight, shows broad, rounded wings with warm-brown panel on primaries, tail with dark terminal band and head with blunt profile. Hunts during daytime in summer months. Feeds mainly on small mammals such as voles, often scanning from vantage point such as dead tree.

Voice Call of male a series of 12 or so hoots, accelerating and dropping in tone towards end.

Habitat Extensive coniferous and mixed forests. Nests in old raptor nest or on tree stump.

Distribution Breeds locally NE Scandinavia and eastwards at similar latitudes.

Occurrence Local and generally uncommon, numbers and breeding success affected by prey abundance.

Ural Owl
Strix uralensis L 60cm

Recalls large Tawny Owl but with proportionately longer tail and pale grey-brown plumage. Eyes dark. Boldly streaked on breast. Extremely aggressive towards human intruders near nest site. Feeds on small mammals and medium-sized birds.

Voice Territorial call of male a booming *woohoo...(pause)...woohoo-owoohoo*.

Habitat Coniferous and mixed forests.

Distribution Breeds E Scandinavia and at similar latitudes eastwards. Also locally in mountains of SE Europe.

Occurrence Rather uncommon resident within range and generally sedentary throughout year.

Hawk Owl

Great Grey Owl

Eagle Owl
Snowy Owl

Ural Owl, female

Long-eared Owl
Asio otus L 36cm

Beautifully marked plumage with streaks, spots and blotches. Has bright-orange eyes and large ear-tufts. These are lowered when bird is resting but raised at slightest agitation or curiosity. Usually sits in rather upright posture and, if alarmed, stretches itself giving rather bizarre, laterally flattened appearance. In flight, ear-tufts are hidden and shows long, rounded wings, looking confusingly similar to Short-eared Owl. Underwing pale and upperwing brown, the outer wing, beyond the dark carpal patch, being paler brown with darker barred wingtips. Exclusively nocturnal species, seldom seen in daytime except when disturbed. However, in winter, sometimes sits prominently on outside of bush or ivy-covered tree with dense cover, seemingly sunning itself. In winter, occasionally roosts in loose groups. Feeds mainly on mice and voles but also takes small birds, especially during winter when it will attack roosts of birds at dusk.

Voice Male's territorial call *hooo*, female's response being *kaah*. Calls of young resemble the squeak of a rusty gate.

Habitat Typically breeds in small clumps of woodland, including conifer plantations, surrounded by more open country. Uses old Crows' nests. Seldom found in woodland where Tawny Owls are resident. In winter, found roosting in similar habitat but also in overgrown hedgerows with ivy-covered trees.

Distribution Occurs throughout Europe in suitable habitats as far north as S Scandinavia. Found locally throughout Britain and Ireland. Some dispersal in winter and most northern birds move south.

Occurrence Fairly common but usually difficult to locate.

T	1–12	N 4–6

Short-eared Owl
Asio flammeus L 38cm

Buffish-brown plumage, heavily marked with white spots and dark blotches. Eyes yellow and staring, the effect enhanced by black eye surround. Ear-tufts short and stubby and often not visible. In flight, has long, rounded wings held stiffly in gliding flight. Underwings white with dark wingtips and carpal patches. Upperwing brown with dark carpal patch, outer wing being buffish with black wingtips. Often seen feeding during daytime but mostly around dawn and dusk. Hence, one of the easiest larger owls to see. Sometimes systematically quarters rodent-rich grassy areas. Regularly perches on fence posts or on tussocks or low mounds. Feeds mainly on small mammals but will take small birds, e.g. Wrens during winter months.

Voice Male courtship call a repeated *doo-doo-doo*, with female response *chee-op*.

Habitat Breeds on northern grassy moors, and extensive heaths and fields. Nests on ground. In winter, found on similar habitats in lowland areas but also on agricultural land.

Distribution Breeds locally in NW Europe including upland Wales, N England and Scotland. Also breeds N and NE Europe, the population migrating south and west in winter and augmenting populations in Britain. Winter range includes most of Europe.

Occurrence Fairly common in suitable habitats within range.

T	1–12	N 4–6

Marsh Owl
Asio capensis L 36cm

Similar appearance to Short-eared Owl but rich dark-brown plumage and almost unmarked upperparts. In flight, shows buff patch at base of primaries.

Voice Frog-like call given in flight.

Habitat Marshes and swamps.

Distribution Range includes much of Africa, nearest location to Europe being NW Morocco.

Occurrence Very rare vagrant to S Iberian peninsula.

Short-eared Owl

Short-eared Owl

Marsh Owl

Long-eared Owl

Long-eared Owl

Tawny Owl
Strix aluco L 38cm

The commonest owl throughout much of Europe. Typical plumage colour warm brown but also occurs as much scarcer grey phase. At rest, looks rather compact, short-tailed and large-headed. White blotches noticeable on wings but otherwise plumage shows darker barring and streaking. Eyes dark. In flight, wings appear relatively short, broad and rounded. Held gently bowed downwards in leisurely flight. Almost exclusively nocturnal in habits. Occasionally seen hunting at dusk but more often heard than seen. During daytime, usually roosts in cover of foliage or pressed close to tree trunk. Roost sites rarely detected by discovery of pellets beneath tree. If discovered roosting by woodland birds, is mobbed vigorously. In spring, downy young sometimes seen sitting conspicuously after having recently left nest. Feeds mainly on voles and mice.

Voice Typical and well-known call of male is *who-WHOOO*, followed by a pause and then *who-who-who-WHOOO*. Female has typical *kew-wick* call.

Habitat Found in well-established broadleaved woodland, parks and mature gardens. Nests in hollow trees but also takes readily to nestboxes.

Distribution Widespread throughout much of Europe as far north as S Scandinavia. Absent from Ireland and Iceland.

Occurrence Generally common resident in range including most of Britain.

R	1–12	N 3–6

Barn Owl
Tyto alba L 36cm

A very pale owl with a heart-shaped face and dark eye. Typical pale race *alba* has beautiful pale-buff and soft grey upperparts and white underparts including underwing. Dark-breasted race *guttata* has orange-buff underparts but retains pale underwing. In flight, has long and rounded wings. Flies with stiffly held wings and legs often dangling. Sometimes seen quartering fields in late afternoon or at dusk for voles and mice. Glides on rigid wings and speed sometimes appears incredibly slow. Occasionally feeds on wide, grassy roadside verges and then often caught in car headlights in flight or perched on fence posts. Feeds mainly on voles and mice.

Voice Territorial call of male a blood-curdling shriek. That of female is softer.

Habitat Feeds over grassland and other open areas where small mammal prey common. Nests in barns, lofts and farm outbuildings. More occasionally in hollow trees. Readily takes to nesting trays and boxes placed in likely-looking rural buildings.

Distribution Widespread in Europe as far north as Denmark. Breeds in Britain and Ireland but absent from Iceland. Race *alba* occurs in W Europe including Britain. Race *guttata* occurs in N and E Europe.

Occurrence Fairly common resident in most of Europe although has declined markedly in some areas, including Britain, owing to loss of feeding habitat and nesting sites.

R	1–12	N 4–7

Barn Owl

Tawny Owl   Barn Owl

Tawny Owl

NIGHTJARS
ORDER CAPRIMULGIFORMES
Family Caprimulgidae

Nocturnal birds with large heads and camouflaged plumage. Small bill but large mouth. Rest on ground during day with eyes closed. Active at night, catching moths and other insects on the wing. Nest on ground.

Nightjar
Caprimulgus europaeus L 28cm
Mottled plumage, mainly grey, brown, black and buff, gives superb camouflage when at rest among fallen leaves and fragments of tree bark. Tiny bill but huge gape. Entirely nocturnal, roosting during daytime with large eyes mostly closed, bird then looking extremely inanimate. Takes to wing at dusk, when long tail and wings with buoyant flight and raptor-like silhouette are visible. Male has white patches on 3 outer primaries and on outer 2 pairs of tail feathers. Catches flying insects in huge mouth.
Voice Typical territorial churring of male starts at dusk and continues for minutes on end without pause. Churring pitched on 2 tones. Flight call *kru-it*. Male also performs a vigorous wing-clapping display.
Habitat Heathland, wide clearings in open woodland and cleared and newly planted conifer plantations.
Distribution Widespread but local summer visitor throughout Europe as far north as S Scandinavia. In Britain, found locally in England, Wales and S Scotland. Local in Ireland. Winters in Africa.
Occurrence Occurs locally from May to August. Presence in suitable area easily determined by listening for churring. In Britain, most likely areas are heathlands of S England.

S	5–8	N 5–7

Red-necked Nightjar
Caprimulgus ruficollis L 30cm
Very similar to Nightjar but slightly larger with paler-grey plumage, rufous neck collar and more conspicuous white on throat. Both sexes have white on wings and tail. Habits and behaviour same as Nightjar.
Voice Song a disyllabic and continuously repeated *ky-tok ky-tok*.
Habitat Open, Mediterranean habitats including maquis and olive groves.

Red-necked Nightjar

Distribution Summer visitor to Iberian peninsula and adjacent areas of N Africa. Winters in Africa.
Occurrence Widespread but seldom common from May to September.

Common Nighthawk
Chordeiles minor L 24cm
Superficially similar to Nightjar but with more pointed wings, extensive white patch on primaries in both sexes and forked tail. Male has white throat and white band on tail. Not exclusively nocturnal and vagrants to Europe occasionally seen flying during daytime.
Voice Vagrants to region mostly silent.
Habitat Open terrain.
Distribution Breeds N America and winters S America.
Occurrence Very rare autumn vagrant to W Europe including Britain.

V	—	—

Nightjar

Nightjar

Common Nighthawk

SWIFTS
ORDER APODIFORMES
Family Apodidae

Spend most of life on wing. Streamlined bodies and scythe-shaped wings. Legs short and almost useless on ground. Feed on aerial insects. Sexes similar.

Swift
Apus apus L 16cm

The most common and widespread swift of the region. Seen mostly in flight with narrow, scythe-shaped wings, uniform dark-brown plumage except for pale throat and slightly forked tail. Feeds on the wing, catching aerial insects. Invariably seen in small to large parties, accompanied by typical swift screaming.

Voice Typical screaming call, uttered both on wing and, occasionally, by nesting individuals.
Habitat Often associated with towns and villages since roof spaces provide most nest sites.
Distribution Summer visitor to most of Europe except Iceland and N Scandinavia.
Occurrence Present from May to August around breeding areas. Large groups of birds may gather over lakes in August prior to migration.

S	4–9	N 5–7

Chimney Swift *Chaetura pelagica* is smaller with cigar-shaped body. Very rare vagrant to Britain from N America.

Pallid Swift
Apus pallidus L 17cm

Very similar to Swift but plumage paler brown. In harsh light, this difference can be difficult to discern although flight feathers usually look rather translucent. Often in mixed flocks with Swifts. Habits and behaviour similar to Swift.

Voice Swift-like screams but lower in pitch.
Habitat Mediterranean coasts and towns.
Distribution Breeds along coast and islands of Mediterranean from S Iberian peninsula to N Greece. Winters mainly in Africa.
Occurrence Common Mediterranean species from March to September. Occasionally seen north of range and very rare vagrant to Britain.

V	—	—

Alpine Swift
Apus melba L 22cm

Considerably larger than Swift, with white underparts divided by dark breast band. White throat not always easy to see in bright light. Wingbeats

slower than Swift. Rapidly switches from rather slow, languid flight to incredibly rapid speeds. Vagrants outside usual range.

Voice Call a trilling scream.
Habitat Towns and rugged upland regions.
Distribution Breeds locally across much of S Europe. Winters in Africa.
Occurrence Fairly common within breeding range from April to September.

V	—	—

Needle-tailed Swift *Hirundapus caudacutus* is slightly smaller with white throat, white horse-shoe shape on rear flanks and undertail, and pale-brown back. Very rare vagrant to Europe.

White-rumped Swift
Apus caffer L 14cm

Smaller than Swift with pale throat, narrow white rump crescent, white trailing edge to secondaries and deeply forked tail, the latter not always clearly visible. Habits and behaviour as Swift.

Voice Twittering screams.
Habitat In limited European range, uses old nests of Red-rumped Swallow.
Distribution In Europe, breeding range restricted to S Spain and there extremely local.
Occurrence In Europe from May to September.

V	—	—

Pacific Swift *Apus pacificus* is similar but larger than Swift. Very rare vagrant to Britain from Asia.

Little Swift
Apus affinis L 12cm

Similar to White-rumped Swift but with square-ended tail and broad white rump.

Voice Twittering call.
Habitat Similar to other swifts.
Distribution Nearest breeding colonies to Europe in N Africa. Winters in Africa.
Occurrence Rare visitor to Europe and very rare vagrant to Britain.

V	—	—

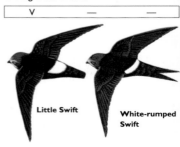

Little Swift

White-rumped Swift

Swift

| Swift | Pallid Swift | Alpine Swift |

KINGFISHERS AND
ALLIED BIRDS
ORDER CORACIFORMES

A group of colourful birds. Kingfishers (family Alcedinidae) have large heads, long bills and short tails. Most dive into water for fish and nest in burrows. Bee-eaters (family Meropidae) are slim birds with pointed wings and long bills. They catch insects on the wing and nest in burrows. Rollers (family Coracidae) are medium-sized birds which catch insects and lizards on the ground. They nest in holes in trees or buildings. Hoopoes (family Upupidae) have long bills for probing ground and large, rounded wings. Hole-nesters.

Kingfisher
Alcedo atthis L 17cm
Amazingly colourful combination of orange-red below and pale blue to greenish-blue above. Metallic-looking sheen especially to feathers on back. Male has all-black bill, female with reddish base to lower mandible. Young birds have pale tip to bill. Seen perching motionless over stream or river, watching for prey such as Minnows, Sticklebacks and Bullheads. Also perches for extended periods in shade or among overhanging foliage and then very difficult to spot. Often seen as flash of blue flying by along river course. Sometimes hovers before plunge-diving.
Voice High-pitched whistling call tzee.
Habitat Typical habitats clear, unpolluted streams and rivers. Steep, sandy banks are essential since Kingfishers excavate long nest tunnels. Also seen on gravel pits, ponds and lakes and occasionally on coast, especially in winter.
Distribution Widespread in suitable habitats in much of S Europe as far north as Baltic. Found throughout Ireland, Wales and England, and just over border into Scotland.
Occurrence Resident species, mostly sedentary but with some dispersal in autumn and winter especially by populations in N and E Europe.

R	1–12	N 5–6

White-breasted Kingfisher
Halcyon smyrnensis L 27cm
Striking bird with blue back, wings and tail, reddish-chestnut head, neck and underparts, and white throat and chest. Large, dagger-like bill is blood-red. In flight, shows pale-blue bases to primaries. Catches fish and amphibians over water but also feeds on land, catching insects and lizards.

Voice Loud, whistling calls.
Habitat Lakes, rivers and neighbouring dry land
Distribution A mainly Asian species with a limited range in S Turkey.
Occurrence Local and scarce within the region.

Pied Kingfisher
Ceryle rudis L 25cm
Unmistakable kingfisher with bold black-and-white plumage. Male has 2 breast bands, female only 1. Perches over water, often at considerable height on overhead wires, but also frequently hovers before plunge-diving.
Voice Shrill, whistling calls.
Habitat Feeds over ponds, lakes and rivers but also on estuaries and brackish pools.
Distribution Main range includes Africa and Asia but occurs locally in S Turkey.
Occurrence Local in S Turkey and rare vagrant to SE Europe.

Belted Kingfisher
Ceryle alcyon L 32cm
A huge kingfisher with blue-grey upperparts and white neck and below. Both sexes have blue-grey breast band but female has reddish-chestnut band below this, the colour extending to the flanks. Frequently perches on overhead wires.
Voice A loud, rattling call.
Habitat Rivers and, more occasionally, estuaries.
Distribution Breeds N America, birds from north of range moving south in winter.
Occurrence Very rare vagrant to W Europe including Britain.

V	—	—

Belted Kingfisher, female

Kingfisher

Pied Kingfisher

White-breasted Kingfisher

Bee-eater
Merops apiaster L 28cm

Adult is unmistakable with long bill, streamlined outline and stunning combination of colours including reddish-chestnut, yellow, blue and green. In flight, shows pointed wings and short tail projections. Juvenile has mostly green upperparts, except for reddish-brown crown, and no tail projections. Soars and glides on outstretched wings but also has direct flight with rapid wingbeats. Catches insects on the wing, notably hoverflies, dragonflies and bumblebees.

Voice Call a rolling *kruup*, a typical early-summer sound in the Mediterranean.

Habitat Feeds over open country and nests colonially in burrows excavated in sandy banks.

Distribution Normal breeding range covers most of lowland S Europe where Mediterranean influence is felt. Widespread in Iberian peninsula and extends further northwards in E Europe. Winters in Africa.

Occurrence Locally fairly common in S Europe from May to September. Migrants often overshoot in spring and occasionally breeds well beyond its usual range. Rare but annual visitor to Britain, mostly in late spring and early summer.

V	5–8	—

Blue-cheeked Bee-eater
Merops superciliosus L 29cm

Silhouette resembles Bee-eater but has much longer tail projections. Plumage almost entirely green with blue on cheeks and supercilium and reddish-orange throat. Could be confused with juvenile Bee-eater but has green not reddish-brown crown. Habits and behaviour as Bee-eater.

Voice Similar to that of Bee-eater.

Habitat Open country.

Distribution Main range Africa and W Asia.

Occurrence Rare vagrant to Europe and has occurred in Britain.

V	—	—

Roller
Coracias garrulus L 30cm

Adult has rather shiny, pale-blue feathers on head, neck and underparts and buffish-brown back. Deeper-blue carpals and underside to flight feathers. Juvenile has washed-out adult colours with more buffish feathering on head and neck. Flight is direct and corvid-like. Often perches on elevated look-out such as dead tree or roadside telephone wire, scanning for prey such as insects and lizards. English name derives from male's display flight during which he dives from a considerable height, performing half-rolls and calling loudly.

Voice Corvid-like *kak-ak*.

Habitat Open country including heaths and agricultural land. Nests in hollow trees.

Distribution Similar to that of the Bee-eater. Widespread in S Europe where the Mediterranean influence is felt but range extends northwards in E Europe to E Baltic coast. Winters in Africa.

Occurrence Rather local and scarce summer visitor from May to September. Rare vagrant to Britain.

V	—	—

Hoopoe
Upupa epops L 27cm

Can be rather unobtrusive but when seen well is unmistakable. Pinkish-buff head and neck and strongly barred, black-and-white wings and tail most conspicuous in flight. Bill long and slightly downcurved and head with erectile crest of long pinkish-buff feathers tipped with black. In flight, wings look disproportionately large and rounded. Flight pattern rather Jay-like but often recalls a giant moth. Feeds on ground, probing soil for insects and other invertebrates, and among rocks for small lizards. Can be difficult to locate, especially if feeding in cultivated fields.

Voice Far-carrying, rhythmic, quick *hoopoopoo*.

Habitat All sorts of open country including farmland, gardens and parks. Nests in holes in trees and walls.

Distribution In summer, found in most of S and central Europe as far north as Baltic. Most birds migrate south of Mediterranean in winter but largely resident in S Iberian peninsula.

Occurrence Common within range from March to September. Often overshoots normal range and scarce but regular visitor to Britain where has bred.

V	3–10	—

Bee-eater

Blue-cheeked Bee-eater

Roller

WOODPECKERS
ORDER PICIFORMES
Family Picidae

Small to medium-sized birds with powerful bills used for drilling into wood, to extract wood-boring insects. Climb tree trunks with strong feet, 2 toes pointing forward and 2 pointing back. Stiff tails used for support. Nest in holes in trees.

Green Woodpecker
Picus viridis L 30cm

Has greenish upperparts and bright-yellow rump, most conspicuous in flight. Both sexes have red crown and black mask and moustachial stripe. Male, however, has red centre to moustachial stripe. Male of Iberian race *sharpei* has moustachial stripe mostly red. Juvenile has dark streaks and spots on head, neck and underparts. Flight is undulating with glides. Often feeds on ground, searching mostly for ants. Can be extremely unobtrusive and, in many areas, heard far more frequently than seen. Seldom drums.

Voice Typical call in spring is well-known laughing yaffle *kyu-kyu-kyu-kyu-kyu*.

Habitat Open woodland, mainly deciduous, and wooded parks with open, grassy spaces.

Distribution Widespread in most of Europe to S Scandinavia. In Britain, occurs as far north as S Scotland. Absent from Ireland and Iceland.

Occurrence Fairly common resident throughout range and generally sedentary.

R	1–12	N 5–7

Northern Flicker *Colaptes auratus* has barred, greenish back, underparts pale with black spots and buffish head and neck with black malar stripe and chest band and red on nape. Very rare vagrant to NW Europe from N America.

Grey-headed Woodpecker
Picus canus L 27cm

Similar to Green Woodpecker but slimmer, smaller and with greyer face, neck and underparts. Black markings on face much less extensive than Green Woodpecker. Black confined to narrow moustachial stripe and marking between eye and base of bill. Male only has limited amount of red on forecrown. Juvenile similar to female but with some dark feathering on underparts. Generally rather shy and elusive.

Voice Similar to Green Woodpecker but higher pitched and more fluty with diagnostic fade and fall at end.

Grey-headed Woodpecker, male

Habitat Breeds in deciduous and mixed woodland and parkland with clumps of trees.

Distribution Found rather locally throughout central and NE Europe including central Scandinavia.

Occurrence Rather uncommon and easily overlooked.

Great Spotted Woodpecker
Dendrocopus major L 22cm

Commonest and most widespread of the black-and-white woodpeckers. Both sexes have large, white shoulder panel and red undertail. White underparts are unstreaked and black moustachial stripe is joined to black on nape. Juvenile has black markings similar to adult but with extensive red on forecrown and pinkish-buff undertail. Underparts dirtier white than adult. Flight typically undulating and often accompanied by loud call. Drums loudly in spring. Feeds on insects but also on seeds and nuts.

Voice Typical call a sharp *chik*, sometimes repeated in agitated succession.

Habitat Deciduous and coniferous woodland, parks and gardens.

Distribution Widespread throughout most of Europe but absent from Ireland and Iceland.

Occurrence Common and rather sedentary.

R	1–12	N 5–7

Middle Spotted Woodpecker
Dendrocopus medius L 20cm

Similar to Great Spotted Woodpecker (especially juvenile) but smaller and with red crown and streaked flanks. Face mostly white with black limited to streak from cheek to side of breast. Pinkish undertail. Sexes similar. Often seen feeding on outermost branches in tree crown. Seldom drums.

Voice Call similar to that of Great Spotted Woodpecker but lower-pitched.

Habitat Deciduous woodland especially where oak and hornbeam predominate.

Distribution Found throughout central, E and SE Europe. Occurs in N Spain.

Occurrence Common resident within range.

Green Woodpecker

Great Spotted Woodpecker, female

Great Spotted Woodpecker, juvenile

Middle Spotted Woodpecker

Syrian Woodpecker
Dendrocopus syriacus L 23cm
Distinguished from Great Spotted Woodpecker by lack of black stripe linking moustachial stripe with black on nape. Undertail is pink rather than red. Male has more extensive red on nape than male Great Spotted. Juvenile has similar patterning to adult but extensive red on crown.
Voice Similar to Great Spotted Woodpecker.
Habitat Villages, parks and agricultural land.
Distribution SE Europe, from E Austria to Turkey.
Occurrence Common resident within range.

White-backed Woodpecker
Dendrocopus leucotos L 25cm
Larger than Great Spotted Woodpecker and distinguished from other similarly sized *Dendrocopus* woodpeckers by white rump and lower back, best seen in flight, and lack of white panels on shoulders. At rest, shows transverse white bars on back, the upper one being broadest and most extensive. Streaking on flanks and red undertail extending as red flush to belly. Both sexes have black moustachial stripe extending to cheeks and flanks but not linking with black on nape. Crown red in male and black in female.
Voice Similar to Great Spotted Woodpecker.
Habitat Mature forests with decaying trees.
Distribution Very local from Greece to S Scandinavia. Also very local in W Pyrenees.

White-backed Woodpecker

Three-toed Woodpecker, right

Lesser Spotted Woodpecker
Dendrocopus minor L 15cm
Smallest European woodpecker. Has barred black-and-white back and no red under tail. Male has red crown, that of female being mostly white. Often extremely unobtrusive. In winter, occasionally seen with mixed flocks of woodland birds.
Voice Calls include a quiet *kik* and subdued but insistent *pee-pee-pee*, like a distant bird of prey.
Habitat Deciduous and mixed woodlands, often favouring wetter areas beside rivers.
Distribution Widespread but local in Europe. Absent from Ireland and Iceland. In Britain, found mainly in S and central England and Wales.
Occurrence Generally rather scarce resident species but often overlooked.

Three-toed Woodpecker
Picoides tridactylus L 22cm
Bold black-and-white stripes on head, white back and barring on flanks. Male has yellow crown. Feeds relatively low down. Mainly insectivorous but also drills for sap. Drums loudly but slowly.
Voice Softer than Great Spotted Woodpecker.
Habitat Forests of spruce and birch.
Distribution Main range from central and N Scandinavia eastwards. Also occurs locally in mountains of SE Europe.
Occurrence Fairly common in N of range.

Black Woodpecker
Dryocopus martius L 45cm
Large size and all-black plumage distinctive. Male has red crown and female has red patch on nape. Flight crow-like. Drums extremely loudly.
Voice Calls include a drawn-out *klee-ee* when perched and *klee-klee-klee* in flight.
Habitat In mature, deciduous, mixed and coniferous forests. Excavates large nest hole.
Distribution Widespread in central and N Europe to tree-line in Scandinavia. Much more local in W and S Europe to N Spain. Absent from Britain, Ireland and Iceland.
Occurrence Fairly common resident in N and central Europe.

Wryneck
Jynx torquilla L 17cm
Distinctive and unusual bird and the least woodpecker-like species of the group. Cryptic plumage a mixture of grey, brown, black and white, closely resembles tree bark and lichens. Bill short and triangular. Feeds almost exclusively on ants. Flight undulating.
Voice Repetitive *teu-teu-teu*, resembling raptor.
Habitat Breeds in parks, gardens and open woodland. Nests in natural holes in trees.
Distribution Breeds across most of mainland Europe except S Iberian peninsula, S Greece and N Scandinavia. Absent from Iceland and Ireland. In Britain, confined as a breeding species to central Scotland. Winters mostly in Africa.
Occurrence Fairly common in most of breeding range from May to August. Has recently colonized Scotland but extremely local. In Britain, seen mostly as passage migrant around coasts.

R	1–12	N 5–7

S	4–10	N 5–6

Syrian Woodpecker

Lesser Spotted Woodpecker

Black Woodpecker, at nest hole

Wryneck

PASSERINES OR PERCHING BIRDS
ORDER PASSERIFORMES

The passerines or perching birds is a large and varied group, both in terms of size and appearance. It includes some of the most familiar and common species of birds in Europe, and all share the ability to perch, having toes pointing forward and pointing back. Another characteristic of the group is that many of its members are accomplished songbirds, and all the birds on the remaining pages of this book belong to this order.

Despite the small size of many of the passerines, a large number of species are long-distance migrants. Some visit Europe to breed during the spring and summer months and herald their arrival with a chorus of song. In the autumn, many of the warblers, for example, fly south, some reaching as far as sub-Saharan Africa. Others move within the boundaries of Europe, breeding in the far north or east and moving south and west in the autumn.

The social behaviour of passerine birds is also remarkably varied. With relatively few exceptions, they are solitary nesting birds but some, such as Fieldfares and Redwings, form large flocks, even mixing with other species, on migration and outside the breeding season. Some of their nests are remarkable constructions. The Long-tailed Tit, for example, weaves a beautiful ball-like creation of moss, lichen and spiders' webs, and lines it with as many as a thousand feathers. The variation in behaviour and habits is also reflected in the habitats occupied by passerines. Different species can be found from sea level to the highest mountains in Europe. Although often associated with wetland habitats, no passerines are truly aquatic. However, the Dipper does dive below the surface of fast-flowing streams and rivers, clasping onto boulders and rocks with its feet as it searches for aquatic invertebrates.

The endearing Robin is among the most familiar of Europe's passerine birds. An accomplished songster, this species is widespread in woods and gardens.

LARKS
Family Alaudidae

Small birds with rather uniform brown plumage. Mainly terrestrial, inhabiting open country. Songs often delivered in flight. Ground-nesting.

Dupont's Lark
Chersophilus duponti L 18cm
Recalls Skylark but lacks crest and has longer, downcurved bill. Shows pale supercilium, relatively short tail with white outer feathers and rather long legs. Prefers to run rather than fly. Has rather upright stance. Usually incredibly difficult to see.
Voice Subdued, fluty whistle of 3 or 4 syllables.
Habitat Breeds on arid steppes and stony plains.
Distribution Main breeding range in N Africa but established populations in central Spain.
Occurrence Extremely local

Dupont's Lark

in central Spain; easy to overlook.

Short-toed Lark
Calandrella brachydactyla L 15cm
A small, compact lark with sandy-brown upperparts and pale, mostly unmarked underparts. Pale supercilium, dark eye-stripe behind eye, rather conical bill and slight crest which is not always obvious. Small, dark patch on side of neck is a good feature but not always visible.
Voice Calls include a Skylark-like *chirp*. Song, given in yo-yo-like flight, fast and spluttering.
Habitat Dry, bare ground including mudflats, semi-deserts and ploughed arable land.
Distribution Breeds across S Europe within area of Mediterranean climate. Winters in N Africa.
Occurrence Fairly common in S Europe from May to September. Seen outside breeding range on passage and rare, regular vagrant to Britain.

V	5, 9–10	—

Lesser Short-toed Lark
Calandrella rufescens L 14cm
Very similar to Short-toed Lark and easily confused. Shows distinctly streaked breast, the streaking extending along flanks, rather stubby bill and primaries extending beyond tertials at rest.

Spanish race *apetzii* has grey-brown upperparts.
Voice Call a buzzing *churrr*. Song contains elements of mimicry, particularly of other larks.
Habitat Stony steppes, dry lake margins.
Distribution Main range N Africa but also locally in S and E Spain and Turkey.

Lesser Short-toed Lark

Occurrence Very local resident in Europe and very rare vagrant to Britain.

V	—	—

Calandra Lark
Melanocorypha calandra L 19cm
Large, stoutly built lark with proportionately large head, large bill and short tail. Large, black neck patches most obvious in spring male. In flight, shows dark underwings and white trailing edge to wing. Wingbeats rather slow.
Voice Harsh call and song containing Corn Bunting-like jingles and elements of mimicry.
Habitat Dry, grassy plains and arable land.
Distribution Mainly S Europe, generally where the influence of the Mediterranean climate is felt.
Occurrence Fairly common within breeding range. Very rare vagrant to Britain, mainly spring.

V	—	—

Shore Lark
Eremophila alpestris L 16cm
Adults have sandy-brown upperparts, pale underparts and bold black and yellow facial markings. In summer, acquires small black 'horns' on crown. In winter, black facial markings are less contrasting. Northern race *flava* has black on cheek separate from breast band. In race *penicillata* from Greece and Turkey the two are joined. Juvenile has back, nape, crown brown with pale spots.
Voice Flight call a trisyllabic *tsee-tsutsu*. Song erratic and tinkling.
Habitat Breeds on northern heaths and mountain tops. Winters on coasts.
Distribution Isolated breeding populations in Scandinavia, Greece and Turkey. Scandinavian population winters on coasts of NW Europe.
Occurrence Rather scarce breeding species. In Britain, small numbers regularly overwinter, especially on E coast of England.

W	10–4	—

Short-toed Lark

Calandra Lark

Shore Lark, winter

Shore Lark, summer male

Desert Lark
Ammomanes deserti L 16cm

Rather dumpy build with uniform and unmarked, sandy-brown plumage. Tail shows diffuse dark band at tip and no white.

Voice Call a subdued *chwee*.

Habitat Arid semi-desert and rocky plains.

Distribution Breeds N Africa to SE Turkey.

Occurrence Common in non-European range.

Crested Lark
Galerida cristata L 17cm

Plumage of most races greyer-brown than Skylark and has characteristic long, pointed crest. Bill relatively long and stout and tail short with reddish-brown outer feathers. Rather diffuse streaking on breast. Runs well. In flight, shows rounded wings without white trailing edge seen in Skylark. Feeds on seeds and insects.

Voice Call *twee-tweeooo*. Song a subdued version of Skylark's with mimetic phrases. Often delivered from perch but sometimes in flight. Seldom perches on bushes.

Habitat Dry, open terrain including town parks, roadside verges, arable fields and derelict land.

Distribution Widespread in lowland mainland Europe north to Baltic coast. Absent from upland regions and Britain, Ireland and Iceland.

Occurrence A common resident species in much of Europe, but a very rare vagrant to Britain.

| V | — | — |

Thekla Lark
Galerida theklae L 17cm

Very similar to Crested Lark with which it overlaps in parts of its range. Distinguished by shorter bill and crest and more distinct streaks on breast. Plumage is generally more richly marked than on Crested Lark. In flight, shows distinctly reddish-brown rump and grey-brown axillaries. Often perches on bushes.

Voice Call similar to that of Crested Lark. Song similar to Skylark but more musical.

Habitat Prefers garigue-type habitat with stony ground and scattered bushes. Choice of habitat is usually a clue to identity.

Distribution Main range includes central and S Iberian peninsula and N Africa, the range, but not necessarily the habitat, overlapping with that of Crested Lark. Also found on Majorca where Crested Lark absent.

Occurrence Fairly common resident in suitable habitats within range.

Skylark
Alauda arvensis L 18cm

The commonest and most widespread lark of the region. Most races have rather warm-brown plumage, rich streaking on breast and pale belly. Tail relatively long with white outer feathers. Has short crest which is not always visible. In flight, shows white trailing edge to wings. Juvenile has rather scaly appearance; lacks crest. In summer months recognized by incessant song mostly delivered in fluttering song-flight. In autumn and winter, seen in small flocks feeding in stubble and ploughed fields.

Voice Continuous stream of high-pitched warbling, musical phrases with elements of mimicry. Song often lasts for up to half an hour. Heard at any daylight hour during spring and summer.

Habitat Breeds in grassy habitats from farmland and meadows to heaths and moorland. In winter, often on arable land.

Distribution Widespread breeding range in Europe north to central Scandinavia. Absent from Iceland. In autumn, withdraws from N and E of range.

Occurrence A very common resident in W and S Europe, numbers augmented from October to March by migrants from N and E Europe.

| R | 1–12 | N 4–7 |

Woodlark
Lullula arborea L 15cm

Superficially resembles a small Skylark but with markedly short tail tipped with white but lacking pale outer feathers. Overall appearance of plumage distinct and contrasting, particularly on head. Shows pale superciliaries which almost meet at nape and contrast with dark crown and reddish-brown ear coverts. Has small crest which is seldom raised. Diagnostic feature is black spot bordered with white on forewing, visible both in flight and at rest. Combination of fluttering wings and short tail produce bat-like appearance in flight. Feeds on ground but also perches in trees.

Voice A musical series of yodelling phrases, descending in pitch and sometimes rendered as *too-de-loo-de-loo*. Usually delivered in song-flight.

Habitat Breeds on heaths and sometimes farmland with scattered clumps of trees. Shows a marked preference for recently burnt areas.

Distribution Widespread but local in mainland Europe north to S Scandinavia. In Britain, confined to S England. Absent from Ireland.

Occurrence A rather scarce resident in W and S Europe. Populations from N and E Europe migrate south and west in autumn.

| R | 1–12 | N 4–7 |

Desert Lark

Crested Lark

Woodlark

Thekla Lark

Skylark

SWALLOWS AND MARTINS
Family Hirundinidae

Streamlined bodies and long, pointed wings. Feed on wing, catching aerial insects. Large mouths but small bills. Swallows have deeply forked tails. Often perch on wires. Legs small. Most species are long-distance migrants.

Sand Martin
Riparia riparia L 12cm
Upperparts dark sandy-brown. Underparts white except for distinct brown breast band and brown underwing. Juvenile is similar but has pale-fringed feathers on upperparts giving scaly appearance. Often seen feeding over water, catching insects in the company of other hirundines. Post-breeding birds roost in reedbeds, often in large numbers.
Voice Call a rasping chatter.
Habitat Nests colonially, excavating burrows in vertical sandy cliffs, e.g. in sand pits or riverbanks.
Distribution Breeding range includes most of Europe including Britain and Ireland. Absent from many upland regions and from Iceland. Winters in Africa.
Occurrence Common summer visitor from April to September. Some arrive as early as March.

S	3–10	N 5–6

Crag Martin
Ptyonoprogne rupestris L 15cm
Larger and broader-winged than Sand Martin and without dark breast band. Upperparts grey-brown and underparts pale sandy-brown. Underwing coverts distinctly darker than brown flight feathers and contrast often visible in flight. When tail is spread, pale spots visible near tip. In suitable habitats, often seen patrolling and circling up and down along cliff face, usually in small groups.

Voice Mostly silent except for weak *chree* call.
Habitat During breeding season, associated with cliffs, rock-faces, gorges and ravines. Usually nests under overhanging rock. In winter, upland birds move south to lower altitudes where often found in the vicinity of water in rugged terrain.
Distribution Breeding range includes most of S Europe. In winter, withdraws from mountainous regions and found around Mediterranean coast although still widespread in Iberian peninsula.
Occurrence Fairly common within range but rather local.

House Martin
Delichon urbica L 13cm
A small but distinctive hirundine. Underparts white and upperparts black except for conspicuous white rump. Head and mantle with blue sheen in certain lights. In flight, tail is slightly but noticeably forked. Hawks over open spaces for insects which are caught in flight. Soon after arrival, can be seen gathering mud from around puddles for nest building. Prior to migration in autumn, can be seen in large flocks resting on overhead wires, often in company of Swallows.
Voice Twittering call. Song, often delivered from overhead wires, a continuous chattering based on the call.
Habitat Feeds over open spaces, usually in proximity to towns and villages. Common nesting site is under eaves of house. Nests colonially and builds cup-shaped nest of mud.
Distribution Widespread breeding species across most of Europe including Britain and Ireland. Absent from Iceland.
Occurrence Common from April to September. New arrivals in early spring are usually seen feeding over open water.

S	3–10	N 5–6

Sand Martin, approaching nest hole

Crag Martin

House Martin, pair at nest

House Martin, collecting mud

Swallow
Hirundo rustica L 20cm
Adult has very long tail streamers, longer in male than female, and all-dark upperparts, lacking white rump. Head and throat dark but with red chin and forehead. Breast and belly white in most birds but tinted reddish in some eastern races. White spots on base of tail. Juvenile similar to adult but has chin and forehead reddish-buff, with similar feathering appearing irregularly on throat and head, and lacks long tail streamers. Feeds on aerial insects. Newly arrived and post-breeding birds gather in large numbers, often with other hirundines, over wetland areas. Perch on overhead wires and roost in reedbeds.
Voice Song a prolonged series of twitters. Call a sharp *twit twit*.
Habitat Open country, often farmland, around villages, farms and rural houses. Builds nest of mud and straw on rafters or under eaves in barns and outbuildings etc.
Distribution Breeds throughout most of Europe except far north of Scandinavia and Iceland. Winters in Africa.
Occurrence Common visitor to the region, most staying from March until August. Early visitors to Britain arrive in March and the occasional bird may linger on, in mild weather, until December.

S	3–10	N 5–7

Red-rumped Swallow
Hirundo daurica L 18cm
Flight silhouette similar to Swallow but tail streamers not as long. Upperparts dark but has conspicuous pale rump with reddish tinge. Has narrow, reddish nape band separating dark back from dark cap. Undertail coverts black, not white as in Swallow. Flight pattern more gliding than that of Swallow. Feeds on aerial insects, often quartering sunny hillsides or ravines.
Voice Song is similar to that of Swallow but more rasping and given in shorter bursts. Call a rasping *tchreep*.
Habitat Warm, open country in S Europe. Nests under bridges, on buildings and under overhangs on cliff-faces. Nest with tunnel entrance built of mud.
Distribution Has a rather limited breeding range with distinct populations in S Iberian peninsula and SE Europe. Very local in Italy. Winters in Africa.
Occurrence Present in breeding range from April to August. Rare but regular vagrant to Britain, mostly April–May and September–October.

V	—	—

Cliff Swallow
Hirundo pyrrhonota L 14cm
Recalls Red-rumped Swallow but with square-ended tail and without long tail streamers. Adult shows dark upperparts, orange-buff rump, reddish-orange nape extending to throat, and white on forehead. Juvenile has much duller plumage compared to adult and lacks white on forehead. Habits and behaviour similar to other hirundines.
Voice Vagrants to Europe mostly silent.
Habitat Open terrain.
Distribution Breeding range covers most of N America. Winters in S America.
Occurrence Very rare vagrant to Britain.

V	—	—

Swallow, male

Swallow, at nest

Red-rumped Swallow, collecting mud

Red-rumped Swallow
Cliff Swallow

PIPITS AND WAGTAILS
Family Motacillidae

Rather slim birds, wagtails especially so, with relatively long tails and thin, pointed bills. Mainly terrestrial, feeding on insects. Wagtails have conspicuous plumage while pipits have brown and streaked plumage.

Tree Pipit
Anthus trivialis L 15cm
Similar to Meadow Pipit but with a cleaner appearance overall and more distinct markings. Most readily identified by voice, however. Upperparts buffish-brown and belly white. Yellow wash on submoustachial stripe and upper breast. Rump only slightly streaked. Streaking distinct on breast, less so on flanks. Parachuting song-flight often starts and finishes from treetop. Alarm call usually given from elevated perch.
Voice Alarm call a repeated *tsit*. Flight call *beezz*. Song is a series of short phrases, delivered in song-flight, accelerating as bird ascends and then slowing down as bird parachutes down on stiff wings. Ends with thin, whistling *seer seer seer*.
Habitat Associated with trees in such situations as wide woodland rides and forest edges.
Distribution Widespread breeding species across most of Europe except the south. Absent from Ireland and Iceland and, as a breeding species, south of the Pyrenees and southernmost SE Europe. Winters in Africa.
Occurrence Present in breeding range from May to August. Seen on passage April–May and September–October.

S	4–11	N 5–7

Olive-backed Pipit
Anthus hodgsoni L 14cm
Similar to Tree Pipit but upperparts olive-brown with darker streaking much less evident. Underparts are boldly marked with yellow wash on breast and flanks. Markings on head offer good identification features. Supercilium broad and buffish in front of eye and white behind. Also shows one black and one white mark

Olive-backed Pipit

behind eye on edge of ear coverts, resembling teardrop. Unstreaked rump.
Voice Call similar to Tree Pipit but thinner.
Habitat Northern taiga forests.
Distribution Breeds Siberia; winters in S Asia.
Occurrence Very rare vagrant to NW Europe including Britain, mostly in autumn.

V	10–11	—

Tawny Pipit
Anthus campestris L 16.5cm
A large, pale wagtail-like pipit with long legs. Adult has sandy-coloured plumage with faint streaking and pale supercilium. Juvenile is more heavily streaked and marked and so then superficially similar to Richard's Pipit. However, these features are mostly lost prior to autumn migration and the species is always told by shorter hind claw, less robust bill and different call.
Voice Call *chilp*, very similar to that of House Sparrow. Song a drawn-out *seerloo*, delivered either from low perch or in song-flight.
Habitat Breeds in dry, open terrain with bare ground such as sandy heaths and bare grassland. Also in upland meadows in S Europe. On migration, often found in ploughed arable fields.
Distribution Widespread but rather local breeding species in S and central Europe as far north as Baltic coast. Absent as a breeding species from Britain and Ireland. Winters south of region.
Occurrence Present within breeding range from May to August. Seen on migration April–May and August–October. Scarce but regular passage migrant to Britain, mostly in the autumn.

M	4–5, 8–10	—

Richard's Pipit
Anthus novaeseelandiae L 18cm
A large pipit with bold markings, upright stance and long legs. Bill is long and large, and has very long hind claw which is not always visible when feeding in long grass. Shows dark streaking on breast and on mantle, especially noticeable in first-autumn birds, i.e. individuals most likely to be seen in W Europe. Sometimes feeds in quite long grass, disappearing from view for long periods.
Voice Call a loud and distinctive *schrruup*.
Habitat Vagrants to Europe usually seen in grassy meadows, mainly coastal.
Distribution Breeds in Asia, wintering south of breeding range.
Occurrence Rare but regular vagrant to W Europe including Britain, mostly autumn.

V	9–11	—

Tree Pipit

Tawny Pipit

Richard's Pipit

Meadow Pipit
Anthus pratensis L 14.5cm
Superficially similar to Tree Pipit but slightly
smaller with grey-brown upperparts and lacking
latter's clean appearance. Distinct streaking on
mantle and slightly streaked rump. Belly dirty
white and streaking on breast extends to flanks.
Dark malar stripe indistinct. White sides to tail. In
spring, performs song-flight rising rapidly and
then parachuting on stiff wings.
Voice Call a thin *seet seet seet*. Alarm call *sitit*.
Song, delivered in flight or from perch, a series of
trilling phrases, accelerating and then slowing.
Habitat Breeds in open, grassy areas including
upland meadows and moors. In winter, more usually on coast and cultivated fields.
Distribution Breeds across central and N Europe from central France north to N Scandinavia.
Widespread breeding species in Britain, Ireland
and Iceland. In winter, northern populations move
south and range extends to most of S Europe.
Occurrence Common and widespread in most
suitable areas. In Britain, absent as breeding
species from many cultivated areas of S England.

R	1–12	N 4–7

Red-throated Pipit
Anthus cervinus L 15cm
In all plumages, differs from Meadow Pipit in over-
all darker upperparts and more contrasting and
distinct dark markings. Heavy streaking on man-
tle and rump as well as on breast and flanks. In
summer, adult has variable amount and intensity
of red on throat and breast. This colouring may
be retained into autumn but is lost in winter.
First-autumn bird resembles winter adult.
Voice Flight call *speee-ah* and alarm call *chup*.
Song similar to Meadow Pipit.
Habitat Breeds in tundra habitats.
Distribution Breeds N Scandinavia and eastwards at similar latitudes. Winters Africa and Asia.
Occurrence Rather local and scarce breeding
species within range, present from May to
August. Seen on passage in W Europe, especially
coastal areas, April–May and September–Octo-
ber. Rare vagrant to Britain.

V	—	—

Pechora Pipit *Anthus gustavi* is similar to first-
autumn Red-throated Pipit with even more distinct streaking, especially on buffish breast and
white underparts. Very rare vagrant to NW
Europe from Asia. Very secretive. Most British
records from Fair Isle.

Water Pipit
Anthus spinoletta L 17cm
A large pipit. In summer, has grey head and brow
mantle with darker-brown wings. Distinct whit
supercilium and wing bars. Underparts wit
inconspicuous streaking confined to flanks, an
pinkish-buff wash to breast. Outer tail feather
white and legs dark. In winter, breast become
streaked and loses pinkish wash but still pale
than winter Rock Pipit with white supercilium
Voice Call *pheeet*, thinner than Rock Pipit. Son
similar to Meadow Pipit.
Habitat Usually found in close proximity t
water. In summer, found above the tree-line. I
winter, found beside rivers and stony lakes a
lower altitudes. In Britain, usually associated wit
watercress beds and marshes.
Distribution Breeds in mountain regions
central and S Europe. In winter, widespread bu
local across much of NW, central and S Europe
Occurrence Locally fairly common breedir
species in suitable habitats. Widespread but ger
erally scarce in winter. Winters in small number
in S England from October to March.

W	10–3	—

Buff-bellied Pipit *Anthus rubescens* is very sim
lar but slightly smaller and shows moustachia
stripe, pale lores, more delicate bill, and deep-bu
underparts. Very rare vagrant to NW Europ
from N America and NE Asia.

Rock Pipit
Anthus petrosus L 17cm
Identical size and shape to Water Pipit wit
which, until recently, considered conspecific. In a
plumages, however, most birds appear darke
and with rather dingy-looking plumage. Legs dar
and, in summer, upperparts dark olive-grey an
heavy streaking on dull underparts. Supercilium
indistinct and outer tail feathers grey. In winter
plumage is more grey-brown.
Voice Call *feest*, more slurred than that o
Water Pipit.
Habitat Invariably associated with the coast. I
summer, breeds on rocky coasts. Feeds amon
rocks and on grassy cliffs, but also along tidelin
debris. On marshes in winter.
Distribution Breeds around coasts of NW
Europe from Brittany to N Scandinavia but con
fined exclusively to rocky coastlines. In winter
some dispersal along coast, especially by bird
from north of range, and reaches S Spain.

R	1–12	N 5–7

Meadow Pipit

Red-throated Pipit, summer plumage

Water Pipit

Rock Pipit

Yellow Wagtail
Motacilla flava L 18cm

Typical wagtail appearance with slim body and long tail. Several distinct races occur in the region where females are similar but males have different colouring on head and neck. Males of all races have greenish-yellow back and yellow underparts. **Yellow Wagtail** *M.f.flavissima* has greenish-yellow head and yellow supercilium and throat. **Blue-headed Wagtail** *M.f.flava* has blue-grey head, yellow throat and white supercilium and moustachial stripe. **Spanish Wagtail** *M.f.iberiae* has greyish head, black ear coverts and white throat and supercilium. **Ashy-headed Wagtail** *M.f.cinereocapilla* has grey head, black ear coverts and white throat. **Black-headed Wagtail** *M.f.feldegg* has black head and white throat. **Grey-headed Wagtail** *M.f.thunbergi* has grey head, black ear coverts and yellow throat. Female similar to male of race *flavissima* but never as bright, having pale-yellow underparts, pale supercilium and greenish-yellow upperparts. Juvenile has buffish upperparts, pale underparts and darker moustachial stripe and markings on neck forming faint gorget. In winter, plumage is variable but most retain some yellow on underparts while losing distinct facial markings in males. First-winter females have buffish-yellow plumage but usually some yellow on vent. In breeding habitat, often seen perched on fence posts or barbed wire. Follow grazing animals for flushed insects.
Voice Call a rising, slurred *sreet*. Song a series of trilling warbles.
Habitat Breeds mainly in wet meadows and grazing pastures, but also occasionally in cultivated areas.
Distribution The species breeds across most of Europe except Ireland and Iceland. Represented in Britain by *M.f.flavissima*, found mainly in S and central England; *M.f.flava* breeds in mainland NW Europe including S Scandinavia; *M.f.iberiae* breeds in the Iberian peninsula, Balearics and SW France; *M.f.cinereocapilla* breeds in Italy and Balkans; *M.f.feldegg* breeds in Balkans and Black Sea area; *M.f.thunbergi* breeds in N Scandinavia. All races winter mainly in Africa.
Occurrence Found on breeding grounds from April to August. Seen on passage, invariably near water, March–April and August–September.

S	3–9	N 5–7

Citrine Wagtail
Motacilla citreola L 18cm

Breeding male is very distinctive with bright yellow head and underparts, black collar on nape, grey upperparts and two conspicuous white wing bars. Female also shows white wing bars but has greyish ear coverts and grey running from crown to mantle. Shows broad yellow supercilium continuing around ear coverts and joining yellow flush on throat and upper breast. Juvenile has similar pattern to female but is pure grey and white, lacking any yellow. Behaviour and habits similar to Yellow Wagtail.
Voice Call a loud and shrill *sreeep*, distinctly different from Yellow Wagtail.

Citrine Wagtail, juvenile

Habitat Marshes, meadows and tundra bogs.
Distribution Breeds central and N Asia, wintering to the south.
Occurrence Rare vagrant to Europe, including Britain, mainly in autumn but occasionally in spring.

V	—	—

Yellow Wagtail, male

Yellow Wagtail, female

Blue-headed Wagtail, male

Black-headed Wagtail, male   **Citrine Wagtail,** male

Grey Wagtail
Motacilla cinerea L 18cm

Has extremely long tail and, in all plumages, shows lemon-yellow on vent and grey upperparts. In summer, male has entirely yellow underparts and black throat, the latter fading to white in winter. In summer, female has white throat, sometimes speckled or margins defined by dark feathers, yellow breast and white belly. Colours on underparts fade in winter. Flight is extremely undulating. Broad, white wing bar and yellow rump easily visible in flight. Perches on rocks and stones, when tail and rear end of body pumped up and down vigorously. Chases after insects near water's edge and sometimes hovers briefly.

Voice Usual call *tsisit*, similar to that of Pied Wagtail but much sharper in tone. Song comprises a series of phrases similar to call.

Habitat Invariably associated with water. During breeding season, occurs beside running water, from lowland chalk streams to mountain torrents. Often nests in cavities under bridges or other man-made structures. In winter, seen beside rivers, watercress beds, lakes, and occasionally on coast.

Distribution Widespread breeding species west of an imaginary line from Denmark to N Greece, including Britain and Ireland. Absent from Iceland.

Occurrence Common and widespread. Generally resident and sedentary but some movement in winter away from upland areas to lower altitudes.

R	1–12	N 4–7

Pied and White Wagtails
Motacilla alba L 18cm,

This single species is represented in Europe by two distinct subspecies, the **Pied Wagtail** *M.a.yarrellii* which occurs throughout Britain, Ireland and adjacent areas of coastal NW Europe, and the **White Wagtail** *M.a.alba* which occurs throughout the rest of Europe. Both have black, grey and white plumage, slim body and long tail which is constantly wagged. Male Pied Wagtail has black cap, nape and back and white face. In summer, shows black chin and throat. In winter, throat becomes white but retains black breast band. Female Pied Wagtail has dark-grey back but black rump, nape and cap. In winter, female has more extensive grey on face. Adults of White Wagtail superficially similar to Pied Wagtails of similar age and same sex but at all times show grey back and, diagnostically, grey (not black) rump too. Juveniles of the two subspecies are effectively indistinguishable, but by first winter, Pied Wagtail has acquired its black rump. Both have plumages similar to faded version of winter female. Black breast band acquired in first-winter plumage. Behaviour and habits identical in both subspecies. Has undulating flight and runs quickly, chasing after insects. Seen singly or in pairs during breeding season. In autumn and winter, sometimes in sizeable flocks, roosting in reedbeds, etc.

Voice Characteristic calls *chizzik* and *tsuwee*. Song comprises a series of call-like twitters.

Habitat All sorts of open country but often associated with habitation and man-made structures. Common around farms but also seen on school fields and car parks. Nests in cavities, from holes in walls to sheds.

Distribution Pied Wagtail breeds throughout Britain, Ireland and locally in coastal mainland Europe from France to Germany. White Wagtail is found throughout rest of Europe including Iceland and N Scandinavia.

Occurrence Pied Wagtails are mostly resident with some dispersal outside breeding season within range. Northern and eastern populations of White Wagtails generally move south and west outside breeding season.

R	1–12	N 4–7

Grey Wagtail, winter

Pied Wagtail, summer male

Grey Wagtail, summer male

White Wagtail, male

Pied Wagtail, juvenile

SHRIKES
Family Laniidae

Small to medium-sized birds with long tails and stout, hook-tipped bills. Feed on insects and occasionally small mammals and birds, sometimes impaling prey on thorns or barbs.

Red-backed Shrike
Lanius collurio L 18cm

Male has reddish-brown back, grey head and black mask through eyes. Underparts white with buffish-pink wash, and tail is black with white sides to base. Female has brown back and head with dark mask through eye. Underparts pale, covered with crescent markings. Tail is dark brown with less white at base than male. Juvenile similar to female but with scaly appearance to upperparts. Sometimes perches on low but prominent lookout, e.g. gorse bush. Occasionally impales prey, such as grasshoppers, lizards and young birds, on thorns, forming a larder for later consumption.

Voice Call a sharp *chew*. Song comprises elements of mimicry.

Habitat Open country with bushes and scattered trees, including heaths and cultivated land such as vineyards.

Distribution Widespread breeding species across central Europe from France eastwards into Asia. Breeds as far north as S Scandinavia but effectively absent as a breeding species from Britain. Winters in Africa.

Occurrence Present within breeding range from May to August. Once widespread in England but now almost extinct with only occasional pairs breeding. May be colonizing Scotland. Seen regularly on migration, however, May–June and August–September.

M	5–6, 8–9	—

Woodchat Shrike
Lanius senator L 19cm

A striking bird with white underparts, black upperparts and white shoulder patches and white rump. White on base of primaries most noticeable in flight but absent in birds of subspecies *badius* from Balearics. Conspicuous orange-brown on nape and crown and black on forehead and mask through eye. Female has more subdued colours on upperparts and more extensive white at base of bill. Juvenile is similar to juvenile Red-backed Shrike with scaly upperparts and cres-

cents on underparts. However, shows suggestion of white shoulder patches and rump. Routinely perches on fence posts and barbed wire, sometimes using the latter to remove stings from bumblebees. Food comprises mainly insects including large beetles and wasps.

Voice Utters harsh, churring call. Song varied and mimetic, including whistles and grating chatters.

Habitat Occurs in a range of Mediterranean-type habitats, particularly maquis with low shrubs and scattered trees. Also common in cultivated country with small fields surrounded by stone walls.

Distribution Breeding range confined mainly to areas where influence of Mediterranean climate is felt. Widespread throughout S Europe, Iberian peninsula and central France. Range extends northwards in E Europe. Winters in Africa.

Occurrence Present within breeding range April to August. Seen on passage April–May and September–October and rare but regular vagrant to Britain between the 2 extreme months.

V	—	—

Masked Shrike
Lanius nubicus L 18cm

Superficially similar to Woodchat Shrike but immediately recognized by black not orange-brown on nape and crown and overall slimmer appearance. Male has upperparts black including rump, but with conspicuous white wing patches and bases to primaries. Forehead white but black mask through eyes. Underparts white but with orange-buff flush to flanks. Female shows patterning similar to male but upperparts duller black. Juvenile similar to juvenile Woodchat Shrike but told by slimmer build, grey not brown upperparts and more conspicuous white wing patches. Perches in the open less frequently than other shrikes and prefers the cover provided by bushes.

Voice Call harsh and grating. Song comprises a series of grating and chattering phrases.

Habitat Breeds in open woodland and overgrown olive groves.

Distribution Breeds in SE Europe, mainly N Greece and Turkey. Winters in Africa.

Occurrence Locally common within limited breeding range from May to August. Seen on migration elsewhere in E Mediterranean region and common on spring migration in Cyprus.

Red-backed Shrike, male

Woodchat Shrike, male

Red-backed Shrike, female

Masked Shrike, female

Masked Shrike, male

Great Grey Shrike
Lanius excubitor L 24cm

Slight plumage variation between races. *L.e.excubitor*, the most widespread race in Europe, has pure-white underparts and soft-grey back, nape and crown. Black on head confined to mask through eyes and does not extend to forehead. Shows white supercilium and black tail with white outer feathers. Black wings have white wing bar formed by white bases to primaries. In some races, wing bar extends to bases of secondaries. *L.e.meridionalis* from Spain has rather dirty-grey upperparts and a pinkish flush to underparts. Juveniles of all races similar to adults but have underparts with crescent markings and with off-white flush. Has undulating and gliding flight. Often perches on exposed dead branch or telegraph wire, looking very white. Catches small birds and mammals, insects and lizards, impaling prey on thorn bushes.
Voice Utters a variety of harsh calls including *schreeik*. Song comprises a series of chattering and warbling phrases.
Habitat Open country and heaths with scattered trees and a supply of likely prey.
Distribution Breeds from SW and central Europe to N Scandinavia. Absent as a breeding species from Britain and Ireland and SE Europe. In winter, retreats from north of range and some penetrate SE Europe.
Occurrence Widespread but rather uncommon breeding species in Europe. In Britain, seen as a scarce winter visitor, October–March.

W	10–4	—

Lesser Grey Shrike
Lanius minor L 20cm

Superficially similar to Great Grey Shrike with smaller black mask extending on to forehead and absence of white supercilium. Pinkish wash to breast contrasts with white throat. Wings are proportionately longer and tail shorter than Great Grey Shrike and usually sits in more upright position. Juvenile has scaly upperparts and lacks black on forehead. Often perches in the open, scanning the ground for prey.
Voice Utters occasional harsh, grating call. Song a mixture of chattering and whistling phrases.
Habitat Open country with scattered trees.
Distribution Breeds in SE Europe and locally in central S Europe. Winters south of region.
Occurrence Found within breeding range from May to August. Occurs as a vagrant elsewhere in Europe and very rare in Britain.

V	—	—

Isabelline Shrike
Lanius isabellinus L 18cm

Plumage rather like a washed-out version of Red-backed Shrike. Upperparts greyish-buff or sandy coloured and underparts off-white. Face shows mask through eyes which is black in male and brown in female. Tail is reddish-brown and proportionately longer than that of Red-backed Shrike. First winter is similar to first-winter Red-backed Shrike but is unmarked, not scaly, with a grey-brown back and strikingly reddish-brown tail. Habits as Red-backed Shrike.
Voice Vagrants to region mostly silent.
Habitat Open country with scattered bushes.
Distribution Breeds in central Asia and winters in Africa and S Asia.
Occurrence Very rare vagrant to Europe including Britain, mostly in autumn.

V	—	—

WAXWINGS
Family Bombycillidae
Plump, medium-sized birds with crests. Outside breeding season, gregarious, feeding mainly on berries. One species in Europe.

Waxwing
Bombycilla garrulus L 18cm

Easily recognized by buffish-pink plumage and long crest. Has black throat and mask through eye, yellow-tipped tail and chestnut undertail. Red, wax-like tips to secondaries give species its name, but absent in some young birds. At rest adults show yellow line along primaries, the tips of which have white margins. Juveniles show pale line along primaries which are dark-tipped. In flight, resembles Starling. In winter, flocks feed on berries, often close to habitation, when usually indifferent to man.
Voice Call a thin and ringing *sirrr*. Song includes call-like phrases and chattering.
Habitat Breeds in northern conifer forests. Winters in areas that have good supplies of berries.
Distribution Breeds N Scandinavia and at similar latitudes eastwards. Winter range depends on food supply but may extend S and W to Britain, NE France and Austria.
Occurrence Breeds from May to August and thereafter flocks form and disperse. Appears in Britain October–March. Numbers, however, are variable and unpredictable.

W	10–3	—

Great Grey Shrike

Lesser Grey Shrike

Isabelline Shrike

Waxwing

ORIOLES
Family Oriolidae

Medium-sized, brightly coloured birds with dagger-like bills and fluty songs. Nest high in trees. One species in Europe.

Golden Oriole
Oriolus oriolus L 24cm
Blackbird-sized bird with slim proportions and distinctive plumage. Adult male is bright yellow with black wings and black on tail. Female and first-year males have greenish-yellow upperparts and whitish, streaked underparts. An extremely retiring species, heard far more often than seen due to excellent camouflage afforded by colouring. Usually glimpsed foraging in treetops or warily watching observer through foliage.
Voice Song is very distinctive and almost tropical. Usually given as *o-weela-weeeoo*, a fluty sound, rising and then falling.
Habitat Breeds in deciduous woodland, copses and mature deciduous (e.g. poplar) plantations.
Distribution Breeding range includes most of Europe as far north as Baltic coast. Very rare breeding species in England. Winters in Africa.
Occurrence Locally common in mainland Europe from May to August. In Britain, rare and local breeding species in E Anglia in mature poplar plantations. Also passage migrant, mostly April–May.

S	5–8	N 5–6

STARLINGS
Family Sturnidae

Medium-sized gregarious birds with short tails and triangular wings. Nest in holes in buildings and trees.

Starling
Sturnus vulgaris L 21cm
A well-known bird throughout Europe. Adult has blackish plumage with green or purple iridescence in some lights. Generally looks rather speckled and especially so during winter months. Legs are reddish and bill is yellow during summer and blackish during winter. Juvenile has brownish plumage with paler throat, dark-reddish legs and dark bill. Feeds very actively on lawns and grassy areas, probing and searching for insects and other invertebrates. Usually seen in flocks, especially from late summer onwards when huge numbers sometimes gather in communal roosts in reedbeds, woods or even on buildings.

Voice Song contains elements of mimicry, thin reedy whistles, clicks and subdued warbles.
Habitat Open country including farmland and parks, but also commonly in gardens and towns. Nests in roofs, buildings and holes in trees.
Distribution Breeding range includes most of Europe including Iceland but absent from Iberian peninsula, Sardinia, Corsica, Sicily and southernmost SE Europe. Northern and eastern populations move south and west in autumn spreading to the whole of S and W Europe.
Occurrence Extremely common and widespread species throughout most of Europe. British birds are resident but numbers augmented in winter by visitors from mainland Europe.

R	1–12	N 4–7

Spotless Starling
Sturnus unicolor L 21cm
Very similar to Starling but, in summer, has uniform dark plumage with violet iridescence and completely lacks white spots. In winter, plumage covered in small pale spots, much less noticeable than on Starling. Juvenile similar to juvenile Starling. Behaviour and habits similar to Starling.
Voice Similar to Starling, plus twangy and screeching notes.
Habitat Similar to Starling.
Distribution Breeding range does not overlap that of Starling, covering Iberian peninsula, Sardinia, Corsica and Sicily. Resident year-round.
Occurrence Common within range. Joined by Starlings during winter months.

Rose-coloured Starling
Sturnus roseus L 21cm
Adult in summer easily identified by pink and black plumage. Legs and bill are pinkish, and has shaggy crest. In winter, pink plumage looks rather grubby. Juvenile resembles very pale version of juvenile Starling with noticeably pale rump and pale-yellow bill. Very gregarious, flocks following locust swarms and nesting where food is plentiful. Habits and behaviour as Starling and vagrants to W Europe often associate with this species.
Voice Song and calls similar to Starling.
Habitat Open country but vagrants sometimes in urban areas when associating with Starlings.
Distribution A mainly Asiatic species that breeds sporadically in SE Europe.
Occurrence Occasionally irrupts westwards; rare vagrant to W Europe including Britain.

V	—	—

Golden Oriole, female

Golden Oriole, male

Starling, juvenile

Starling, adult

Spotless Starling

Rose-coloured Starling, juvenile

Rose-coloured Starling, adult

CROWS
Family Corvidae

Successful and varied group with extensive global distribution. Omnivorous diet includes carrion, nuts, eggs and young birds. Most have broad wings and stout bills. Vocal range limited. Sexes similar.

Jay
Garrulus glandarius L 35cm

Stocky and distinctive bird with pinkish plumage and blue wing panel. White on wings and white rump seen best in flight when disturbed feeding along forest ride or roadside verge through woodland. In flight, shows broad wings and rather exaggerated wingbeats interspersed with glides. Generally rather shy and retiring, especially so in areas where persecuted. In autumn, seen gathering acorns which are buried in woodland floor.

Voice Has a variety of harsh calls, notably *kraar*.

Habitat Mostly deciduous and coniferous forests, but also found in town parks and mature gardens.

Distribution Found throughout most of Europe except N Scandinavia and Iceland.

Occurrence Resident and sedentary in most areas. Northern populations sometimes irrupt to the south and west. In Britain, common and widespread in England and Wales. Occurs in lowland regions of Scotland and more local in Ireland.

R	1–12	N 5–7

Siberian Jay
Perisoreus infaustus L 28cm

Grey-brown plumage with darker-brown head and rusty-orange in wings, tail and undertail. These elements of colour are best seen in flight which has long glides interspersed with rapid wingbeats. Usually seen in small groups and is sometimes inquisitive towards human visitors. Omnivorous diet, taking seeds and nuts but also eggs and invertebrates.

Voice Mostly silent but occasionally utters harsh, Jay-like calls.

Habitat Northern conifer forests.

Distribution Central and N Scandinavia and at similar latitudes eastwards.

Occurrence Fairly common resident within range and mostly sedentary.

Magpie
Pica pica L 46cm

Easily recognized by black-and-white plumage and extremely long tail. At close range and in certain light, black feathers have a green sheen. Juvenile similar to adult but with much shorter tail. In flight, shows relatively short, rounded wings with rapid, shallow wingbeats and glides. On the ground, walks with rather curious high-stepping gait and often hops. Often seen in pairs and, during winter, may gather in larger flocks. Generally rather wary of man but, where not persecuted, can become bold. Diet comprises a wide range of items from seeds and fruits to eggs and young birds. Also feeds extensively on carrion and frequently seen feeding on animal road casualties.

Voice Utters loud, chattering call but also a range of subdued whistling sounds.

Habitat A wide range of habitats from farmland with scattered woods to urban parks and gardens. Builds large, domed nest of twigs in dense tree cover.

Distribution Found throughout the whole of Europe except Iceland and a few islands in the Mediterranean.

Occurrence Common throughout most of range and mostly sedentary.

R	1–12	N 5–7

Azure-winged Magpie
Cyanopica cyana L 35cm

Typical magpie proportions with long tail and rounded wings. Plumage distinctive with pinkish-buff body, blue wings and tail, black hood and white throat. Flight is undulating, often with long glides. Usually seen in parties of up to 10 birds moving through the trees.

Voice Utters a whistling *zchreee*.

Habitat Mainly found in native Stone Pine woodlands but also in mature plantations.

Distribution Found only in the Iberian peninsula. Has a curious global distribution, the nearest populations being in E Asia.

Occurrence Fairly common but rather local. Resident and generally rather sedentary.

Siberian Jay

y

Magpie

Azure-winged Magpie

Nutcracker
Nucifraga caryocatactes L 33cm
Has dark-brown plumage covered with large, white teardrop spots. White-tipped black tail is made more prominent by white on rump and undertail. In flight, tail looks proportionately short and wings are broad and rounded. Bill is long but dimensions vary according to race. Siberian subspecies has slender bill whereas those from central Europe have thicker bill. Rather secretive during breeding season but otherwise perches prominently. Pine seeds form major part of diet but also takes fruits, nuts, eggs and invertebrates.

Voice Calls include a crow-like croak and a buzzing alarm call.

Habitat Mainly associated with conifer forests. In the north, prefers Arolla Pine with Hazel.

Distribution Separate breeding populations in mountainous regions of central and SE Europe and in S Scandinavia and at similar latitudes eastwards.

Occurrence Fairly common resident within breeding range. Mainly sedentary but some movement south and west by northern populations when food in short supply. In some years, irrupts and reaches Britain as rare vagrant.

V	—	—

Chough
Pyrrhocorax pyrrhocorax L 40cm
Adult has shiny-black plumage, long curved, red bill and red legs. Juvenile has yellowish bill. Very distinctive flight silhouette with broad wings and primaries forming distinct 'fingers'. Tail relatively short and square-ended. Extremely aerobatic, performing rolls, tumbles and dives, often while part of larger flock. Flocks seen patrolling cliff faces and feeding on steep, grassy slopes. Uses long bill to probe for insects and other invertebrates.

Voice Calls include a Jackdaw-like version of its name, *cheahh*, with a ringing tone.

Habitat Steep rocky and grassy slopes. Inland, in mountainous regions but also coastal in W and S Europe.

Distribution Widespread in Iberian peninsula and S Europe. Also in NW Europe including Brittany and W coasts of Britain and Ireland.

Occurrence Fairly common and resident breeding species in S and W Europe. Much more local in NW Europe. In Britain, best seen on some of the Welsh seabird islands, coastal headlands in SW Scotland and a few Scottish islands including Islay. Widespread on W coast of Ireland.

R	1–12	N 4–7

Alpine Chough
Pyrrhocorax graculus L 38cm
Superficially similar to Chough but smaller and with shorter, yellow bill. Plumage much less shiny and can even look rather dowdy and unkempt. In flight, 'fingers' on wingtips are less prominent than Chough's, and shows proportionately longer tail with rounded end. No less aerobatic than Chough and flocks soar effortlessly over mountain slopes, instantly spotting potential source of food. Will probe for invertebrates but much more inclined to search for scraps around sites of human activity.

Voice Utters Chough-like calls but usually with a ringing, metallic tone.

Habitat High mountain areas, usually around the snow-line. In winter, sometimes visits villages and ski-resorts at slightly lower altitudes.

Distribution Occurs in high mountain regions of S Europe including Pyrenees, Alps, Dolomites and mountains of SE Europe.

Occurrence Fairly common resident within limited range and altitude requirements. Visit any ski-centre or high pass in mountains of S Europe and Alpine Choughs are almost sure to be present. If not, the mere sight of a packed lunch will attract a flock of inquisitive birds, usually within a few seconds.

Jackdaw
Corvus monedula L 33cm
Much smaller than Crow or Rook and with relatively stubby bill, grey nape and pale iris. Thickset neck is apparent at rest and in flight. Invariably seen in flocks which are highly aerobatic and vocal, especially towards dusk when preparing to return to communal roost. Feeds on ground in flocks and associates with other species. Walks with rather quick, rolling gait. Alert and quite wary but can become bold and inquisitive in areas where not persecuted such as town parks. An opportunistic feeder, taking invertebrates, seeds, etc. in the wild but also scavenging around farms and in urban environments.

Voice Typical call a loud and sharp *chak*.

Habitat Found in all sorts of open country, breeding in woodland, buildings and even on sea-cliffs.

Distribution Occurs throughout Europe as far north as S Scandinavia. Absent from Iceland.

Occurrence Common resident species in most areas. Mostly sedentary but northern populations move west in autumn.

R	1–12	N 4–7

Nutcracker

Chough

Alpine Chough

Alpine Choughs

Jackdaw

Rook

Corvus frugilegus L 46cm

Adult has black plumage with violet sheen. Long bill is exaggerated by pale, bare skin at base. Fore-crown usually looks peaked. Shows shaggy 'trousers'. Immature lacks sheen to feathering and pale base to bill, consequently looking rather Crow-like. However, feathering at base of bill and on head produce a more peaked-crown appear-ance than Carrion Crow. Flight is purposeful, often with intervals of gliding. Tail looks relatively long and sometimes rather wedge-shaped. On the ground, has a rather rolling, shuffling gait. Feeds in flocks in fields and nests in large colonies in treetops, nest-building activity starting from late winter onwards. Has a rather varied diet, tak-ing worms and invertebrates from the soil but also occasionally eggs and young birds.

Voice Typical call a harsh *cah*.

Habitat Generally associated with farmland with scattered copses and woodland.

Distribution Breeding range includes most of central and NW Europe, including Britain and Ire-land, as far north as Baltic coast but at more northerly latitudes further east. Northern and eastern populations migrate south and west, swelling numbers in NW Europe. Winter range extends to most of S Europe.

Occurrence Common resident species in most of lowland NW Europe including Britain and Ireland.

R	1–12	N 3–6

Carrion and Hooded Crows

Corvus corone L 47cm

Carrion Crow and Hooded Crow *c.c.cornix* are races of the same species. Carrion Crow has all-black plumage and is superficially similar to imma-ture Rook. However, has stouter bill and smoother head profile, lacking peaked fore-crown. Hooded Crow has mainly grey body with black hood, wings and tail. Hybrids occur where the ranges of the two races overlap. Occasionally associates with others of the same species but does not flock habitually like Rook. Will search for invertebrates but frequently feeds on carrion and takes eggs and young birds.

Voice Utters a harsh croaking *craar*.

Habitat Found in a wide variety of open habi-tats from farmland to town parks and seashores. Builds large, untidy nest of twigs in tree.

Distribution Carrion Crow occurs throughout W Europe from Iberian peninsula and Austria north to Baltic coast. Also found in England, Wales and S Scotland. Hooded Crow replaces Carrion Crow throughout rest of E Europe from Italy and SE Europe north to N Scandinavia. Also occurs in N Scotland, Isle of Man and Ireland.

Occurrence Common and widespread throughout most of Europe. Carrion Crows are mostly sedentary residents. Northern and east-ern populations of Hooded Crow migrate south and west in autumn.

R	1–12	N 4–6

Raven

Corvus corax L 65cm

Distinguished by large size (Europe's largest passerine), massive bill and rather peaked fore-crown. Wedge-shaped tail is a distinguishing fea-ture of this species. In flight, has powerful wingbeats and often soars like bird of prey. Also performs spectacular aerobatic displays including rolls and tumbles. Usually seen in pairs, even out-side the breeding season. Generally rather wary of humans. Feeds on carrion but will also take small live prey and eggs where available.

Voice Call a very loud and distinctive cronking *krruup*.

Habitat Found in mountainous and upland regions and on rocky coasts.

Distribution Widespread in Europe but absent from lowland regions of central and NW Europe. In Britain, found only in the west and north, and essentially absent from S and E England. Present in Ireland and Iceland.

Occurrence Fairly common where habitat suit-able. Mostly sedentary resident.

R	1–12	N 2–5

Rook

Carrion Crow

Raven

Hooded Crow

Raven

DIPPERS
Family Cinclidae

Dumpy birds with powerful legs and feet. Always associated with running water. Feed immersed in water. Sexes similar. One species in Europe.

Dipper
Cinclus cinclus L 18cm

Can usually be identified by dumpy appearance and habitat choice alone. Plumage mainly greyish-black with dark-brown head. Throat and breast pure white. Black plumage on underparts grading into brown on belly. In British birds this is bright chestnut but on continental birds belly is very dark indeed. Juvenile birds are rather greyish with an almost scaly appearance. Flies low over water with direct flight and whirring wingbeats. Sits on rocks in fast-flowing water, bobbing and dipping constantly. Makes frequent forays into the water.
Voice Utters a penetrating and grating *zrritt* as it flies along watercourse. Song rasping and subdued.
Habitat Beside fast-flowing rivers and streams. Nests under bridges and among tree roots etc.
Distribution Widespread in upland areas of central and S Europe as well as N Europe. In Britain, mainly confined to west and north.
Occurrence Fairly common along suitable watercourses. Mostly sedentary resident but northern birds sometimes forced to move if rivers freeze. Dark-bellied continental birds are rare winter visitors to Britain.

R	1–12	N 4–6

WRENS
Family Troglodytidae

Small, dumpy birds with brown plumage and invariably cocked tail. Retiring habits and flight with whirring wingbeats. Sexes similar.

Wren
Troglodytes troglodytes L 10cm

One of the smallest birds of the region and almost mouse-like in its habits. Has compact body shape, reddish-brown plumage and habit of cocking tail vertically. Races occur on several Scottish islands, such as St Kilda and Shetland, which are larger and have richer-brown plumage. Moves through undergrowth and low vegetation, presence often given away by tell-tale call.
Voice Alarm call an insistent and repeated *chek*. Also utters a lengthy rattle. Song is a surprisingly loud mixture of ringing warbles and trilling rattles.
Habitat Any habitat with low cover from moors to cliffs, but mostly scrub and woodland.
Distribution Found throughout Europe including Iceland, except for N Scandinavia.
Occurrence Common and widespread resident throughout most of range. Mostly sedentary but some movement west and south in winter.

R	1–12	N 4–7

ACCENTORS
Family Prunellidae

Small and rather unobtrusive birds. Thin bills and rather subdued plumage. Insectivorous. Sexes alike.

Dunnock
Prunella modularis L 15cm

Has warm-brown upperparts, slate-grey face and underparts, slender, pointed bill and beady, red eye. Usually unobtrusive but singing males perch in exposed positions. Forages for invertebrates and seeds on ground or among low vegetation.
Voice Song comprises a series of warbling phrases and jingling rattles. May recall more musical version of Wren's song but with Blackcap-like phrasing and tone. Call a loud and clear *seeh*.
Habitat A wide variety of habitats with dense undergrowth, including woods and gardens.
Distribution Breeds across most of Europe except Mediterranean region, Iceland and far N Scandinavia. In winter, northern populations withdraw south.
Occurrence Common and widespread in Europe. Mostly sedentary.

R	1–12	N 4–7

Alpine Accentor
Prunella collaris L 18cm

Superficially similar to Dunnock with grey head and underparts and brown back. Larger and dumpier, however, and shows dark wing bar fringed with white dots, chestnut streaking on flanks and black-and-white barring on throat. Base of lower mandible yellow.
Voice Song musical and trilling. Call a chirping whistle and *chup-chup-chup*.
Habitat Mountain in S Europe, mostly above tree-line but at lower altitudes in winter.
Distribution Breeds in most mountain chains of central and S Europe. In winter, limited dispersal away from mountains.
Occurrence Fairly common breeding species and best seen around ski-resorts and high passes in Alps. Very rare vagrant to Britain, mostly early spring and S England coast.

V	—	—

Dipper

Wren

Dunnock

Alpine Accentor

WARBLERS
Family Sylvidae

Represented in Europe by 7 genera of warblers and 1 of crests. Small birds with thin bills used for feeding on insects. Songs often powerful and species-specific, and useful in identification. Many species are long-distance migrants.

Cetti's Warbler
Cettia cetti L 14cm

Relatively large and stocky warbler, better known for its song than its appearance. Reddish-brown upperparts and greyish-white underparts. Tail broad and rounded, often flexed or cocked, and pale supercilium. Generally rather shy and retiring and even sings from the cover of reeds or bushes.

Voice Song a loud and explosive *chetti chetti chetti, chip chip chip* and so on. Sometimes sings outside breeding season. Calls include a loud *pech*.

Habitat Marshes, swamps and overgrown wet ditches.

Distribution Throughout most of S and W Europe in suitable habitats. Has colonized England in recent years and now local in S England.

Occurrence Fairly common resident species especially in south of range. Sedentary, staying in same habitat throughout year. In England, very local but easily heard, for example, at Radipole Lake in Dorset.

R	1–12	N 5–6

Savi's Warbler
Locustella luscinioides L 14cm

Upperparts uniform and unstreaked warm grey-brown and underparts pale and unmarked. Shows brownish wash on breast, pale supercilium and long, rounded tail with pale-tipped brown undertail coverts. Rather secretive and difficult to locate unless singing. Generally feeds low down near base of reeds in dense reedbeds.

Voice Song is buzzing and insect-like. Rather similar to that of Grasshopper Warbler but faster and deeper in tone. Usually sings from within cover of reedbed and most vocal at dawn and dusk.

Habitat Preferred habitat is dense and extensive reedbeds.

Distribution Breeds in suitable habitats in central and S Europe, and also NW Europe including Britain where very rare. Winters in Africa.

Occurrence Present within breeding range from May to August. In Britain, best looked for (or listened for) at classic sites such as Stodmarsh in Kent or coastal reedbed reserves in E Anglia in May.

S	5–8	N 5–6

River Warbler
Locustella fluviatilis L 14cm

Superficially similar in appearance to Savi's Warbler but with greyer-brown upperparts and lightly spotted or streaked breast. Tail broad and rounded, the undertail coverts with very pale tips. Generally rather secretive and retiring but sings from elevated and often exposed perch.

Voice Song recalls that of Field Cricket. Rather mechanical and prolonged with rhythmic sewing-machine quality.

Habitat Breeds in riverine forest, wet alder woodland and overgrown wooded tangles beside rivers and canals.

Distribution Breeds in E Europe as far north as Baltic coast. Winters south of the region.

Occurrence Present in breeding range from May to August. Very rare vagrant to W Europe, including Britain.

V	—	—

Grasshopper Warbler
Locustella naevia L 13cm

Song and manner of delivery are best identification features. Upperparts olive-brown and heavily streaked and underparts whitish or pale yellowish. Shows indistinct supercilium and faint streaking or spotting on breast, rear flanks and undertail coverts. Feeds unobtrusively low in vegetation and difficult to flush.

Voice Song is high-pitched, insect-like reeling, performed for minutes or even hours on end with few or no pauses. Sometimes sings from low perch affording the observer good views. Most vocal from dusk onwards. Call a sharp *stik*.

Habitat Breeds locally in damp meadows, overgrown ditches and areas of low, rank vegetation. Winters in Africa.

Distribution Breeds across most of central Europe as far north as S Scandinavia. Range includes most of Britain and Ireland except far north.

Occurrence Present in breeding range from mid-April to August. Rather local in Britain.

S	4–8	N 5–6

Cetti's Warbler

Savi's Warbler

River Warbler

Grasshopper Warbler

Sedge Warbler

Acrocephalus schoenobaenus L 13cm

Upperparts buffish-brown to grey-brown with lightly streaked mantle. Has dark eye-stripe and crown and conspicuous off-white supercilium. Rump is warm buffish-brown and unstreaked. Juvenile has diffuse pale centre to crown and a suggestion of streaking on breast. Retiring but sings from exposed position in reedbed.

Voice Song a series of alternating bursts of grating, rasping, tuneful and mimetic phrases. Song occasionally performed in flight. Call a sharp *tchek* and alarm a buzzing *trrrr*.

Habitat Breeds in reedbeds, tangled swampy vegetation beside rivers and lakes.

Distribution Breeds across most of central and N Europe. Occurs throughout Britain and Ireland. Winters in Africa.

Occurrence Present in breeding range from May to August. Common in much of range.

S	5–8	N 5–7

Moustached Warbler

Acrocephalus melanopogon L 12.5cm

Superficially similar to Sedge Warbler but plumage more reddish-brown. Has dark cap, eye-stripe and ear coverts and pure-white supercilium. Flanks and breast washed with reddish-brown. Tail sometimes bobbed in alarm or held raised.

Voice Song rather similar to that of Reed Warbler with short grating and musical phrases. Included, however, are characteristic whistling phrases recalling Nightingale or distant Redshank.

Habitat Reedbeds and marshes with Reedmace.

Distribution Breeds in S Europe, mostly

Moustached Warbler

within range of influence of Mediterranean climate. Occurs in SE Europe as far north as E Austria.

Occurrence Sedentary resident in much of range; birds in SE Europe move E in winter.

V	—	—

Aquatic Warbler

Acrocephalus paludicola L 12.5cm

Rather similar to Sedge Warbler but has yellowish-brown plumage. Mantle has dark centre bordered by pale stripes. Has dark and pale stripes on head: supercilium and centre of crown are

Aquatic Warbler

buffish-white and has dark stripes through eye and on sides of crown. Mantle and rump are streaked. Rather retiring habits and usually difficult to see.

Voice Song similar to Sedge Warbler but more subdued and flowing.

Habitat Breeds in wet, sedgy meadows.

Distribution Very local in SE Europe and E central Europe. Winters south and east of region.

Occurrence Scarce in breeding range from May to August. Rare early-autumn visitor to Britain.

V	8–9	—

Lanceolated Warbler

Locustella lanceolata L 12cm

Very similar to Grasshopper Warbler, but smaller and with more distinct streaking on olive-brown or grey-brown upperparts. Throat and flanks also lightly streaked. Extremely skulking.

Voice Song similar to Grasshopper Warbler but not heard in the region.

Habitat Breeds in marshy scrub with rushes. Migrants to Europe likely to favour similar habitats.

Distribution Breeds E Siberia, winters S Asia.

Occurrence Very rare vagrant to NW Europe but probably also overlooked. In Britain, most records from Fair Isle, in September.

V	9	—

Fan-tailed Warbler

Cisticola juncoides L 10cm

Often recognized at a distance by habits and song alone. At close range, note small size and yellow-brown, heavily streaked upperparts. Tail is short and rounded; seen from below, shows distinct black-and-white tips to feathering. Rather secretive and difficult to see on the ground but obvious in bouncing song-flight, as if bird were on a yo-yo.

Voice Song a continually repeated *zip-zip-zip*, each note corresponding to one bounce of the yo-yo.

Habitat Grassy areas including the fringes of marshes, arable fields and meadows.

Distribution Widespread in S and W Europe as far north as Normandy.

Occurrence Resident species, common in south of range, less so further north. Very rare vagrant to Britain.

V	—	—

Sedge Warbler

Fan-tailed Warbler

Sedge Warbler

Lanceolated Warbler

Reed Warbler
Acrocephalus scirpaceus L 12.5cm

Upperparts are warm-brown and unstreaked and underparts pale and unmarked. Supercilium indistinct, rump reddish-brown and legs dark. When skulking in cover, often adopts an elongated posture. Feeds mainly on insects gleaned from reed stems and tangled undergrowth. Builds a superbly constructed deep, cup-shaped nest, woven among reeds.

Voice Song a series of short phrases repeated in succession, some of which may be mimetic. Typically *cherr cherr cherr, chek chek chek, chirric chirric chirric.* Rather similar to Sedge Warbler but lacks harsh extremes of this species. Call a subdued, almost hissing scold.

Habitat Typically found in extensive reedbeds but also in other wetland habitats on migration.

Distribution Breeding range includes most of lowland Europe as far north as S Scandinavia. Absent from Ireland, Iceland and N Britain. Winters in Africa.

Occurrence Present in breeding range from late April to August. Common in suitable habitats throughout most of range.

S	4–8	N 5–6

Marsh Warbler
Acrocephalus palustris L 13cm

Very similar to Reed and Blyth's Reed Warblers and best separated by song. Upperparts including rump are buffish-brown, with slight greenish hue, and underparts pale. Shows pale eye-ring and indistinct supercilium.

Voice Song a rich medley of phrases, many or most of which are mimetic and uncannily accurate. Not uncommonly includes imitations of African species from wintering range such as orioles and boubous.

Habitat Usually associated with rank, overgrown vegetation usually in the vicinity of water. A typical site would be dense stands of Stinging Nettles growing beside a wet ditch or slow-flowing river.

Distribution Breeds across central Europe as far north as S Scandinavia. Very rare breeding species in Britain. Winters in Africa.

Occurrence Present within breeding range from May to August. In Britain, very small breeding population in S England but also seen on migration, usually in spring, when located by song.

S	5–8	N 5–6

Blyth's Reed Warbler
Acrocephalus dumetorum L 12.5cm

Very similar to Marsh and Reed Warblers. Upperparts grey-brown and underparts pale. Shows pale eye-ring and supercilium most noticeable in front of eye. Wings relatively short and rounded compared with close relatives.

Voice A superb mimic, song comprises a series of phrases, each one repeated 5–7 times. Most vocal at night. Call a sharp *chek.*

Habitat Overgrown marshes and tangled clearings and rides in damp woodland.

Distribution Breeding range from E coast of Baltic eastwards at similar latitudes. Winters south of region.

Occurrence Fairly common within limited European breeding range. Very rare vagrant to W Europe including Britain.

V	—	—

Great Reed Warbler
Acrocephalus arundinaceus L 19cm

Similar to Reed Warbler in plumage and appearance but the size of a thrush. Supercilium pale and prominent and bill noticeably large and stout. Clambers up reed stems and often sings from prominent position for short periods before disappearing again.

Voice Song a loud and croaking version of Reed Warbler's song. Usually a series of repeated phrases *kurr kurr kurr, karra karra karra, kirk kirk kirk.*

Habitat Mainly in extensive reedbeds but also on reed-fringed margins of lakes.

Distribution Breeds in suitable habitats throughout most of lowland central and S Europe. Absent as breeding species from Britain, Ireland, Iceland and most of Scandinavia. Winters in Africa.

Occurrence Fairly common breeding species within range. Rare vagrant to Britain, mostly in spring where overshooting birds may sing in suitable habitat for a few days.

V	—	—

Reed Warbler

Great Reed Warbler

Marsh Warbler

Reed Warbler

Icterine Warbler
Hippolais icterina L 13cm

Upperparts usually greyish-green and underparts pale with clean, yellow wash. At first glance, may recall outsize juvenile Willow Warbler but note stout bill and sloping forecrown. Shows pale eye-ring but lacks eye-stripe. Pale panel on closed wing created by pale edges to secondaries. Legs greyish. Compared with *Phylloscopus* warblers, feeds in slower, more deliberate manner and perches in more upright position. On passage, often feeds within cover of bushes and prolonged observation sometimes necessary to get identifiable views.
Voice Song recalls that of Marsh Warbler, a series of repeated phrases, many of which are mimetic. Calls include a pure *deet-lueet* and a sharp *chek*.
Habitat Scrub and undergrowth along woodland rides and edges. Also in mature parks and gardens.
Distribution Breeds in E Europe as far north as central Scandinavia. Absent from S, SW and W Europe including Britain and Ireland.
Occurrence Fairly common breeding species, present within range from May to August. Seen in Britain as a scarce passage migrant, mainly in autumn.

M	5, 8–10	—

Melodious Warbler
Hippolais polyglotta L 13cm

Similar to Icterine Warbler but lacks pale wing panel on closed wing and often with more yellowish underparts. Legs often brownish and primaries markedly shorter than Icterine Warbler. Habits and behaviour similar to Icterine Warbler.
Voice Song a series of chattering and musical phrases, a few of which may be mimetic. Delivery faster than Icterine Warbler. Calls include a sparrow-like chirp.
Habitat Breeds in overgrown woodland rides, parks and gardens.
Distribution Replaces Icterine Warbler in SW Europe, from Iberia to N France. Absent from Britain and Ireland. Winters in Africa.
Occurrence Fairly common breeding species within range, present from May to August. In Britain, seen as a scarce passage migrant, mainly August–September.

M	5, 8–10	—

Olive-tree Warbler
Hippolais olivetorum L 15.5cm

Structure, and in particular bill size and head shape, obviously that of *Hippolais* warbler. Large size separates it from its relatives. Upperparts rather greyish and underparts dirty-white. Shows pale wing panel on closed secondaries. Bill dull orange and legs greyish. Has rather retiring habits, feeding among cover of foliage.
Voice Song a loud and harsh series of repeated phrases. Call a sharp *tek*.

Habitat Preferred habitats include olive groves and oak woodlands.

Olive-tree Warbler

Distribution Breeds in SE Europe and winters in Africa.
Occurrence Rather scarce and local within limited breeding range from May to August. Fairly easy to see in suitable habitats in coastal N Greece.

Olivaceous Warbler
Hippolais pallida L 13cm

Plumage recalls Garden Warbler but structure obviously that of *Hippolais* warbler. Upperparts pale-grey to buffish-grey and underparts pale. Shows pale eye-ring and supercilium. Bill is dull orange with broad base.
Voice Song recalls that of Reed Warbler. Calls include a sharp *chak*.
Habitat Breeds in a wide variety of habitats including mature parks and gardens, Mediterranean maquis and open woodland.
Distribution Breeds in S Spain and SE Europe. Winters in Africa.
Occurrence Common breeding species within limited range, present from April to August. Very rare autumn vagrant to Britain.

V	—	—

Icterine Warbler, spring

Melodious Warbler, spring

Olivaceous Warbler, at nest

Booted Warbler
Hippolais caligata L 11.5cm

Recalls a small version of Olivaceous Warbler but with finer bill and relatively short wings. At a glance, *Phylloscopus* warbler-like. Upperparts pale sandy-grey and underparts pale but with warm hue. Outer tail feathers have pale fringe, and tips to tail feathers also pale. Rather secretive.

Voice Song a fairly rapid series of chattering and warbling phrases. Call a repeated, sharp *chek*.

Booted Warbler

Habitat Breeds in scrub and mature gardens.

Distribution Breeding range just reaches NE Europe but mainly an Asiatic species.

Occurrence Fairly common within breeding range but very rare vagrant to W Europe including Britain, mostly in autumn.

V	—	—

Barred Warbler
Sylvia nisoria L 15cm

A large and robust *Sylvia* with stout bill and relatively long tail. Adult has grey-brown upperparts and paler underparts suffused by soft, crescent markings. Shows 2 pale wing bars and white-tipped tail. Iris yellow, brightest in male. Juvenile lacks crescent markings, has dark eye and pale fringes to greater coverts and tertials. Rather shy.

Voice Song recalls that of Garden Warbler but slower and including grating *chrrrr* call note.

Habitat Prefers open, scrubby areas, overgrown hedgerows and tangled woodland edge.

Distribution Breeds across most of E Europe north to Baltic coast. Winters south of region.

Occurrence Scarce breeding species, present May to August. In Britain, scarce passage migrant.

M	9–10	—

Orphean Warbler
Sylvia hortensis L 15cm

Adult recalls an outsize Sardinian Warbler but with pale-yellow iris. Has dark hood, greyish-brown upperparts and pale underparts, lightly suffused pink on breast. Outer tail feathers white. Female duller than male. Juvenile has uniform greyish upperparts and pale underparts. Lacks adult's dark head markings. Generally rather shy and retiring.

Voice Song varies with geographical location. W European birds have repetitive series of short phrases, sung with thrush-like tone. In E Europe song recalls Blackbird. Sharp *chak* call.

Habitat Woodland, olive groves and maquis.

Distribution Breeds across most of S Europe, within limits of Mediterranean climate.

Occurrence Fairly common breeding species, May to August. Very rare vagrant to Britain.

V	—	—

Blackcap
Sylvia atricapilla L 14cm

A robust *Sylvia* warbler with greyish-brown upperparts and pale underparts. Male has black cap while that of female is reddish-brown. Juvenile similar to female. Easiest to see before trees are in full leaf; thereafter requires patient observation to see well.

Voice Song similar to Garden Warbler but usually faster and with more scratchy elements. Includes rich, warbling phrases. When alarmed, utters *chek chek chek* call.

Habitat Breeds in open woodland, especially with tangled or coppiced understorey.

Distribution Breeding range includes most of Europe as far north as S Scandinavia. Absent from Iceland. Some birds winter south of region but many winter around Mediterranean. S European breeding birds mostly resident.

Occurrence Common and widespread breeding species. Present all year in S Europe. Further north, birds present from April to August. Small numbers winter in N Europe including Britain.

S	4–9	N 5–7

Garden Warbler
Sylvia borin L 14cm

A rather nondescript *Sylvia* warbler, lacking any distinctive features. Upperparts uniform grey-brown and underparts pale. Head has rather rounded appearance. Bill is short and pointed and legs are greyish-brown. Behaviour rather skulking and presence usually first detected by song.

Voice Song recalls that of Blackcap but usually lacks excited and rapid quality of that species. Tone usually Blackbird-like. Call a sharp *chek*.

Habitat Woodland with dense undergrowth such as mature coppice, and mature gardens.

Distribution Breeds across most of central Europe as far north as central Scandinavia and including Britain and Ireland. Absent from much of S Europe. Winters south of region.

Occurrence Common breeding species, present within breeding range May to August.

S	5–8	N 5–6

Barred Warbler

Orphean Warbler

Blackcap, male

Blackcap, female

Garden Warbler

Whitethroat

Sylvia communis L 14cm

Adult male has grey head, white throat and red-dish-brown wings. Pale underparts have pinkish wash to breast. Adult female has duller plumage than male but still shows reddish-brown wings. Both sexes have rather pale flesh-brown legs and light-brown iris. Juvenile similar to adult female but with darker iris. Feeds actively on and in tangled undergrowth. Male usually sings from exposed position and sometimes in song-flight.

Voice Song a scratchy and energetic series of warbling phrases.

Habitat Breeds in overgrown hedgerows, scrub-covered hillsides and extensive, open areas of bramble patches.

Distribution Breeds throughout most of Europe but absent from N Scandinavia and Iceland. Winters in Africa.

Occurrence Common and widespread breeding species, present from April to August. In Britain, common breeding species except in far north. On passage, sometimes seen in uncharacteristic habitats and as late as September–October.

S	4–10	N 5–7

Lesser Whitethroat

Sylvia curruca L 13.5cm

Superficially similar to Whitethroat but with grey-brown upperparts and uniformly pale underparts. Ear coverts are noticeably dark grey. Lacks bright reddish-brown aspects of Whitethroat's wings. Legs dark grey. Juvenile similar to adult but has duller, washed-out plumage. Has rather retiring habits, usually even singing from cover.

Voice Song distinctive and recalls Cirl Bunting. A dry rattle, usually preceded by a short burst of *Sylvia*-type warbling. Call a sharp *chett.*

Habitat Old hedgerows, scrub with sizeable bushes and open woodland.

Distribution Breeds in central and E Europe as far north as S Scandinavia. Absent from SW and much of S Europe, Ireland and Iceland. In Britain, confined mostly to southern counties of England and Wales.

Occurrence Fairly common breeding species, present within range from April to August. In Britain, seen also on passage, especially around the coast.

S	4–8	N 5–7

Rüppell's Warbler

Sylvia rueppellii L 14cm

Male is distinctive with black head and black throat, separated by white moustachial stripe. Upperparts grey-brown and underparts pale. Adult female has grey-brown upperparts with darker hood, pale underparts and dark feathering on throat, highlighting white moustachial stripe. Both sexes have red eyes, orbital ring and legs. Male often sings from exposed position but otherwise keeps to cover.

Voice Song a repetitive, chattering warble, rather similar to Sardinian Warbler but containing harsh, scolding notes and rattles. Call a rattling *chrrr.*

Habitat Mediterranean habitats including maquis and open woodland with tangled undergrowth.

Distribution Breeds locally in SE Europe, mainly S Greece and W Turkey. Winters in Africa.

Occurrence Locally fairly common from April to August within breeding range. Common on migration in E Mediterranean, e.g. Cyprus, in spring. Very rare vagrant to Britain.

V	—	—

Sardinian Warbler

Sylvia melanocephala L 13cm

Male is distinctive with grey-brown upperparts, black hood with conspicuous red orbital ring, and pale underparts. Iris and legs reddish-brown. Adult female has brownish upperparts, grey cap and pale underparts. Orbital ring red and legs and iris reddish-brown. Juvenile similar to female but orbital ring pale brown.

Voice Song a series of rapid phrases comprising warbling, harsh and tuneful bursts. Typical call is a loud 5-syllable chatter.

Habitat Found in all sorts of Mediterranean habitats including maquis, open woodland and mature gardens.

Distribution Found all round the Mediterranean region and inland where influence of climate is felt.

Occurrence Common in Mediterranean and the typical warbler of the region. Mostly a sedentary resident but very rare vagrant to Britain.

V	—	—

Cyprus Warbler *Sylvia melanothorax* is possibly a subspecies of Sardinian Warbler. Similar but male with black speckling on underparts. Only found on Cyprus.

Whitethroat

Lesser Whitethroat

Rüppell's Warbler, male

Cyprus Warbler

Sardinian Warbler, female

Sardinian Warbler, male

Subalpine Warbler
Sylvia cantillans L 13cm

Male has blue-grey upperparts, pinkish-orange on throat and breast and conspicuous white moustachial stripe. Orbital ring and legs reddish. Adult female plumage a pale and washed-out version of male but orbital ring and legs pale orange and white moustachial stripe usually evident. Juveniles and some females are very pale. Unobtrusive but not over-shy. Song from exposed site or in song-flight.
Voice Song a rapid series of chattering, scratchy warbles. *Chett* call similar to Lesser Whitethroat.
Habitat Breeds in scrub-rich Mediterranean habitats from sea-level to foothills of mountains.
Distribution Breeds in S Europe within influence of Mediterranean climate. Winters in Africa.
Occurrence Common within breeding range from March to August. Rare vagrant to Britain.

V	—	—

Spectacled Warbler
Sylvia conspicillata L 12cm

Recalls a tiny Whitethroat. Male has grey head grading to grey-brown back, well-defined white throat with grey lower edge and pinkish-buff underparts. Wings are reddish-brown, the tertials with black centres. White orbital ring creates spectacled effect, accentuated by black lores. Bill has yellow base and legs are yellowish-orange. Female plumage is duller and paler than male. Usually sings from prominent perch or in flight. Otherwise rather secretive.
Voice Song recalls a short, higher-pitched version of Whitethroat's song. Call a dry rattle.
Habitat Breeds in steppe and garigue habitats with short vegetation and scattered, low bushes.
Distribution Breeds in SW Europe from S Iberian peninsula to S Italy. Winters in N Africa.
Occurrence Present in breeding range from March to September.

V	—	—

Desert Warbler
Sylvia nana L 11.5cm

Recalls a tiny and very pale Whitethroat. Upperparts pale sandy-brown, tail rusty and underparts whitish, the white throat usually noticeable. Legs and base of bill yellow. Iris yellowish and eye surrounded by pale orbital ring. Sings in flight and from bush. Otherwise skulks in low bushes.
Voice Thin warbling song. Rattling call.
Habitat Breeds in deserts and arid steppes.
Distribution Mainly N Africa and central Asia.
Occurrence Very rare vagrant to Europe.

V	—	—

Dartford Warbler
Sylvia undata L 12cm

A typical small *Sylvia* warbler which, in poor light, looks rather dark. Male has dark blue-grey upperparts and deep reddish-purple underparts. Shows white flecks on throat feathers, red orbital ring and dull-orange legs. Female and juvenile have similar but much duller plumage. Often perches briefly on top of gorse bush with tail cocked almost vertically. Sings from top of bush or sometimes in song-flight. Otherwise rather skulking.
Voice Song is rapid, scratchy warble given in short bursts. Call a hissing *cheer-chh*.
Habitat In Britain, invariably associated with heathland and mature, but not rank, gorse bushes. In S Europe, occurs in maquis and garigue.
Distribution Breeds in SW Europe from S Italy to Iberian peninsula, and in W Europe as far north as S Britain.
Occurrence Fairly common resident species in suitable habitats. In Britain, most birds sedentary but some birds move to coasts in winter. Population plummets during severe winters.

R	1–12	N 5–7

Marmora's Warbler
Sylvia sarda L 13cm

Resembles an all-grey Dartford Warbler. Male has dark-grey upperparts with underparts slightly paler. Shows reddish base to bill and red orbital ring, eye and legs. Female and juvenile have slightly browner plumage, duller bare parts, and inconspicuous paler orbital ring. Sings from bush or in flight but otherwise extremely skulking.
Voice Song a high-pitched version of Dartford Warbler's song. Call a sharp *chrrr*.

Marmora's
Warbler

Habitat Breeds in open Mediterranean habitats including maquis and garigue, mainly coastal.
Distribution Very local in W Mediterranean. Breeds E coast of Spain, Balearics, Sardinia and Corsica. Mostly sedentary.
Occurrence Fairly common within local and limited range. Extremely rare vagrant to Britain.

V	—	—

Subalpine Warbler, male

Spectacled Warbler, female

Dartford Warbler

Spectacled Warbler, male

Desert Warbler

Willow Warbler

Phylloscopus trochilus L 11.5cm

Adult has upperparts grey-brown with olive tinge and underparts whitish, usually with yellow wash on breast. Legs flesh-coloured to brown. Very similar to Chiffchaff and best distinguished by song. Juvenile shows more yellow on underparts. Feeds actively among foliage in search of insects.

Voice Song a descending series of clear, tuneful whistles. Call a soft but insistent, disyllabic *hoo-eet*.

Habitat Most types of open woodland and even in small areas of birch and willow scrub.

Distribution Breeds across most of N Europe from S central France to far north of Scandinavia. Found throughout Britain and Ireland but absent from Iceland. Winters in Africa.

Occurrence Very common in breeding range and present from April to September.

S	4–9	N 5–7

Chiffchaff

Phylloscopus collybita L 11cm

Very similar to Willow Warbler and best distinguished by song. Upperparts olive-brown and underparts dirty-white. Plumage usually lacks yellowish hues of Willow Warbler in both adult and juvenile. Legs always dark, often appear black.

Voice Song *chiff chaff chiff chaff*, sometimes rendered *sip sap sip sap*. Occasionally *chiff chiff chaff*. Sometimes heard singing in autumn. Call *hweet*.

Habitat All types of deciduous and mixed woodlands with tangled undergrowth.

Distribution Breeding range includes most of Europe except far north of Scandinavia and Iceland. Winters from S Europe to Africa. Small numbers occasionally overwinter in SW England.

Occurrence Very common breeding species throughout most of range. Present in many areas, including Britain, mid-March to August. Seen and heard on passage in atypical habitats.

S	3–9	N 5–6

Wood Warbler

Phylloscopus sibilatrix L 12cm

Larger than Willow Warbler with clean-looking plumage. Upperparts greenish-yellow. Underparts pure white except for bright-yellow wash on throat and breast. Shows bright-yellow eye-stripe and flesh-coloured legs. Usually active high in tree canopy.

Voice Song a beautiful trilling that accelerates and ends in a vibrating flourish. Sometimes likened to a coin spinning on a plate. Call *peeuu*.

Habitat Favours mature woodland, especially beech, with high-vaulted leafy canopy.

Distribution Breeds across N Europe from S France to S Scandinavia and including Britain. Absent from Iceland. Winters in Africa.

Occurrence Fairly common but rather local due to precise and restricted habitat preference. Present from April to August.

S	4–8	N 5–6

Bonelli's Warbler

Phylloscopus bonelli L 11cm

Head and mantle pale grey (especially head), contrasting with wings and tail feathers which are dark conspicuously fringed with greenish-yellow. Rump yellowish and underparts whitish.

Voice Song a short, soft Wood Warbler-like trill without acceleration. Call *hoo-eet*.

Habitat Mature deciduous woodlands.

Distribution Breeds in central, S and SW Europe. Winters in Africa.

Occurrence Fairly common breeding species, April to August. Rare vagrant to Britain.

V	—	—

Radde's Warbler

Phylloscopus schwarzi L 12cm

A large, thickset *Phylloscopus* warbler with a stout bill. Upperparts brown and underparts whitish with buff wash. Shows dark eye-stripe and conspicuous long, pale supercilium, sometimes buffish in front of eye. Feeds low down in vegetation and sometimes on ground.

Voice Call a soft *chuk*.

Habitat Vagrants usually seen in tangled cover around coast.

Distribution An Asiatic species.

Occurrence Very rare autumn vagrant to NW Europe including Britain. N Norfolk coast and Scilly Isles are likely locations.

V	10	—

Dusky Warbler

Phylloscopus fuscatus L 11cm

Has Willow Warbler proportions but plumage recalling that of Radde's Warbler. Upperparts dark brown, underparts greyish-white and bill slender. Shows dark eye-stripe and long, pale supercilium, whiter in front of eye than behind.

Voice Call a sharp *chak*.

Habitat Vagrants skulk in low vegetation.

Distribution An Asiatic species.

Occurrence Very rare vagrant to NW Europe including Britain.

V	10	—

Willow Warbler

Chiffchaff

Bonelli's Warbler

Wood Warbler

Radde's Warbler

Greenish Warbler
Phylloscopus trochiloides L 11cm
Recalls Willow Warbler with its grey-green upperparts and pale underparts but shows narrow, pale wing bar. Legs flesh-coloured, and has long, prominent pale supercilium. Feeds actively, often in tree canopy.

Voice Song a disyllabic call followed by trill. Call *tsu-wee*.

Greenish Warbler

Habitat Deciduous and mixed woodland.
Distribution Breeds from E Baltic coast and at similar latitudes eastwards.
Occurrence Fairly common in breeding range, May to August. Rare vagrant to NW Europe.

V	5–6, 9–10	—

Arctic Warbler
Phylloscopus borealis L 12cm
Upperparts greyish-green, underparts pale and wings showing one conspicuous pale wing bar and a second less obvious one, not always visible. Shows dark eye-stripe and long, pale supercilium. Larger than Greenish Warbler with proportionately larger head and stouter bill.
Voice Song a rapid trill. Call a Dipper-like *tsit*.
Habitat Northern birch forests, Arctic scrub.
Distribution Breeds from N Scandinavia eastwards at similar latitudes. Winters in SE Asia.
Occurrence Fairly common in breeding range, June to August. Rare vagrant to NW Europe.

V	9–10	—

Yellow-browed Warbler
Phylloscopus inornatus L 10cm
A small and highly active *Phylloscopus* warbler with greyish-green upperparts and pale underparts. Distinctive features include 2 pale wing bars and very long, pale-yellow supercilium. Tertials show whitish fringes, and sometimes shows faint impression of pale crown stripe.
Voice Call a disyllabic *tss-weet*.
Habitat Wooded areas.
Distribution An E Asiatic species.
Occurrence Scarce but regular autumn visitor to NW Europe, including Britain.

V	9–11	—

Pallas's Warbler
Phylloscopus proregulus L 9.5cm
Smallest *Phylloscopus* of the region. Recalls Yellow-browed Warbler with its greenish upperparts, pale underparts and 2 pale-yellow wing bars. Also shows pale-yellow rump, especially noticeable when hovering and flitting between branches. Shows long, pale-yellow supercilium and pale-yellow crown stripe.
Voice Call a disyllabic *hoo-et*.
Habitat Woodland and scrub.
Distribution An E Asiatic species.
Occurrence Regular vagrant to NW Europe.

V	10	—

Goldcrest
Regulus regulus L 9cm
Together with Firecrest, Europe's smallest bird. Upperparts olive-green and underparts paler. Shows pale area around eye and dark-bordered crown stripe, orange in male and yellow in female. Juvenile lacks crown stripe. Wings show 2 pale wing bars and dark base to flight feathers. Incredibly active, hovering and flitting in search of insects.
Voice Song high-pitched, thin notes ending in a flourish. Call a thin and high-pitched *see-see-see*.
Habitat Usually associated with woodlands or mature gardens often where conifers present.
Distribution Widespread in Europe as far north as central Scandinavia but mostly absent from SW and SE Europe as a breeding species.
Occurrence Common resident within range. Winter range withdraws from far north.

R	1–12	N 4–7

Firecrest
Regulus ignicapillus L 9cm
Size of Goldcrest and superficially similar. Differs, however, in having black eye-stripe and broad white supercilium as well as black-bordered crown stripe, orange in male and yellow in female. Good views reveal bronze tinge to shoulders and overall appearance cleaner than that of Goldcrest.
Voice Song a series of high-pitched notes, similar to Goldcrest but accelerating and without final flourish. Call similar to Goldcrest.
Habitat Breeds in mixed and coniferous woodland. In Britain, often associated with unusual conifers in parkland or arboretum settings.
Distribution Breeds central, S and SW Europe, birds from north of range moving south in winter.
Occurrence Fairly common breeding species in suitable habitats within range. In Britain, scarce migrant, and rare breeding species in S England.

R(M)	1–12 (10–11)	N 5–7

Arctic Warbler

Yellow-browed Warbler

Goldcrest

Pallas's Warbler

Firecrest

FLYCATCHERS
Family Muscicapidae

Small, insectivorous birds that feed by making aerial forays from exposed perches in trees. Nest in recesses or holes in trees. Long-distance migrants. Sexes dissimilar except for Spotted Flycatcher.

Pied Flycatcher
Ficedula hypoleuca L 13cm

In breeding plumage, male has black or dark-grey upperparts and pure white underparts. Shows small patch of white on base of otherwise black forecrown, white edging to greater coverts producing wing bar, and white on tertials. Female has brown upperparts and white underparts. Female shows similar pattern of white on wing to male but lacks white on forecrown. After moult, often in July, male closely resembles female. Regularly flicks and pumps tail.

Voice Song a tuneful variation on *tsree tsree tsree wachorr weechorr tsee tsuu*. Call a sharp *wit*.

Habitat Open woodland with sunny clearings. Nests in holes in trees but takes to nestboxes.

Distribution Breeds locally in W and N Europe from Iberia to N Scandinavia. Absent from Ireland; in Britain, found only in west and north.

Occurrence Fairly common breeding species, from May to August. In Britain, classic locations are Sessile Oak woodlands of Wales.

S	5–8	N 5–6

Collared Flycatcher
Ficedula albicollis L 13cm

Breeding male recalls Pied Flycatcher but has broad white collar, large white patch on base of forecrown and white bases to primaries forming conspicuous patch. Also shows whitish rump. Female shows suggestion of greyish rump and

Collared Flycatcher, male

neck collar. Pale bases to primaries usually more noticeable than in female Pied Flycatcher.

After post-breeding moult, male resembles female but still shows large patch formed by white bases to primaries. Habits and behaviour same as Pied Flycatcher.

Voice Song unlike that of Pied Flycatcher, a subdued series of squeaky phrases. Call a sharp *eerp*.

Habitat Woodlands, parks and gardens.

Distribution Breeds in central and SE Europe, range just overlapping with Pied Flycatcher.

Occurrence Fairly common breeding species. Common on spring migration in E Mediterranean.

V	—	—

Semi-collared Flycatcher
Ficedula semitorquata L 13cm

Plumage of breeding male contains elements of Pied and Collared Flycatchers. Shows narrow, white half-collar and white bases to primaries form conspicuous patch. Also shows second white wing bar formed by edging to median coverts. Female similar to female Collared Flycatcher and shows second white wing bar. In post-breeding plumage, male resembles female. Habits and behaviour similar to Pied Flycatcher.

Voice Similar to Pied Flycatcher.

Habitat Woodlands, parks and gardens.

Distribution Very local in E Mediterranean.

Occurrence Seen on spring migration in E Mediterranean with Pied and Collared Flycatchers.

Spotted Flycatcher
Muscicapa striata L 14cm

Upperparts uniform grey-brown with streaking on crown and underparts pale with conspicuous streaking on breast. Sexes similar and juveniles show pale spots on upperparts. Perches prominently in upright position watching for insects.

Voice Call sharp *tsee* used as basis for song.

Habitat Sunny clearings and mature gardens.

Distribution Breeds across most of Europe as far north as N Scandinavia. Occurs throughout Britain and Ireland but absent from Iceland.

Occurrence Fairly common and present within breeding range from May until August.

S	5–8	N 5–7

Red-breasted Flycatcher
Ficedula parva L 11.5cm

In all plumages has white patches on base of tail, best seen when tail cocked. Upperparts greyish-brown, underparts pale and shows pale orbital ring. Male has reddish-orange flush on throat. Females and first-year males have buffish breasts.

Voice Trilling song recalls that of Wood Warbler, and ends in a flourish. Robin-like call, *tic*.

Habitat Deciduous woods and mature parks.

Distribution Breeds E Europe as far north as Baltic coast and winters in Asia.

Occurrence Fairly common breeding species, present within range May to August.

V	9–10	—

Pied Flycatcher, female

Red-breasted Flycatcher, female

Pied Flycatcher, male

Spotted Flycatcher

WHEATEARS, CHATS AND THRUSHES
Family Turdidae

Small to medium-sized birds, many with a rather dumpy appearance. Diet varies throughout group. Some feed exclusively on invertebrates. Others, such as thrushes, have more varied diet including berries and fruit. Many species are long-distance migrants.

Wheatear
Oenanthe oenanthe L 15cm

Most striking feature is white rump, emphasized by black tail with white on sides, and seen best in flight. Breeding male has grey upperparts, black mask bordered by white, blackish wings and pale underparts with yellowish-buff wash on throat and breast. Female similar to male but with duller, browner plumage and lacking black mask. Both sexes of Greenland race *leucorrhoa* are larger and brighter. Winter male similar to female but retains black mask. Juvenile has scaly upperparts and bars and crescents on underparts. Adopts rather upright posture on ground and often perches on stone walls.

Voice Call a loud and sharp *chack*. Song comprises short bursts of warbling, chattering phrases.

Habitat Open country with low vegetation including grazed coastal grassland, moors, heaths and tundra. Nests in burrows, among boulders and in stone walls.

Distribution Breeding range includes the whole of Europe including Iceland. Range also extends to Greenland. Winters in Africa.

Occurrence Common breeding species in suitable habitats, present from April to September. Rather local in central Europe and in Britain found mostly in west and north. Also seen as passage migrant and in Britain, often the first migrant to appear in spring (from March onwards) and the last to leave (October–November).

S	3–10	N 5–7

Black-eared Wheatear
Oenanthe hispanica L 14.5cm

Generally slimmer appearance than Wheatear, male occurring in two colour forms. Eastern race *melanoleuca* has black throat and ear coverts while western race *hispanica* has black on head confined to mask through eye to ear coverts. Both races have pale-buff upperparts, often much paler in *melanoleuca*, pale underparts and black wings.

Rump white and tail with black central band, black on outer tail feathers and tip of tail, but otherwise white. Female has dark to reddish-brown upperparts, paler underparts with reddish tone to breast, dark wings and similar tail pattern to male. Female *hispanica* usually shows pale supercilium and female *melanoleuca* may show faint dark feathering on throat. Often perches prominently. Alert and often rather wary and quick to fly.

Wheatear, male   **Black-eared Wheatear**, male

Voice Song a series of warbling and grating phrases. Calls include a sharp *sschak*.

Habitat Open Mediterranean habitats including maquis and garigue-covered slopes and dry, stony areas.

Distribution Breeds throughout S Europe within range of Mediterranean climate. Race *hispanica* occurs mainly Iberian peninsula and S France, being replaced eastwards by race *melanoleuca*.

Occurrence Fairly common breeding species, present within range from April to August. Very rare vagrant to Britain where often very short-staying and difficult to see.

V	—	—

Isabelline Wheatear
Oenanthe isabellina L 16cm

A large, pale wheatear most resembling female Wheatear of northern race. Plumage pale buff to sandy-coloured, effect added to by pale-buff fringes to wing feathers. Markings on head pale and washed-out but showing pale supercilium. Adopts noticeably upright posture, otherwise habits and behaviour similar to Wheatear.

Voice Loud and whistling song, containing elements of mimicry. Call a thin and whistling *cheep*.

Habitat Breeds on stony steppe country, semi-deserts and plains with minimal grass cover.

Distribution A mainly Asiatic species but breeding in N Greece and European Turkey. Winters south of region.

Occurrence Fairly common in suitable habitats and present from April to September. Very rare vagrant to NW Europe including Britain.

V	—	—

Wheatear, female

Black-eared Wheatear, male

Wheatear, male

Black-eared Wheatear, female

Isabelline Wheatear

Pied Wheatear
Oenanthe pleschanka L 14.5cm

Summer male has white cap and nape, the centre of which may appear rather grubby. Shows black face, throat, mantle and wings, and white underparts sometimes with buffish tone to breast. Shows white rump and tail pattern similar to Black-eared Wheatear. In Autumn, pattern of male plumage obscured by buffish feather fringes. Upperparts including crown to breast look generally brown, and shows pale supercilium. Female has dull grey-brown upperparts and head, and often throat and breast too, with whitish underparts. Shows faint pale supercilium. Very similar to eastern-race female Black-eared Wheatear. Often perches on bare branch or post.

Voice Song resembles that of Black-eared Wheatear. Call a sharp *tsak*.

Habitat Rocky slopes, cliffs and arid hillsides.

Distribution W Asiatic breeding species, wintering in Africa. (See also Cyprus Pied Wheatear.)

Occurrence Scarce passage migrant in E Mediterranean. Very rare vagrant to Britain.

V	—	—

Cyprus Pied Wheatear
Oenanthe cypriaca L 14cm

Male very similar to Pied Wheatear, of which this may be a subspecies. Summer female has dark upperparts, including head and throat, and pale underparts with buffish tone. Shows pale supercilium extending back to nape.

Voice Similar to Pied Wheatear but more repetitive. Call a sharp *tsak*.

Habitat Similar to Pied Wheatear.

Distribution Breeds only on Cyprus. Winters south of region.

Occurrence Present on Cyprus from March to September.

Desert Wheatear
Oenanthe deserti L 15cm

Summer male has sandy-buff plumage with black ear coverts and throat continuous with black wings. Shows white rump and all-black tail, and faint pale supercilium. Winter male has greyish-buff plumage and black areas of plumage largely subdued by buffish feather fringes. Female is pale sandy-buff with dark wings, brown ear coverts and a faint pale supercilium. Occasionally shows darker feathering on throat. All-black tail is a distinguishing feature in all plumages.

Voice Song a short series of whistling phrases. Whistling call.

Habitat Arid plains and semi-deserts.

Distribution Breeds in Asia and N Africa.

Pied Wheatear, male   Desert Wheatear, male

Occurrence Very rare vagrant to Europe including Britain, with records from late autumn and early winter.

V	—	—

Black Wheatear
Oenanthe leucura L 18cm

A large and dumpy wheatear, easily told by all-dark plumage except for white rump, vent and base of outer tail. At close range, female and juvenile have very dark brown plumage, not black as in male. Sometimes perches on high lookouts.

Voice Song comprises a mixture of musical and harsh phrases.

Black Wheatear, male

Calls include a whistling *peee-peee*.

Habitat Rocky slopes and gorges.

Distribution Breeds S and central Iberian peninsula, locally in S Pyrenees.

Occurrence A mainly sedentary resident.

White-crowned Black Wheatear
Oenanthe leucopyga L 17cm

Adult has all-black plumage except for white crown and white rump and undertail. Tail white except for central black bar and black tips to outer feathers. Juvenile and first-winter birds have black crowns and only told from Black Wheatear by tail pattern.

Voice Song short bursts of musical phrases.

Habitat Deserts and semi-deserts.

Distribution Breeding range mainly N Africa to Middle East.

Occurrence Very rare vagrant to Britain.

V	—	—

Pied Wheatear

Cyprus Pied Wheatear

Desert Wheatear
White-crowned Black Wheatear

Whinchat

Saxicola rubetra L 12.5cm

Male has dark-brown upperparts, the feathering with blackish centres. Ear coverts and cheeks blackish, and shows conspicuous pale supercilium. Wings blackish with white on scapulars and bases of primaries. Underparts pale with rich orange-buff wash on throat, breast and flanks. Throat bordered by white stripes. Female plumage a washed-out version of male plumage. In winter, sexes are similar, both with dull-brown feathering which suggests the patterning of summer plumage. Perches prominently on low dead bush, barbed wire or post.

Voice Song a rather subdued and rapid series of scratchy warbles interspersed with musical notes. Alarm call *yu tik-tik*.

Habitat Damp meadows, rough commons and grassy heaths.

Distribution Breeds most of central and N Europe from Pyrenees northwards to N Scandinavia. Absent from Iceland.

Occurrence Fairly common breeding species, present within range from April to August. Rather local in Britain and also seen on passage in spring and autumn.

S	4–8	N 5–6

Stonechat

Saxicola torquata L 12.5cm

At a glance, could be confused with Whinchat but never shows pale supercilium. Summer male has all-black head and blackish upperparts with paler, reddish rump. Shows white on scapulars and on side of neck. Underparts with rich orange-red tone. Tail all-dark. Female has brownish upperparts including head and throat. Underparts with orange-red wash on breast. Winter male browner and closer to female plumage but still shows distinct white half-collar on side of neck and dark throat. Winter female has warmer brown upperparts than in summer, looking a more uniform colour above and below. Eastern subspecies, so-called **Siberian Stonechat**, *S.t.maura*, shows almost pure-white rump in all plumages. Winter birds and females have pale throats. Summer males look very black-and-white with whiter underparts and more extensive white half-collar on side of neck. Stonechats, especially males, characteristically perch prominently on high gorse bushes, calling and flicking tail.

Voice Song a rapid series of warbling and twittering phrases, recalling Dunnock in tone. Call a sharp and loud *chak chak*, like two pebbles being hit together.

Habitat Often occurs where gorse is plentiful and so prefers heathy areas, rough grassland, sloping sea cliffs and moors. In Britain, a characteristic bird of southern heathlands. In S Europe, often found in upland areas.

Distribution Breeds across W, S and central Europe. Absent from many areas of Britain because of lack of suitable habitat.

Occurrence A rather common breeding species within range and given habitat preferences. Birds from W and S Europe mostly resident but those from central Europe move S and W in autumn. Siberian Stonechat is a very rare vagrant to Britain.

R	1–12	N 5–7

Whinchat, female

Whinchat, male

Stonechat, summer male

Stonechat, male, winter

Stonechat, female

Rock Thrush
Monticola saxatilis L 19cm

In profile, resembles dumpy, short-tailed thrush with relatively long bill. Summer male is attractive and distinctive with grey-blue head, back and breast and orange-red underparts. Wings are dark brown, tail orange-red and shows conspicuous white patch on lower back. Female has brownish plumage with pale spots on back and crescent markings on underside. Tail orange-red. Winter male resembles female but with faint suggestion of summer plumage colours on head and upperparts. Usually rather shy and wary, often skulking among boulders. Feeds on relatively large prey including lizards and crickets.

Voice Song a musical warbling with thrush-like quality. Usually delivered from high, rocky perch but sometimes in flight. Calls include a loud *chack-chack*.

Habitat Rocky slopes, boulder fields and gorges, often at considerable altitudes.

Distribution Breeding range includes most of S Europe. Winters in Africa.

Occurrence Fairly common breeding species, present within breeding range from April to August. Seen on migration passing through most parts of the Mediterranean region, pausing to feed in stony fields and valleys. Very rare vagrant to Britain, mostly in spring.

V	—	—

Blue Rock Thrush
Monticola solitarius L 20cm

Similar dumpy profile to Rock Thrush but with noticeably larger and longer bill. Male has entirely deep-blue plumage during summer months, tinged grey-brown during the winter. Female recalls female Rock Thrush with pale spots on upperparts and crescent markings on underparts. Background colour is darker brown, however, and tail is dark brown and not orange-red as in Rock Thrush. Presence usually detected first by song. Males discovered by systematic scanning of suitable rocky perches from which song delivered. Shy and retiring and usually will not allow a close approach. Feeds on lizards, insects and other small invertebrates.

Voice Song rather rapid and musical, recalling that of Blackbird. A typical sound of Mediterranean cliffs and rocky slopes. Calls include a loud *chuck*.

Habitat Sunny, rocky slopes, usually with sheer rock-faces, and Mediterranean coastal cliffs.

Distribution Breeds in S Europe, mostly within regions influenced by the Mediterranean climate.

Occurrence Fairly common breeding species in suitable habitats. Mostly resident but some altitudinal migration during winter.

Rock Thrush, male

Blue Rock Thrush, male

Rock Thrush, female   **Blue Rock Thrush,** female

Redstart
Phoenicurus phoenicurus L 14cm
Summer male is distinctive with steely-grey upperparts, white forecrown, black throat and orange-red underparts and tail. Prior to autumn migration, feathers have buffish fringes which make throat look greyish and upperparts brown. The pale fringes are subsequently abraded during the winter months revealing full adult plumage. Female has brown upperparts, paler underparts with an orange hue and orange-red tail. Male in particular perches on dead branches and flicks tail. Feeds mainly on insects.
Voice Song comprises short bursts of melancholy notes starting *tchuee-tchuee-tchuee*. Sings from dawn onwards. Calls include a loud *hueeet*.
Habitat Breeds in open, deciduous woodland, mature parks and wooded heaths.
Distribution Breeding range includes most of Europe except far south, Ireland and Iceland. Winters in Africa.
Occurrence Fairly common breeding species, present within range from May to August. In Britain, breeds mainly in west and north but seen also on passage.

S	5–8	N 5–6

Black Redstart
Phoenicurus ochruros L 14cm
Male has mostly sooty-grey plumage with black face and throat. Shows white panel on wings and orange-red tail. Female has rather uniform greyish-brown plumage but with orange-red tail. Juvenile similar to female and first-summer male is like female but with suggestion of black on throat.
Voice Song a short burst of musical warbling followed by a sound like ball bearings being ground together. Calls include *tsep* and *tik-tik*.
Habitat In many parts of W Europe, including Britain, usually associated with man-made habitats and artefacts. Seen around towns, factories and derelict industrial sites. In central Europe, also common in mountainous areas where associated with boulders and scree.
Distribution Breeds across S and central Europe north to Baltic coast. Rare breeding species in Britain. Southern populations resident but birds from north of range move south and west in winter.
Occurrence Fairly common in S Europe but scarcer in north of range. In Britain, seen mostly as a winter visitor, mainly to coastal regions.

R(M)	1–12 (9–11)	N 5–6

Bluethroat
Luscinia svecica L 14cm
In all plumages, has reddish sides to base of tail and pale supercilium. In summer, male is distinctive with shining blue throat, bordered on breast by distinct black band and more diffuse band of orange-red. Males of Scandinavian subspecies *svecica* have red patch on throat while southern Continental race *cyanecula* has white spot on breast, absent in some birds. Buffish fringes to feathers in autumn may obscure the bright colouring. Female has brownish upperparts, pale underparts, the pale-buff throat outlined by dark feathering. Juvenile recalls juvenile Robin with pale spots and streaks on brown upperparts but shows reddish base to tail. Hops unobtrusively on the ground, pausing momentarily and adopting upright posture.
Voice Song is rich and full, including ringing notes. Calls include *chak-chak*.
Habitat Breeds in damp scrub and woodland.
Distribution Breeds in N Scandinavia and NE Europe, with scattered distribution in central and SW Europe in wetland and upland areas.
Occurrence Fairly common breeding species in north of range but less so further south. In Britain, seen as scarce passage migrant, both spring and autumn and mainly on E coast.

M	5–6, 9–10	—

Red-flanked Bluetail
Tarsiger cyanurus L 14cm
Adult male has blue upperparts including head and tail, white throat and pale, streaked underparts with orange-red flanks. Female and first-winter male have brownish upperparts and breast, pure-white throat, pale underparts with reddish flanks and blue tail. In all plumages blue tail can simply look dark. Shy and retiring.
Voice Song a musical warble. Call a thin *hoeet*.

Red-flanked Bluetail,
summer male

Habitat Breeds in northern conifer forests.
Distribution Breeds mainly N Asia but very local in Finland. Winters in S Asia.
Occurrence Very rare vagrant to Britain.

V	—	—

Redstart, female

Redstart, male

Black Redstart, winter

Black Redstart, male

Bluethroat, female

Bluethroat, male

Red-flanked Bluetail

Robin

Erithacus rubecula L 14cm

Adult is distinctive with orange-red breast, face and forecrown, brown upperparts and white belly. Juvenile has brownish plumage, paler beneath, the upperparts with pale yellowish-buff spots and the underparts with crescent markings. In woodland habitat, can be rather unobtrusive and retiring, especially during breeding season. Can become remarkably bold and tame. Hops on ground, pausing and adopting upright posture. **Voice** Song a cascade of musical warblings. Heard at most times of the year, in winter sounding distinctly melancholy. Call a sharp *tic*. **Habitat** Woodlands, mature gardens and parks. **Distribution** Breeds throughout most of Europe. Resident in W, central and S Europe but NE European birds migrate to S Europe in autumn. **Occurrence** Common breeding species in suitable habitat. Resident in Britain but numbers augmented in autumn by continental migrants.

R	1–12	N 4–7

Rufous Bush Robin

Cercotrichas galactotes L 16cm

Underparts pale and upperparts grey-brown in subspecies *syriacus* and reddish-brown in subspecies *galactotes*. Shows pale supercilium and long, graduated tail with characteristic black-and-white markings on tip. Tail often fanned and pumped. **Voice** Song short bursts of thrush-like phrases, sung from perch or in flight. Call a sharp *chek*. **Habitat** Dry scrub, overgrown olive groves and clumps of prickly pear. **Distribution** Subspecies *galactotes* occurs S Iberian peninsula and N Africa to Israel while *syriacus* occurs mainly Greece and Turkey. Winters in Africa. **Occurrence** Fairly common in limited range, from May to August. Very rare vagrant to Britain.

Nightingale

Luscinia megarhynchos L 16.5cm

Much more often heard than seen. Upperparts warm brown grading to reddish-brown tail. Underparts pale greyish-white and unmarked. Juvenile has pale buffish spots on upperparts similar to juvenile Robin but shows reddish-brown tail. Generally rather shy and retiring, usually even singing from dense cover. **Voice** Song extremely loud and musical. Repertoire varies from bird to bird, but song often begins with a series of thin, pure whistles and continues with deep warbling phrases and including a rapid *chuc-chuc-chuc-chuc-chuc*. Often sings at night. Calls include a sharp *chac* and a thin *hoeet*. **Habitat** Breeds in wooded habitats with dense undergrowth. In mainland Europe, breeds in a wide variety of habitats but in Britain more restricted to mature coppiced woodland and birch and willow thickets on heaths and commons. **Distribution** Breeds across most of central and S Europe as far north as N France and S Britain. Winters in Africa. **Occurrence** Fairly common breeding species but rather local in Britain. Present in breeding range from May to August.

S	5–8	N 5–6

Thrush Nightingale

Luscinia luscinia L 16.5cm

Very similar to Nightingale and best distinguished by contrast between grey-brown upperparts and reddish-brown tail, and by pale grey-brown spots on breast. Juvenile effectively indistinguishable from juvenile Nightingale. Habits and behaviour as Nightingale. **Voice** Song similar to Nightingale but if anything even louder, though with less variation. Calls include a thin *hweet*. **Habitat** Breeds in dense cover in wooded areas, often close to water. **Distribution** Breeds in E Europe as far north as S Scandinavia. Winters in Africa. **Occurrence** Fairly common breeding species in range, present from May to August. Very rare vagrant to Britain.

V	—	—

Siberian Rubythroat

Luscinia calliope L 16.5cm

In all plumages, shows grey-brown upperparts, dark tail and pale grey-buff underparts. Male has red throat bordered with black, and white moustachial stripe and supercilium. Female has white throat, moustachial stripe and supercilium. Shy and retiring habits. **Voice** Song musical with Nightingale-like phrases and elements of mimicry. Calls include a sharp *chat* and *tee-lu*. **Habitat** Breeds in dense woodland undergrowth. **Distribution** Breeds in Siberia; winters in S Asia. **Occurrence** Very rare vagrant to NW Europe including Britain.

V	—	—

Robin, juvenile

Robin, adult

Rufous Bush Robin

Nightingale
Thrush Nightingale   **Siberian Rubythroat**

Blackbird

Turdus merula L 24cm

Male all-black with yellow-orange bill and eye-ring. Female uniform dark brown with suggestion of mottled streaking on throat and breast. Juvenile paler brown than female with buffish streaks on upperparts and mottled underparts. Feeds mostly on ground, searching for earthworms, insects and other invertebrates. Characteristically hops and then stands motionless, peering at ground.

Voice Song is rich and musical without phrase repetition of Song Thrush. Call a tongue-clicking, ringing *clak-clak-clak*, becoming louder, more metallic and repeated incessantly when alarmed, e.g. by presence of cat or Tawny Owl.

Habitat Parks, gardens and woodland.

Distribution Breeds throughout most of Europe, including Britain and Ireland, as far north as central Scandinavia.

Occurrence Mostly resident throughout range although northernmost populations move south and west in winter.

R	1–12	N 4–7

Ring Ouzel

Turdus torquatus L 24cm

Size and shape of Blackbird but male blackish with conspicuous white crescent on breast. Shows whitish fringes to feathers on wing and also on underparts. Bill yellowish with black tip. Female brownish, white crescent on the breast showing subtly darker fringes to feathering giving scaly appearance. Juvenile brown with pale throat and rather scaly underparts but no pale crescent on breast. First-autumn birds resemble adult female but pale feather fringes give greyer, more scaly appearance. Much more wary than Blackbird. On migration in autumn, sometimes feeds in small flocks in berry-bearing bushes.

Voice Song a simple and short series of musical whistles followed by a soft twittering. Calls include a hard *chek-chek-chek*.

Habitat Breeds on open moors with rocky outcrops and in mountainous regions, sometimes in areas with sparse conifer cover.

Distribution Scattered breeding range including N and W Scandinavia, N and W Britain and Ireland and mountains of central and S Europe. Winters around Mediterranean region.

Occurrence Fairly common breeding species within limited range, present from April to September.

S	4–9	N 5–7

Swainson's Thrush

Catharus ustulatus L 18cm

Smaller than European *Turdus* thrushes, with relatively large-headed appearance. Uniform olive-brown upperparts, buff lores and conspicuous buffish eye-ring. Breast is rich buff with dark spots. Feeds on ground.

Voice Call a sharp *whik*.

Habitat Vagrants seen in typical thrush habitats.

Distribution Breeds N America and winters northern S America.

Occurrence Very rare autumn vagrant to Britain.

V	10	—

Gray-cheeked Thrush

Catharus minimus L 18cm

Similar to Swainson's Thrush but with grey-brown upperparts, indistinct eye-ring, greyish ear coverts and pale breast with dark spots grading into greyish flanks. Habits and behaviour as Swainson's Thrush.

Voice Call a slurred *wee-err*.

Habitat Vagrants favour typical thrush habitats.

Distribution Breeds northern N America and winters in S America.

Occurrence Very rare autumn vagrant to Britain, mostly Cornwall and Scilly Isles.

V	10	—

Hermit Thrush

Catharus guttatus L 17cm

Upperparts show contrast between olive-brown or grey-brown head and mantle, and reddish-brown tail. Has whitish, narrow eye-ring and pale breast with dark spots. Rather shy and retiring.

Voice Call a low *chook*.

Habitat Vagrants prefer tangled undergrowth.

Distribution Breeds northern N America and winters southern N America to Central America.

Occurrence Very rare autumn vagrant to Britain.

V	10	—

Veery

Catharus fuscescens L 17cm

Warm-brown upperparts, looking almost reddish-brown on rump. Underparts whitish with grey flanks and only pale and subtle spotting on throat and breast. Lacks pale eye-ring.

Voice Call a thin, whistling *wheew*.

Habitat Vagrants seen in typical thrush habitat.

Distribution Breeds in N, winters S America.

Occurrence Very rare autumn vagrant to Britain.

V	10	—

Blackbird, female

Blackbird, male

Ring Ouzel, female

Ring Ouzel, male

Hermit Thrush

Veery

Song Thrush
Turdus philomelos L 23cm

Upperparts warm brown and underparts pale with dark spots and yellow-buff tinge to breast. Underwing orange-buff, easily seen in flight. Feeds on ground, searching for earthworms etc. Also feeds on berries and fruits, especially in winter.
Voice Song a medley of fluty phrases, each one usually repeated 2–4 times. Call a sharp *zik*.
Habitat Breeds in woodland, parks and gardens. In winter, sometimes in open fields.
Distribution Breeds throughout most of central and N Europe from N Spain to N Scandinavia. Absent from Iceland. Northern populations move S and W in autumn, winter range extending throughout S Europe.
Occurrence Common breeding species throughout range.

R	1–12	N 4–7

Mistle Thrush
Turdus viscivorus L 28cm

Adult has uniform grey-brown upperparts with whitish fringes to wing feathers. Outer tail feathers have white tips, most noticeable in flight. Underparts pale with dark spots and slight buffish wash to breast. Juvenile has conspicuous white spots on back and can look almost scaly above. Habits and behaviour similar to Song Thrush but generally more wary and often seen feeding in pairs.
Voice Song loud, musical and rather slow, with Blackbird-like quality. Regularly sings on rainy days and towards dusk, as well as at more usual songbird times of day. Typical alarm call a dry rattle.
Habitat Breeds in woodlands, parks and mature gardens. In winter, also seen in fields and hedgerows.
Distribution Breeds throughout Europe except far north and Iceland. Northern populations retreat south and west in autumn.
Occurrence Fairly common breeding species throughout range.

R	1–12	N 4–7

Eye-browed Thrush
Turdus obscurus L 22cm

Male has grey head and neck with conspicuous white supercilium, olive-brown upperparts and white underparts with orange-buff wash on flanks. Female and first-winter male have uniform olive-brown upperparts, including head, with white supercilium and throat and white underparts with buffish wash on flanks.
Voice Call a drawn-out *seee*.
Habitat Feeds in open areas.

Eye-browed Thrush, summer male   **Dusky Thrush,** summer male

Distribution An Asiatic species.
Occurrence Very rare vagrant to Britain.

V	—	—

Dusky Thrush
Turdus naumanni L 24cm

Occurs as two races. Dusky Thrush *T. n. eunomus* has blackish-brown upperparts and face blackish with white supercilium and throat. Underparts white with black breast band and large spots on flanks. Naumann's Thrush *T. n. naumanni* has uniform grey-brown upperparts, buff supercilium, orange-red breast and tail and white belly. Female more subdued than male.
Voice Calls include a Fieldfare-like *geeh*.
Habitat Vagrants seen in open, grassy areas.
Distribution Both races are Asiatic in origin.
Occurrence Both races are very rare vagrants to Europe including Britain.

V	—	—

Black-throated Thrush
Turdus ruficollis L 23cm

Occurs as two races. Male Black-throated Thrush *T. r. atrogularis* has grey upperparts, black throat and white underparts. Female and first-winter male have grey upperparts, white underparts and dark spots on breast. Red-throated Thrush *T. r. ruficollis* has red, not black, throat and reddish supercilium. Female and first-winter male have greyish upperparts, white underparts, reddish spotting on breast and reddish supercilium.
Voice Call a subdued *seep*.
Habitat Vagrants seen in fields and open areas.
Distribution Both races Asiatic distributions.
Occurrence Rare vagrant to NW Europe including Britain.

V	—	—

Black-throated Thrush, summer male   **Red-throated Thrush,** summer male

Song Thrush

Mistle Thrush

Redwing
Turdus iliacus L 21cm

Slightly smaller than Song Thrush with dark grey-brown upperparts, white or buffish supercilium and pale underparts with dark streaks and red on flanks and underwing. In winter, seen feeding in flocks in fields or along hedgerows in berry-bearing bushes such as Hawthorn. Sometimes feeds alongside Fieldfares.

Voice Song comprises musical, fluty phrases followed by chattering twitter. Flight call a thin *sheeef*, heard at night from flocks flying overhead.

Habitat Breeds typically in northern birch woodland. In winter, feeds in open habitats such as fields, as well as along hedgerows.

Distribution Breeds throughout Scandinavia and at similar latitudes eastwards. Also in Iceland and rare breeding species in N Scotland. Winter range covers most of W and S Europe.

Occurrence Fairly common breeding species within range. In winter, usually common but appearance, distribution and abundance rather erratic. Winter visitors to Britain seen from October to March.

W	10–3	—

Fieldfare
Turdus pilaris L 25cm

Distinctive with grey head and rump, chestnut-brown back and pale underparts covered with dark arrowhead spots. In flight, shows white underwing. In winter, feeds in flocks in fields and also in berry-bearing trees and bushes. Often feeds alongside Redwings and other thrushes.

Voice Song a series of grating, chattering notes and phrases. Calls a chattering *chak chak chak* and a nasal *ee-eep*.

Habitat Breeds in northern and upland woodland, both deciduous and coniferous. In winter, usually seen in open fields, hedgerows and woodland edge, but occasionally visits gardens.

Distribution Breeds from central Europe to N Scandinavia and at similar latitudes eastwards. Very rare breeding species in Britain. In autumn, northern populations move south and west and winter range covers most of S, W and central Europe.

Occurrence Common breeding species within range. Common winter visitor to Britain, mostly from October to March.

W	10–3	⊥

American Robin
Turdus migratorius L 25cm

Distinctive with dark grey-brown upperparts, orange-red breast, conspicuous broken, white eye-ring and pale throat with dark streaking. Habits and behaviour as Blackbird.

Voice Calls include *tut-tut*.

Habitat Vagrants to Europe usually seen in open, grassy areas.

Distribution Breeds across N America, northern birds moving south in winter.

Occurrence Very rare vagrant to Britain, mainly in winter.

V	—	—

Siberian Thrush
Zoothera sibirica L 22cm

Adult male all-black with conspicuous white supercilium. Sub-adult male has buffish feathering on throat and ear coverts. Female has warm-brown upperparts and pale, heavily spotted underparts. Shows pale supercilium, throat and ear coverts. All plumages have yellowish legs and striking black-and-white bands on underwing.

Voice Typical call *zit*.

Habitat Vagrants seen in typical thrush habitats.

Distribution An Asiatic species.

Occurrence Very rare vagrant to NW Europe, including Britain.

V	—	—

Siberian Thrush, summer male   **White's Thrush,** summer male

White's Thrush
Zoothera dauma L 28cm

A striking thrush with pale background colour, heavily marked all over with black crescent-shaped marks. At first glance, may recall juvenile Mistle Thrush. In flight, shows distinctive black-and-white bands on underwings. Rather shy and retiring.

Voice Call resembles Mistle Thrush.

Habitat Wooded areas with plenty of cover.

Distribution An Asiatic species.

Occurrence Very rare vagrant to NW Europe, including Britain.

V	—	—

Fieldfare, pair at nest

Redwing   **American Robin**

TITS
Family Paridae

Small, active birds with stubby bills. Forage among branches for insects. Most species will visit artificial feeders. Join mixed-species flocks outside breeding season. Most are hole-nesters, taking to nestboxes.

Sombre Tit

Marsh Tit
Parus palustris L 12 cm

Has brownish upperparts including uniformly coloured wings, shiny black cap, small black bib and pale-buffish underparts. Sexes similar. Very similar to Willow Tit and best distinguished by call. Feeds on insects, seeds and nuts. Sometimes accompanies mixed flocks.

Voice Characteristic call a sharp, explosive *pitchoo* but also *cheeoo-cheeoo* and *chickadee-dee-dee*. Typical song a repeated *cheeip-cheeip-cheeip*.

Habitat Deciduous and mixed woods, parks and mature gardens.

Distribution Breeds central and NW Europe from Mediterranean coast of France to Black Sea and northwards to S Scandinavia. Absent from Ireland and in Britain confined mainly to England and Wales.

Occurrence Rather sparse breeding species within range. Resident and mostly sedentary.

R	1–12	N 4–7

Willow Tit
Parus montanus L 12cm

Very similar to Marsh Tit. Distinguished by call and by presence of pale wing panel formed by pale fringes to secondaries. Cap is matt black and black bib marginally more extensive than Marsh Tit. British race *P. m. kleinschmidti* has buffish flanks while northern race *P. m. borealis* has grey-brown upperparts and whitish underparts and flanks.

Voice Characteristic call a nasal *te-chay chay*. Usual song *tsiu-tsiu-tsiu*.

Habitat Coniferous and mixed woodland, in Britain preferring damp, deciduous woods.

Distribution Breeds central and N Europe. Absent from W Europe including Ireland and in Britain, mainly in England and Wales.

Occurrence Sparse breeding species. Resident and mostly sedentary.

R	1–12	N 4–7

Sombre Tit
Parus lugubris L 13.5cm

At first glance, recalls Willow Tit with Great Tit proportions. Upperparts grey-brown and underparts dull greyish-white. Head markings distinctive with very dark brown cap and large bib separated by white cheek. Bill relatively large.

Voice Song similar to that of Great Tit and calls include *churr-rr-rr*.

Habitat Deciduous woodland.

Distribution Breeds SE Europe, mainly Greece and Turkey.

Occurrence Fairly common breeding species within range. Resident and mainly sedentary.

Siberian Tit
Parus cinctus L 13cm

Recalls large Willow Tit but has dull-brown cap and back, extensive black bib, white cheek and panel on wings and buffish flanks.

Voice Rather similar to Willow Tit. Typical calls include *chee-err chee-err* and *tseep*. Song a rapid series of call-like phrases.

Habitat Northern conifer and birch forests.

Distribution Breeds from N Scandinavia eastwards at similar latitudes.

Occurrence Fairly common breeding species. Some birds move slightly south during winter months.

Marsh Tit

Willow Tit

Marsh Tit

Siberian Tit

Blue Tit
Parus caeruleus L 12cm
Adult has yellow underparts, greenish back and
blue wings and tail. Head is white with dark-blue
lines and pale-blue cap. Juvenile has much more
subdued colouring than adult with buffish-yellow
face and dull cap. Feeds actively among twigs and
branches, searching for insects. Also visits feeders
in gardens, taking nuts and fat.
Voice Song a clear *tsee-tsee-tsirrr*. Calls include
an agitated *cherrr-err-err-err*.
Habitat Breeds in woodland, parks and mature
gardens. Nests in holes in trees but readily takes
to nestboxes. In winter, also visits reedbeds.
Distribution Found throughout most of
Europe wherever there is suitable habitat, as far
north as central Scandinavia. Absent from Iceland.
Occurrence Common breeding species. Most
are sedentary residents but populations from
north and east of range move south and west in
winter.

R	1–12	N 4–7

Great Tit
Parus major L 14cm
Adult has yellow underparts and green back.
Head is black with conspicuous white cheeks.
Black continues down centre of breast as distinct
band which on male is wider and darker than on
female and extends to belly. Juvenile has underparts and cheek buffish-yellow with dark markings looking greyish rather than black. Frequently
visits garden feeders but otherwise forages for
insects among branches and twigs. Occasionally
feeds on ground.
Voice Typical song a clear, piping *tee-chew tee-
chew tee-chew*. Often starts singing in late winter.
Calls varied but include a loud *pink* and *tsee-twee-
twee*. Great Tits have a notoriously varied repertoire. Once an observer is familiar with common
woodland bird calls, anything unusual is most
likely to be a Great Tit.
Habitat Woodland, parks and mature gardens.
Distribution Occurs throughout Europe
except Iceland and far north of Scandinavia.
Occurrence Common woodland and garden
bird throughout Europe. Mostly resident and
sedentary.

R	1–12	N 4–7

Coal Tit
Parus ater L 11cm
Distinctive features include black head with white
cheeks and white patch on nape. Underparts are
pale buff and upperparts are brownish-grey.
Feeds very actively among higher branches and
often associates with mixed flocks of small woodland birds in winter. Also visits bird feeders.
Voice Song a thin *tee-cha tee-cha tee-cha*, recalling that of Great Tit. Calls include very high-
pitched *tsee* and thin Great Tit-like notes.
Habitat Prefers conifer and mixed woodlands
but also widely in deciduous woodland and
mature gardens.
Distribution Found throughout Europe except
Iceland and N Scandinavia.
Occurrence Fairly common resident breeding
species. Mostly sedentary but birds from north
and east of range move south in winter.

R	1–12	N 4–6

Azure Tit
Parus cyanus L 13cm
At first glance, could be taken for leucistic Blue
Tit. Plumage mostly white with dark markings on
head, blue wings and tail and soft-grey back.
Shows white on tail and 2 white wing bars.

Azure Tit

Voice Calls include a sharp *tsirr*.
Habitat Deciduous and mixed woodland, usu-
ally near water. In winter, also visits reedbeds.
Distribution Occurs in central Asia.
Occurrence Resident and mostly sedentary. A
very rare vagrant to E Europe.

Blue Tit

Great Tit

Great Tit

Coal Tit

Crested Tit
Parus cristatus L 12cm
Easily recognized by black-and-white crest. Head
has black-and-white markings. Upperparts grey-
brown and pale, greyish-white underparts with
buffish wash on flanks. Very active feeder.
Voice Utters a trilling call *prurrurrit*. Song comprises call-like trilling phrases.
Habitat Found mainly in coniferous woodland.
In Britain confined exclusively to Caledonian pine
forests in Scotland. Nests in holes in decaying pine
trunks.
Distribution Occurs locally throughout SW,
central and N Europe, from Iberian peninsula to
central Scandinavia. In Britain, only found in Highland region of central Scotland.
Occurrence Fairly common breeding species.
Resident and mostly sedentary.

R	1–12	N 5–6

LONG-TAILED TIT
Family Aegithalidae

Similar to tits of family Paridae but with very long
tail. Domed nest built amongst foliage. Sexes similar.

Long-tailed Tit
Aegithalos caudatus L 14cm
Very long tail and body looking fluffy and sometimes almost spherical. Represented by several
subspecies. Those from Britain (*A.c.rosaceus*) and
central mainland Europe (*A.c.europaeus*) have
whitish underparts and head with a broad, black
stripe running above eye to nape. Shows pinkish-
brown feathering on back and rump but otherwise
wings and tail black. Northern subspecies *caudatus*
has head and underparts pure white, and white on
wings. Iberian subspecies *ibericus* resembles *A.c.
rosaceus* but duller. Seen in flocks in winter.
Voice Calls include a Wren-like *tserrr* and thin,
colourless zee zee zee. Song is quiet and subdued.
Habitat Occurs in deciduous and mixed woodland, scrub, hedgerows and wooded heaths.
Builds oval nest made of lichens, feathers and spi-
der's silk, often in gorse or bramble.
Distribution Occurs throughout Europe
except far north of Scandinavia and Iceland.
Occurrence Fairly common breeding species.
Mostly sedentary but northern subspecies espe-
cially may wander south in winter.

R	1–12	N 4–7

BEARDED TIT
Family Timalidae

Similar to true tits but with very long tail. Nests
woven among reeds. Sexes dissimilar.

Bearded Tit
Panurus biarmicus L 16.5cm
Has orange-buff plumage and a long tail. Male has
bluish-grey head with conspicuous black, drooping
moustache and black undertail coverts. Female
and juvenile male lack these features, having uniform grey-buff head and orange-buff head with
black lores respectively. Feeds on insects among
reeds, sometimes on ground. Flight is weak and
often accompanied by characteristic calls.
Voice Typical call is a sharp *ping*. Subdued, song.
Habitat Confined to extensive reedbeds that
are not inundated by tide or flooding.
Distribution Scattered and local distribution
across central and S Europe, mostly in areas
where extensive networks of reedbeds exist.
Occurrence Local but fairly common. Mostly
sedentary but some migrate or disperse in autumn.
In Britain, best seen at southern reed-bed reserves.

R	1–12	N 4–6

PENDULINE TIT
Family Remizidae

Superficially similar to true tits but with sharp,
pointed bill. Constructs hanging, flagon-shaped
nest among branches. Sexes similar.

Penduline Tit
Remiz pendulinus L 11cm
A small, fairly long-tailed tit. Male plumage recalls
that of male Red-backed Shrike with greyish head
and black mask, reddish-brown back and pale
underparts. Female is more uniformly brown but
shows slightly reduced black mask. Juvenile lacks
mask and has buffish-brown upperparts and pale
underparts. Often first noticed by call.
Voice Call a long, fading, thin *tseeee*. Song subdued and based on call.
Habitat Prefers scrubby thickets of willows,
alders and other wetland trees around lake margins and in reedbeds. Builds flagon-shaped nest.
Distribution Main range includes E and S
Europe; range is expanding north and west.
Occurrence Locally fairly common breeding
species. Easy to see at Neuseidler See in Austria.
Very rare but increasing vagrant to Britain.

V	—	—

Crested Tit

Long-tailed Tit

Bearded Tit, female   **Bearded Tit,** male   **Penduline Tit**

NUTHATCHES
Family Sittidae

Small, rather compact birds with dagger-like bills. Powerful feet enable them to walk down as well as up tree trunks. Hole-nesters. Sexes similar.

Nuthatch
Sitta europaea L 14cm

Upperparts blue-grey and underparts varying from buffish-orange, in subspecies *caesia* from W Europe, to white in Scandinavian subspecies *europaea*. Males of both races have feathers of vent orange-chestnut, tipped white. Male *europaea* has flanks orange-chestnut. Routinely climbs head-first down trunk. Collects insects.

Voice Song a loud, whistling *wee-wee-wee-wee*. Calls include a sharp *pseet*.
Habitat Deciduous woodlands, parks and mature gardens. Nests in hole in tree trunk.
Distribution Occurs across Europe north to S Scandinavia. Absent from Ireland and Iceland. In Britain, confined mainly to S and central England and Wales.
Occurrence Fairly common breeding species. Resident and mostly sedentary.

R	1–12	N 5–6

Rock Nuthatch
Sitta neumayer L 15cm

Similar to Nuthatch but larger and paler and with proportionately longer bill. Underparts show buffish wash towards rear and undertail feathers lack any white. Climbs rocks with ease.

Voice Piping song starts with trill and then recalls Tree Pipit. Calls loud and piping.
Habitat Rocky hillsides, cliffs and ruins.
Distribution Breeds SE Europe, mainly Greece and Turkey.
Occurrence Fairly common in suitable habitats. Resident and mostly sedentary.

Corsican Nuthatch *Sitta whiteheadi* is a tiny nuthatch confined to forests of Corsican Pine on the island of Corsica.

WALLCREEPER
Family Tichidromadidae

Long, downcurved bill and broad, rounded wings. Always associated with rocks.

Wallcreeper
Tichidroma muraria L 16cm

Distinctive with long, downcurved bill and mainly soft-grey plumage. Shows red patches on wings and white spots on primaries. Flight is flapping and moth-like. Throat black in summer but pale in winter. Finds insects among rock-crevices.

Voice Call thin and piping. Song comprises whistling phrases.
Habitat Mountains and gorges.

Distribution Very local, breeding in mountain ranges in S Europe.
Occurrence Local and rather uncommon.

Wallcreeper

TREECREEPERS
Family Certhiidae

Thin, downcurved bills. Feet and stiff tail used for climbing tree trunks. Sexes similar.

Treecreeper
Certhia familiaris L 12.5cm

Distinctive bird with long, thin and slightly downcurved bill, mottled brown, almost mouse-like, upperparts and white underparts. Shows pale supercilium, whitish in front of and behind eye. Climbs up tree trunks in a spiral, searching for insects in bark.

Voice Song a series of thin jingles, ending in a trill. Call a thin and reedy *sreet*.
Habitat Deciduous and coniferous woodland.
Distribution Breeds across Europe but absent from many western regions, Iceland and N Scandinavia. Occurs throughout Britain and Ireland.
Occurrence Common and mostly sedentary.

R	1–12	N 5–6

Short-toed Treecreeper
Certhia brachydactyla L 12.5cm

Very similar to Treecreeper. Shows buffish wash to flanks, and supercilium buffish in front of eye. Behaviour and habits as Treecreeper.

Voice Call short, louder and more piping than Treecreeper. Song loud and abrupt.
Habitat Prefers established deciduous woodland in most of range but in conifers in Mediterranean.
Distribution Occurs throughout central and S Europe as far north as Baltic coast. Absent as breeding species from Britain and Ireland.
Occurrence Fairly common within range. Very rare vagrant to Britain.

V	—	—

Nuthatch

Treecreeper

Rock Nuthatch

Short-toed Treecreeper

SPARROWS
Family Passeridae

Small birds with thick, stubby bills and most with rather subdued plumage. Mainly seed-eaters. Gregarious, most nesting in loose colonies.

House Sparrow
Passer domesticus L 15cm

At first glance, a fairly nondescript bird with brown upperparts and greyish-buff underparts. Male, however, has grey crown, bordered with chestnut-brown which runs to nape, and black bib. Female and juvenile have face and entire underparts uniformly pale grey-buff, brown crown and dark eye-stripe. All stages have grey rump, best seen in flight or when sunning. Sociable at all times of year, including when nesting.

Voice Calls include the familiar sparrow *chirrp*. Song comprises call-like notes.

Habitat Invariably found around human habitation, preferring farmyards, gardens and even town centres. Nests under roofs etc., but also occasionally in bushes.

Distribution Found throughout Europe except Iceland, N Scandinavia and Sardinia. Exact distribution tied to human settlements.

Occurrence Common in almost all towns cities, villages and farmyards. Mostly resident.

R	1–12	N 4–7

Tree Sparrow
Passer montanus L 14cm

Distinguished from male House Sparrow by chestnut-brown crown, smaller black bib and black cheek patch on whitish cheeks. Sexes similar but juvenile has greyish forecrown and cheek patch rather faint. May associate with mixed flocks of finches, larks and buntings in winter, feeding in fields.

Voice Calls include a House Sparrow-like *chirrp* and *tet-tet-tet*, given in flight. Song similar to House Sparrow.

Habitat More associated with farmland than House Sparrow and often seen around old-style hayricks and grain spillages. Also breeds in woodland. Nests in holes in trees and takes to nestboxes.

Distribution Occurs throughout Europe as far north as S Scandinavia. Absent from SW Europe and Iceland and effectively absent from SW England and S Ireland.

Occurrence Fairly common but rather local, especially in Britain.

R	1–12	N 5–6

Spanish Sparrow
Passer hispaniolensis L 15cm

Male is boldly marked with chestnut-brown crown, white cheeks and extensive black bib. White belly and back with black streakings. Female and juvenile similar to female and juvenile House Sparrow and effectively indistinguishable except by association with male.

Voice Calls and song similar to House Sparrow.

Habitat Open country with scattered houses and outskirts of villages. Sometimes nests in White Stork nests, occasionally in company of other sparrow species.

Distribution Despite its name, it has a highly restricted distribution in the S central Iberian peninsula. More widespread in SE Europe, S Italy and Sardinia.

Occurrence Very scarce in Spain but fairly common in rest of range where mostly resident.

V	—	—

Dead Sea Sparrow
Passer moabiticus L 12cm

A small sparrow, the male with grey head and underparts and brown back, heavily marked with black. Has black eye-stripe, bordered in front of eye with white, pale supercilium and black throat. Female is like a miniature female House Sparrow with greyish head, pale-buff supercilium, greyish underparts and pale-brown back, heavily streaked with black.

Voice Calls similar to House Sparrow.

Habitat Dry open country and fields and grassland bordering oases and drying water bodies.

Distribution Occurs mainly in Middle East but has bred on Cyprus.

Occurrence Very local and rather scarce.

Rock Sparrow
Petronia petronia L 14cm

At first glance, a rather nondescript bird most resembling a female House Sparrow with brown upperparts and pale, buffish underparts. Has broad, pale supercilium and dark crown with pale central stripe. Yellow spot on breast is difficult to see. Tail has pale tip best seen in flight.

Voice Calls similar to House Sparrow.

Habitat Dry, rocky terrain, often with stony fields beside rocky outcrops or eroded cliff-faces.

Distribution Most of S Europe.

Occurrence Fairly common but rather local and sometimes unexpectedly absent from apparently suitable areas.

V	—	—

House Sparrow, male

House Sparrow, female

Tree Sparrow

Spanish Sparrow

Dead Sea Sparrow, male

Rock Sparrow

FINCHES
Family Fringillidae

Small to medium-sized birds. Seed-eaters with conical-shaped bills. Precise bill shape varies according to diet of particular species. Sexes usually dissimilar. Cup-shaped nests constructed among branches.

Chaffinch
Fringilla coelebs L 15cm

Both sexes have white wing bar, shoulder and outer tail feathers, all most conspicuous in flight. Male is distinctive with blue-grey head, reddish-buff face and underparts, reddish-brown back and greenish rump. Bill blue in summer but pinkish-grey in winter, when plumage also duller. Female and juvenile have grey-brown plumage. Often feeds on ground and in winter seen in flocks sometimes with Bramblings and other finches.
Voice Song is a descending, musical trill ending in a flourish. Calls include characteristic, sharp *pink* and a softer *hweet*.
Habitat A wide range of habitats including woods, forests, gardens and parks. Almost anywhere with a degree of tree cover.
Distribution Occurs throughout most of Europe except far north of Scandinavia. Absent from Iceland. N and NE European populations migrate south and west in winter.
Occurrence Common and widespread. One of the commonest birds in Britain.

R	1–12	N 4–7

Brambling
Fringilla montifringilla L 15cm

In all plumages, and both sexes, shows white wing bars, white rump and orange-buff on breast. Summer male has black head and back and white belly with dark spots on flanks. In winter, black is replaced by grey-buff and then resembles female. Often feeds on ground and winter flocks particularly fond of beech mast.
Voice Song a repeated, wheezing *zwee*, recalling Greenfinch. Calls include a loud *zweerp*.
Habitat Breeds in northern birch forests and taiga. In winter, found in open woodlands, fields and parks, especially where beech and hornbeam present.
Distribution Breeds from central Scandinavia northwards and eastwards. In winter, found throughout central, S and W Europe.
Occurrence Common breeding species within range. Very rare breeding species in N Britain and mainly seen as local winter visitor from October to March.

W	10–3	—

Bullfinch
Pyrrhula pyrrhula L 16cm

An attractive and distinctive finch with black cap, grey back, red underparts and white rump. Rump and white wing bar most obvious in flight. Bill stubby and black. Plumage of female duller than male. Juvenile plumage brownish and without black cap. Generally shy and unobtrusive. Often seen in pairs. Feeds on seeds, fruits and berries, and, in spring, on flower buds.
Voice Song is subdued and warbling. Call a characteristic soft, piping *pewp*.
Habitat Woodland, hedgerows, scrub and mature gardens.
Distribution Widespread in Europe but absent from most of Iberian peninsula, N Scandinavia and Iceland.
Occurrence Fairly common breeding species. Mostly resident but birds from N Europe move south and west in winter.

R	1–12	N 5–6

Hawfinch
Coccothraustes coccothraustes L 18cm

A large finch with a massive bill which is blue-grey in summer and buffish in winter. Plumage of male is a mixture of pinkish-buff, chestnut and dark brown. Broad white wing bar and white-tipped, rather short tail most obvious in flight. Female has duller plumage than male and greyish not white wing panel. Juvenile is rather uniform buffish-brown but shows broad white wing bar. Shy and retiring habits, most easily seen in winter. Massive bill can crack cherry stones and hornbeam seeds, of which this species is especially fond. Occasionally visits woodland pools to drink.
Voice Song is subdued and warbling. Typical call a loud *pik* recalling that of Robin.
Habitat Deciduous and mixed woodlands. In winter, attracted to clumps of Hornbeam trees, sometimes in parkland settings.
Distribution Scattered distribution in Europe as far north as S Scandinavia. Absent from Ireland and Iceland and from much of Iberian peninsula as a breeding species.
Occurrence Generally rather scarce and local. Mostly resident but north-eastern populations migrate south and west in autumn. In Britain, mostly confined to S and central England.

R	1–12	N 5–6

Chaffinch, female

Chaffinch, male

Brambling, female

Brambling, male

Bullfinch, male and female

Hawfinch

Citril Finch
Serinus citrinella L 12cm
A small finch, recalling a miniature Greenfinch with yellow-green underparts and greyish-green upperparts. Plumage rather uniform and unmarked. Has yellow wing bars and unstreaked rump, both best seen in flight. Sexes are similar although female plumage duller with faint streaking on back. Juvenile has brown plumage with streaked upperparts. Feeds on seeds of conifers and alpine meadow flowers. Seen in small flocks outside breeding season. Feeds on ground and in trees.
Voice Song a rapid twittering, recalling that of Goldfinch. Call a thin *chee*.
Habitat Breeds around the tree-line but moves to lower altitudes in winter.

Citril Finch

Distribution Mountains of central S and SW Europe, Corsica and Sardinia.
Occurrence Fairly common within rather restricted range. Best looked for along mountain passes at, or just below, the tree-line.

Serin
Serinus serinus L 11cm
A tiny finch with short, stubby bill. Male has lemon-yellow head and breast, brownish back and wings and white underparts. Female has duller plumage and heavier streaking. Both sexes show pale-yellow rump and 2 faint, pale wing bars, both features best seen in flight. Juvenile has brown, heavily streaked plumage. Often feeds on ground and visits pools to drink.
Voice Song a rapid series of twittering jingles, delivered from treetop or prominent perch. Somewhat recalling rapid and high-pitched jingles of Corn Bunting. Call a thin *zrrr-litt*.
Habitat Prefers open terrain such as parks with scattered clumps of trees.
Distribution Resident of S Europe and summer visitor as far north as Baltic coast.
Occurrence Common and widespread in south of range becoming less so further north. In Britain, spring to autumn visitor; has bred.

| V | 4–6, 8–10 | — |

Red-fronted Serin
Serinus pusillus L 11cm
Shares the proportions of Serin but male with much darker plumage and almost black head with red forecrown. Female is similar but plumage duller. Juvenile is heavily streaked but has unmarked, orange-buff face.
Voice Call a tinkling *zrrrt*.
Habitat Mountain valleys and pastures.
Distribution An Asiatic species whose range extends to mountains of S Turkey.
Occurrence Common resident within range.

Greenfinch
Carduelis chloris L 15cm
Male has yellowish-green plumage, darker above than below. Female has slightly duller, grey-green plumage. Bright-yellow patches on wings and sides of tail base are most noticeable in flight. Juvenile has brownish-green plumage and is heavily streaked below. Flight is undulating.
Voice Song rapid and trilling, delivered from perch or butterfly-like song-flight. Utters wheezing *zzwheee-esh* and typical flight call *jurrrp*.
Habitat Open terrain, usually with trees or bushes, such as hedgerows, parks and gardens.
Distribution Found throughout Europe as far north as central Scandinavia. Absent from Iceland.
Occurrence Fairly common in range. Common in Britain and Ireland; scarce in N Scotland.

| R | 1–12 | N 5–6 |

Siskin
Carduelis spinus L 12cm
Male is attractive with greenish-yellow plumage, streaked back and black on forecrown and chin. Female has duller plumage and heavy streaking. Both sexes have bright yellow on wings and on sides to base of tail, features most conspicuous in flight. Juvenile is brownish and heavily streaked but still shows yellow on wings and tail. Feeds on conifer seeds during summer. During winter, extremely fond of alder seeds. Feeds with Redpolls.
Voice Song a rapid twittering ending in a wheezy sigh. Calls include a drawn-out *jeez*.
Habitat Breeds in conifers. In winter, favours birch and alder.
Distribution Breeds in central and N Europe, range extending to central Scandinavia. Northern populations move south in autumn.
Occurrence Fairly common breeding species. In Britain, breeds locally in north but in winter found throughout in small numbers.

| T | 1–12 | N 5–6 |

Serin

Greenfinch, juvenile

Greenfinch, male

Siskin, female

Siskin, male

Goldfinch
Carduelis carduelis L 14cm

Adult is distinctive with red face, the rest of head being black and white. Back is buffish and wings are black with broad yellow wing bar, noticeable both at rest and in flight. White rump best seen in flight along with white on tail. Juvenile has brownish plumage but shows black wings with yellow wing bar. The young are fed a diet of insects but adults feed mainly on seeds of meadow and wasteground plants such as thistles and knapweeds. Particularly attracted to teasels and seen in flocks in winter, even visiting garden flower borders if teasel heads have been left.

Voice Flocks utter tinkling *tikalik* calls. Song high-pitched and tinkling, including call notes.

Habitat All kinds of open country including farmland wasteground. Nests in hedges and along woodland borders.

Distribution Found across most of Europe as far north as S Scandinavia. Common throughout Britain but scarce in N Scotland.

Occurrence Common breeding species, resident in most of range including Britain and Ireland. Populations from NE Europe move south in winter.

T	1–12	N 5–7

Linnet
Carduelis cannabina L 13cm

In some plumages, appears rather nondescript. Summer male, however, is distinctive with reddish-brown back, grey head with red forecrown and pale underparts with red breast. Female has grey-brown back, greyish head and pale underparts. Winter male similar to female but with slightly richer colours. In flight, shows conspicuous white wing patches on primaries. Both sexes and all plumages have grey-brown bill and streaked throat. Forms flocks outside breeding season, often mixing with other species.

Voice Song is a rapid twittering with occasional reedy notes. Call *tett-terrett*, similar to Greenfinch.

Habitat Open country with bushes and hedgerows for breeding. In winter, all kinds of open ground, including fallow and ploughed fields and coastal grazing marshes.

Distribution Found throughout most of Europe as far north as S Scandinavia. Common in Britain except far north of Scotland.

Occurrence Common breeding species throughout range. Mostly resident but populations from NE Europe move S in winter.

T	1–12	N 5–7

Twite
Carduelis flavirostris L 13cm

Similar to Linnet but with rather undistinguished brown plumage, heavily streaked except for throat and underparts. Male has dull, pinkish rump, best seen in flight, and both sexes show pale wing bar. Feeds on ground and, although not especially wary, can be difficult to see among vegetation and undulations in fields.

Voice Typical call a sharp *tweeit*, from which it gets its name. Song a twittering chatter.

Habitat Breeds on moors and coastal areas in the north. In winter, found on coastal meadows and ploughed fields, saltmarshes.

Distribution Breeds NW Europe: N Britain and Ireland and W Scandinavia. In winter, found around coasts of NW Europe.

Occurrence Fairly common breeding species in upland habitat. In winter, rather local in suitable habitats.

T	1–12	N 5–7

Goldfinch

Linnet, female   **Linnet,** male   **Twite**

Redpoll
Carduelis flammea L 12.5cm

A small finch with brown, heavily streaked upper-parts, pale underparts, pale, streaked rump and buffish bill. Adults have red forecrown and black bib. Male in summer has reddish flush to breast. Female has more sombre colouring. Juvenile does not acquire red forecrown until first autumn. In flight, all plumages show pale wing bar. Three races occur in Europe. *C.f.cabaret* from W Europe is smallest and has warm-brown plumage. *C.f.flammea* from Fennoscandia is medium-sized with grey-brown plumage. *C.f.rostrata* from Greenland is largest with dark-brown, heavily streaked plumage and a heavy bill. In winter, seen in flocks feeding in alders and birches, often with Siskins.
Voice Flight call a sharp *chek-chek-chek*, also included in song which has characteristic trill and is often delivered in flight.
Habitat Breeds in birch and conifer woodland, willow scrub and mature gardens. In winter, often in damp woodland comprising birch and alder.
Distribution Breeds NW Europe, mainly Britain, Ireland, Iceland, Scandinavia, as well as the Alps. Winter range extends to central and E Europe.
Occurrence Fairly common breeding species in range. In Britain, breeds mainly in north. In S England mostly seen as a winter visitor.

T	1–12	N 5–6

Arctic Redpoll
Carduelis hornemanni L 12.5cm

Told from Redpoll by white, unstreaked rump. Adult generally looks paler on head and back than Redpoll and shows much less streaking on flanks. First-winter birds also show pale, unstreaked rump but

Arctic Redpoll

plumage is browner than adult. Habits and behaviour as Redpoll, with which it may associate.
Voice As Redpoll.
Habitat Breeds in northern birches and willows. In winter, in similar habitats to Redpoll.
Distribution Breeds from N Scandinavia eastwards and also in Greenland. In winter, moves south to central Scandinavia and similar latitudes eastwards.

Occurrence Rarely seen south of usual range but very rare winter vagrant to Britain.

V	—	—

Trumpeter Finch
Bucanetes githagineus L 13cm

Breeding male is greyish-buff with pink flush and stubby, red bill. Female lacks pink flush and has yellowish bill. Winter male similar to female.
Voice Call resembles a toy trumpet.
Habitat Breeds in arid terrain and semi-deserts.
Distribution Main range is N Africa and Asia but small population in SE Spain.
Occurrence Rare breeding species in Europe. Very rare vagrant to Britain.

V	—	—

Scarlet Rosefinch
Carpodacus erythrinus L 14cm

Superficially bunting-like with thick, stubby bill. Plumage rather variable but always shows 2 pale wing bars. Adult male has red head, breast and rump, with brown back and tail and pale underparts. Extent of red increases with age, first-year male being largely brown and resembling female. Elusive, especially during breeding season.
Voice Song a spirited *teeju-teeju-tju*. Call a subdued *tueet*.
Habitat Breeds in areas of dense scrub with scattered clumps of trees.
Distribution Mainly Asian but spreading into central and N Europe as far as E Scandinavia.
Occurrence Scarce but increasing breeding species in NE Europe. In Britain, mainly a scarce passage migrant but has bred.

M	5–6, 9–10	—

Pine Grosbeak
Pinicola enucleator L 20cm

A large finch with large bill and 2 pale wing bars. From a distance, could be mistaken for Two-barred Crossbill. Male has red plumage while female is greenish-yellow. Juvenile resembles female. Feeds on berries and seeds, both in trees and on ground. Unobtrusive but not shy.
Voice Call a loud whistle, *tu-lee-lu*. Song a loud and rapid series of whistles.
Habitat Breeds in northern taiga forests of conifers and birch.
Distribution Breeds from N Scandinavia eastwards. Winter range extends to NE Europe.
Occurrence Rather scarce breeding species. Very rare vagrant to Britain.

V	—	—

Redpoll, male

Arctic Redpoll

Trumpeter Finch, male

Scarlet Rosefinch

Pine Grosbeak, male and female

Crossbill

Loxia curvirostra L 16cm

A large and bulky finch with tips of mandibles overlapping. Male has reddish plumage including red rump and female yellowish-green with yellowish rump. Juvenile has brown, heavily streaked plumage. Size of bill is best feature for separating Crossbill from Parrot and Scottish Crossbills. That of Crossbill is the most slender of the 3 species although considerable variation occurs. Uses bill to extract conifer seeds from cones. Prefers spruces but will take other conifers. Often seen on ground, drinking at pools. In invasion years, Crossbills in unusual habitats will resort to feeding on atypical foods such as thistle seeds. Outside breeding season, seen in flocks.

Voice Metallic *glip-glip* call heard in flight and among feeding flocks. Twittering song includes call notes.

Habitat Invariably found in conifer forests, preferring stands of spruces. Nests early in the year, often February or March.

Distribution Occurs locally throughout Europe wherever extensive conifer forests (particularly spruces) are found. Absent from Ireland and, in Britain, occurs as far north as S Scotland.

Occurrence Locally fairly common in suitable habitats. Outside breeding season, flocks roam widely in search of new sources of food.

R	1–12	N 3–5

Scottish Crossbill

Loxia scotica L 17cm

Britain's only endemic species. Superficially very similar to Crossbill in appearance but with bill larger and closer in size to Parrot Crossbill. Feeds on seeds of Scots Pine in Caledonian pine forests of central Scotland. Habits and behaviour as Crossbill.

Voice Similar to Crossbill.

Habitat Scots Pine forests.

Distribution Central Scotland, particularly the Highland region.

Occurrence Sedentary and not irruptive. Can be seen at RSPB Loch Garten reserve and other nearby Caledonian pine forests in Cairngorm region.

R	1–12	N 3–5

Parrot Crossbill

Loxia pytyopsittacus L 18cm

Slightly more bulky than Crossbill but with very similar plumage. Male is reddish while female is dull yellow-green. Best feature for identification is bill shape which appears massive and almost outsized when compared to Crossbill. Feeds mainly on seeds of pines and, like Crossbill, regularly visits woodland pools to drink.

Voice Flight call *chup-chup*, similar to Crossbill but deeper. Song contains call-like notes and distinctive *tchee-urr*.

Habitat Pine forests.

Distribution Main range from central and S Scandinavia eastwards but small numbers have bred in Britain.

Occurrence Mostly sedentary but movements do occur, hence breeding records in Britain, including N Norfolk coast. Otherwise a rare vagrant to Britain.

V(R)	1–12	(N 3–5)

Two-barred Crossbill

Loxia leucoptera L 15cm

Two broad, white wing bars and white tertial tips are distinctive and diagnostic. Bill is comparatively slender. Male has pinkish-red plumage and female is dull yellow-green. Juvenile is brownish and heavily streaked. Feeds primarily on larch cones but will also take cones of other conifers as well as berries. Vagrants often associate with Crossbills.

Voice Calls include a Crossbill-like *chip-chip* and a tuneful *teet*.

Habitat Mainly associated with larches in Siberian taiga.

Distribution Main breeding range Siberia but occasionally nests in Scandinavia.

Occurrence Mainly sedentary but irrupts occasionally and then rare vagrant to Britain.

V	—	—

Two-barred Crossbill, male

Crossbill, male

Crossbill, female

Parrot Crossbill, female

Parrot Crossbill, male

BUNTINGS
Family Emberizidae

Small birds with thick bills, the lower mandible of which is larger than the upper. Feeds mainly on seeds but insects offered to young in nest. Some species are attractive songsters. Sexes usually dissimilar.

Corn Bunting
Miliaria calandra L 18cm

A robust and bulky bunting, lacking distinctive features. Upperparts sandy-brown and heavily streaked. Underparts pale and heavily streaked on breast and flanks. Sexes similar. Occasionally dangles legs in flight. Male sings from fence posts and overhead wires. Each male may pair with several females.

Voice Song has been likened to jangling keys. An accelerating hissing jingle *tuk-tuk-tuk-te tshhh tshhh*. Call a sharp *tec*.

Habitat Open country including farmland and fields. In Britain, usually associated with arable land and chalk downland.

Distribution Found throughout Europe as far north as Baltic coast. Occurs locally throughout Britain.

Occurrence Fairly common resident in suitable habitats.

R	1–12	N 4–7

Little Bunting
Emberiza pusilla L 13cm

A small bunting, in summer with largely chestnut-brown head, especially on crown, cheeks and chin. Shows pale eye-ring and black borders to chestnut crown stripe. In winter, recalls juvenile Reed Bunting but distinguished by call and brown crown stripe, bordered with black. Chestnut-brown ear coverts are framed with black, the black not extending to bill as in Reed Bunting. Upperparts grey-brown and underparts white with dark streaking. At close range, culmen straight not curved. Vagrants sometimes mix with other buntings.

Voice Song a jingling twitter. Call a sharp *tic*.

Habitat Breeds in northern scrub comprising birch and willow. Vagrants often in fields and hedges.

Distribution Breeds mainly N Asia with a few in NE Europe. Winters S Asia.

Occurrence Rare vagrant to NW Europe including Britain, mainly autumn and winter.

V	—	—

Rustic Bunting
Emberiza rustica L 15cm

Summer male superficially recalls Reed Bunting but shows mainly black head with white throat

Rustic Bunting,
breeding male

and broad, white stripe behind the eye. Upperparts brown and underparts white except for chestnut breast band and flanks. Female and winter male are similar and easily confused with female Reed Bunting. However, show reddish-brown not black on breast and flanks, pale eye-stripe behind eye only and pale spot on rear of ear coverts. At close range, note straight culmen and call.

Voice Song is fast and warbling. Call a sharp *tik* unlike Reed Bunting.

Habitat Breeds in marshy northern forests.

Distribution Breeds from central and N Scandinavia eastwards at similar latitudes. Winters in S Asia.

Occurrence Fairly common breeding species in limited European range. Rare vagrant to Britain, mainly autumn.

V	—	—

Rock Bunting
Emberiza cia L 16cm

Male has blue-grey head with black stripes on sides of crown, through eyes and around ear coverts. Upperparts brown and underparts warm reddish-brown. Female has duller plumage than male but both show reddish-brown rump and white outer tail in flight. Juvenile has warm-brown underparts, reddish rump and white in outer tail. Feeds on ground and perches on rocks and in branches.

Voice Song a rapid, buzzing warble. Call a sharp, elusive *zip*.

Habitat Mountains, rocky slopes and outcrops.

Distribution Breeds in S Europe.

Occurrence Fairly common resident in suitable habitats with some altitudinal movement in winter. Very rare vagrant to Britain.

V	—	—

Corn Bunting

Little Bunting

Rock Bunting, female

Rock Bunting, male

Ortolan Bunting
Emberiza hortulana L 16.5cm

Male has brown back, pinkish-orange belly and greenish-grey head and breast with pale-yellow throat, moustache and eye-ring. Female is similar to male but plumage much duller with browner head and streaked breast. Juvenile similar to female but with more streaking on underparts. Bill and legs pink in both sexes and all plumages.

Voice Song a series of melancholy ringing notes. Calls include *seee* and a thin *tsit*.

Habitat Breeds in open country with scattered trees from lowland farmland and vineyards to lower slopes of mountains. Migrants often seen in ploughed fields or on bare ground.

Distribution Breeds locally throughout Europe from Mediterranean to S Scandinavia. Absent as a breeding species in Britain and Ireland. Winters in Africa.

Occurrence Present in breeding range from May to August. In Britain, seen as scarce passage migrant May–June and August–September.

M	5–6, 8–9	—

Cretzschmar's Bunting
Emberiza caesia L 16cm

Very similar to Ortolan Bunting but male has blue-grey head and breast with orange-red throat and moustache, concolorous with belly. Female has more subdued colouring than male and streaking on crown and breast. Juvenile is even more heavily streaked on head and underparts than female and very similar to juvenile Ortolan Bunting. Both sexes and all ages have pink bill and legs.

Voice Song a series of ringing notes, shorter in duration than Ortolan. Call a sharp *ship*.

Habitat Rocky slopes, stony vineyards etc.

Distribution Breeds SE Europe, mainly Greece and Turkey. ·

Occurrence Migrant, present in breeding range May to August and fairly common in suitable habitats. Very rare vagrant to Britain.

V	—	—

Pine Bunting
Emberiza leucocephalos L 16.5cm

Male has chestnut face with white crown and white stripe below eye. Upperparts brown and underparts white except for chestnut breast band and streaking on flanks. Female similar to female Yellowhammer but yellow replaced by white.

Voice Song and calls similar to Yellowhammer.

Pine Bunting, breeding male

Habitat Conifer forests.

Distribution Breeds in Siberia.

Occurrence Very rare vagrant to NW Europe including Britain.

V	—	—

Cinereous Bunting
Emberiza cinereacea L 16.5cm

Distinctive with very pale grey-brown plumage, male with yellowish head. Female shows more streaking and yellow on throat only. Juvenile is browner with heavy streaking. Similar to juvenile Ortolan and best distinguished by greyish not pink bill, a feature shared by adults of both sexes.

Voice Song a short series of ringing notes. Call a sharp *chip*.

Habitat Rocky slopes.

Distribution Breeds mainly in Turkey but very rare breeder on Aegean island of Lesbos.

Occurrence Seen in SE Europe mostly on migration.

Yellow-breasted Bunting
Emberiza aureola L 15cm

Male has chestnut-brown upperparts and crown with black face and yellow underparts with chestnut breast band. Has white wing patches, most noticeable in flight. Female has brown, heavily streaked upperparts and pale-yellow underparts. Shows pale supercilium and throat, suggestion of pale crown stripe and white wing bar. Juvenile similar to female.

Voice Jingling song recalls that of Ortolan. Call a sharp *tsip*.

Habitat Wetland scrub and damp woodland.

Distribution Breeds from NE Europe eastwards into Asia. Winters SE Asia.

Occurrence Present in breeding range May to August. Very rare vagrant to Britain, mostly in autumn in far north.

V	—	—

Ortolan Bunting, male

Ortolan Bunting, female

Cretzschmar's Bunting, male

Cinereous Bunting, male

Yellow-breasted Bunting, male

Reed Bunting
Emberiza schoeniclus L 15.5cm

Male in summer has black hood and throat and white moustache. Hood separated from brown back and wings by white collar. In winter, head of male appears browner. Female lacks male's black on head and shows pale supercilium, pale throat bordered by black malar stripes and dark streaking on flanks. Juvenile similar to female. Both sexes and all ages show white in outer tail and close view reveals convex culmen on dark bill. In winter, sometimes mixes with flocks of other buntings and finches.

Voice Song is a simple *twink twink twititirr*. Call a thin *tseeup*.

Habitat Reedbeds, wetland scrub and marshes but sometimes in drier habitat such as field borders.

Distribution Breeds throughout most of central and N Europe including Britain and Ireland. Absent from Iceland. N and NE European populations move south in autumn and winter range extends to most of S Europe.

Occurrence Common breeding species. British breeding birds mostly resident but numbers boosted by winter visitors from mainland Europe.

R	1–12	N 4–7

Yellowhammer
Emberiza citrinella L 16.5cm

In all plumages, shows reddish-brown rump, white outer tail feathers and at least some yellow in plumage. Male in summer has yellow head with dark feathering bordering crown and ear coverts and through eye. Underparts yellow and back brown. Winter male has duller yellow plumage, particularly on head. Female has buffish-yellow plumage and streaking on breast, throat and crown. Juvenile is similar to female but with even less yellow in plumage and more distinct streaking. Perches in bushes during breeding season. Often feeds on ground and sometimes seen in flocks during winter.

Voice Song a breezy series of notes, *tse-tse-tse-tse-tse-tse tse tsi tsu*, often rendered 'a little bit of bread and no cheese'. Call a sharp *twikt*.

Habitat Open country with bushes and scrub and farmland with hedgerows.

Distribution Breeds throughout most of Europe except Mediterranean regions and central and S Iberian peninsula. Populations from N Europe move south in autumn, wintering range including all of S Europe.

Occurrence Common breeding species, resident in Britain and most of NW Europe.

R	1–12	N 5–7

Cirl Bunting
Emberiza cirlus L 16.5cm

In all plumages and both sexes, rump is grey-brown and unstreaked. Male has black throat and eye-stripe, and grey-green crown and breast band. Otherwise underparts are yellow except for chestnut on flanks. Back and wings brown. Female and juvenile similar to Yellowhammer female and juvenile respectively and best distinguished by rump colour. Female sometimes has suggestion of grey breast band. Habits and behaviour similar to Yellowhammer.

Voice Song a dry rattle, recalling that of Lesser Whitethroat or Bonelli's Warbler. Call a subdued *zeet*.

Habitat Hedgerows, open country with scattered bushes. In winter, seen in fields.

Distribution Breeds in S and W Europe as far north as SW England.

Occurrence Fairly common in S Europe but rather more scarce further north. Very local and decidedly uncommon in Britain, with last stronghold in S Devon.

R	1–12	N 5–6

Black-headed Bunting
Emberiza melanocephala L 16.5cm

Male is distinctive with black hood, yellow underparts and brown back and rump. Female has pale-brown upperparts, pale yellowish, unmarked underparts and sometimes a suggestion of a darker hood. Both sexes lack white in tail.

Voice Song a rapid series of harsh whistles, beginning with sharp *tzit-tzit-tzit* phrase. Calls include a sharp *tzupp*.

Habitat Mediterranean habitats including olive groves and small fields, hedges and scattered bushes.

Distribution Breeds in SE Europe from S Italy to Turkey. Winters in Asia.

Occurrence A fairly common and conspicuous bird, present in breeding range May to August. Rare vagrant to Britain, mainly in spring.

V	—	—

Reed Bunting, female

Reed Bunting, male

Yellowhammer, juvenile
Cirl Bunting, female

Yellowhammer, male
Cirl Bunting, male   **Black-headed Bunting,** male

Red-headed Bunting
Emberiza bruniceps L 16.5cm

Male has orange-red face and breast, yellow underparts and streaked, greenish-brown back. Female very similar to female Black-headed Bunting but has greenish-brown rump. All plumages and both sexes lack white in tail. Habits and behaviour as Black-headed Bunting.

Red-headed Bunting, breeding male

Voice Similar to Black-headed Bunting.
Habitat As Black-headed Bunting but often near water.
Distribution An Asiatic species.
Occurrence Rare vagrant to Europe. Records from Britain all suspected of being escapes.

V	—	—

Lapland Bunting
Calcarius lapponicus L 16cm

Male in breeding season is distinctive with black face, throat and breast separated from chestnut nape by white border. Shows pale buff stripe behind eye, white underparts and streaked, grey-brown back. In winter, male's distinctive colours are muted by pale fringes to feathers. Female has dull chestnut nape and pale supercilium which continues as pale border around ear coverts. Upperparts streaked and brown, underparts white. Adults of both sexes have dull-yellowish bill. First-winter birds have pinkish-buff bill and dull-chestnut panel on wings bordered by 2 pale wing bars. Feeds on ground and rather unobtrusive. In winter, seen in flocks.

Voice Tinkling song, sometimes delivered in flight. Calls include *pr-rr-t* and *teu* given in flight.
Habitat Breeds on tundra and northern moorland. In winter, seen in fields, mainly coastal in NW Europe.
Distribution Breeds from W and N Scandinavia eastwards through Siberia. Winters locally coastal NW Europe and central Asia.
Occurrence Fairly common breeding species in range. In Britain, very rare breeding species and seen mainly as winter visitor October to March.

W	10–3	—

Snow Bunting
Plectrophenax nivalis L 16cm

Both sexes and all plumages show considerable amount of white in wings although more in male than female and more in adult than juvenile. Breeding male is pure white except for black back, wingtips and on tail. Female has black feathering on back with pale-brown fringes and brown on face and crown. Male in winter has pale fringes to feathering on back and orange-buff wash to head and upperparts. Juvenile and winter female appear even more buffish. In winter, seen in often large flocks, taking to the wing with characteristic calls and flashes of white in wings.

Voice Song is simple, tinkling and musical. Typical flight calls *trrrrit* and *tchuu*.
Habitat Breeds on rocky tundra, boulder slopes and mountains. In winter, found on fields, sand-dunes and coastal meadows.
Distribution Breeds from W and N Scandinavia eastwards. Also breeds Iceland and Scottish mountains. In winter, occurs around coasts of NW Europe and eastwards to central Asia.
Occurrence Common breeding species in Arctic and sub-Arctic. Rare breeding species in Britain but widespread and regular winter visitor to coasts from October to March.

Mainly W	10–3	—

SPARROWS
Family Passeridae

For identification purposes the Snow Finch has been placed alongside the Snow Bunting.

Snow Finch
Montifringilla nivalis L 18cm

Despite its name, a sparrow not a finch. Superficially resembles Snow Bunting but ranges never overlap. Has soft-grey head, white underparts and grey-brown back. Wings are largely white with black tips (white more extensive in male than female) and tail is white with black centre. These features most noticeable in flight. Male has black chin in summer only. Bill black in summer but yellow in winter. Seen in flocks outside breeding season and often visits ski-resorts in winter.

Voice Calls include a sharp *peeu*. Song short and twittering.
Habitat Rocky mountain slopes.
Distribution Mountain ranges of S and SE Europe.
Occurrence Fairly common in suitable habitats. Fairly easy to see around high passes in the Alps.

Snow Bunting, winter

Snow Bunting, summer male

Lapland Bunting, female

Lapland Bunting, winter male

Lapland Bunting, male
Snow Finch, non-breeding

NORTH AMERICAN PASSERINES

With increasing numbers of observers and improved identification skills, a surprising number of American passerines are found as vagrants in NW Europe. Most occur in autumn as immature birds after periods of strong westerly winds associated with low pressure systems moving across the Atlantic. The following are some of the more regularly observed or easily identified species. They belong to the following families: vireos (Vireonidae); American wood warblers (Parulidae); Tanagers (Thraupidae); American sparrows (Emberizidae); Bobolink and orioles (Icteridae).

White-throated Sparrow
Zonotrichia albicollis L 17cm
Bunting-like appearance with grey bill, adult with striking markings on head. Pure-white throat and whitish supercilium and crown stripe, the supercilium yellow in front of eye. Shows black eyestripe and black borders to crown. Upperparts brown and underparts greyish. Juvenile has greyish throat and subdued markings on head with no yellow.
Voice Typical call *pink*.
Habitat Vagrants likely to favour coastal scrub.
Distribution Breeds northern N America and winters in southern states.
Occurrence Very rare vagrant to NW Europe including Britain.

V	—	—

White-crowned Sparrow
Zonotrichia leucophrys L 18cm
Similar to White-throated Sparrow but with pinkish-orange bill and lacking the latter's distinct white throat. Upperparts brown and underparts greyish. Has black cap with broad white supercilium and crown stripe.
Voice Call a sharp *pink*.
Habitat Vagrants likely to favour coastal grassland.
Distribution Breeds northern N America and winters southern USA and Central America.
Occurrence Very rare vagrant to NW Europe including Britain.

V	—	—

Savannah Sparrow
Passerculus sandwichensis L 14cm
Widespread and variable species in N America, occurring as several races. So-called Ipswich Sparrow *P. s. princeps* has occurred in Britain. Superficially resembles female bunting with streaked brownish plumage recalling pipit or lark. Shows pale supercilium which is yellowish in front of eye, and suggestion of pale crown stripe.
Voice Call a thin *tseep*.
Habitat Vagrants likely to favour coastal grassland.
Distribution Occurs throughout most of N America but *P. s. princeps* breeds in the north-east and winters along E coast.
Occurrence Very rare vagrant to Britain.

V	—	—

Song Sparrow
Melospiza melodia L 16cm
Another widespread and variable species found throughout most of N America. Tail is rounded and lacks any white. Typically shows greyish supercilium, ear coverts and sides of neck. Upperparts brown, often with grey as well. Underparts pale, sometimes grey on breast, heavily streaked and usually with dark central spot on breast. Pumps tail in flight.
Voice Musical song ends in a nasal trill. Typical call *chimp*.
Habitat Scrub and grassland.
Distribution Breeds throughout most of N America, wintering in southern states.
Occurrence Very rare vagrant to Britain.

V	—	—

Dark-eyed Junco
Junco hyemalis L 16cm
Variable species but so-called Slate-colored Junco is typical. Male has grey head, upperparts and breast clearly separated from white belly. Female has grey aspects of plumage brown instead. Both sexes have pinkish-buff bill and white outer tail feathers, most noticeable in flight.
Voice Call a sharp *tsit*.
Habitat Woodland and scrub.
Distribution Breeds across northern and western N America, wintering in southern states.
Occurrence Very rare vagrant to NW Europe including Britain.

V	—	—

White-throated Sparrow

White-crowned Sparrow

Song Sparrow

Savannah Sparrow

Dark-eyed Junco

Rose-breasted Grosbeak
Pheucticus ludovicianus L 20cm
Has noticeably large bill. Adult male has dark head and upperparts, white rump and white underparts with reddish breast. Female has streaked brown plumage with pale supercilium and faint, pale crown stripe. First-autumn birds are similar to female, males sometimes with warm buffish-pink wash to breast. Both sexes and all plumages show white wing bars. Males have red on underwing only visible in flight.
Voice Call a sharp *eerk*.
Habitat Vagrants to Europe likely to prefer coastal hedgerows and bramble thickets.
Distribution Breeds N America and winters S America.
Occurrence Rare vagrant to NW Europe including Britain.

V	—	—

Rufous-sided Towhee
Pipilo erythropthalmus L 22cm
Variable species, male of eastern form with black upperparts, head and breast showing clear cut-off from white underparts and orange-red flanks. Female has black in plumage replaced by brown. Both sexes have conspicuous white patches in wings and on corners of tail, most obvious in flight. Juvenile has streaked, brown plumage but white in wings and tail as adult. Feeds on ground.
Voice Call *tow-hee*.
Habitat Woodland clearings and open areas in scrub.
Distribution Breeds across USA and winters from southern states southwards.
Occurrence Very rare vagrant to Britain.

V	—	—

Red-eyed Vireo
Vireo olivaceus L 15cm
Olive-green upperparts, whitish underparts and bold head markings. Shows grey cap and white supercilium bordered above and below with black. Adult has beady red eye. First-autumn bird has brown eye and faint yellow wash to flanks.
Voice Calls include a harsh *chrrr*.
Habitat Vagrants likely to favour hedgerows and scrub.
Distribution Breeds northern and eastern N America, winters S America.
Occurrence Rare vagrant to NW Europe including Britain. One of the most regularly recorded Nearctic passerines.

V	—	—

Black-and-white Warbler
Mniotilta varia L 13cm
Plumage a striking mixture of black and white, particularly on head with white supercilium and black cap with white central stripe. Adult male has black ear coverts while in female and immature these are grey. Immature female has buffish wash to flanks and face. Feeds actively among foliage but also behaves like Treecreeper, searching bark for insects.
Voice Call a sharp *sip*.
Habitat Woodlands.
Distribution Breeds eastern half N America and winters Central and S America.
Occurrence Very rare vagrant to NW Europe including Britain.

V	—	—

Northern Parula
Parula americana L 11cm
A small, delicate warbler with blue-grey upperparts, whitish underparts, broken white eye-ring and 2 white wing bars. Throat and breast are yellow. In male, these are broken by breast band of black and reddish feathering. In female and immature, breast band is subdued or even absent. Very active.
Voice Vagrants mostly silent.
Habitat Vagrants likely to favour hedges and scrub in coastal areas.
Distribution Breeds eastern states of N America, winters in Central and S America.
Occurrence Rare vagrant to NW Europe including Britain.

V	—	—

Yellow Warbler
Dendroica petechia L 13cm
Striking yellow plumage, slightly darker and duller above than below. Breeding male has pure-yellow head and chestnut streaks on breast and flanks. Female and immature are paler yellow and unmarked.
Voice Call a subdued *tsip*.
Habitat Vagrants likely to favour damp woodland and scrub.
Distribution Breeds throughout most of N America and winters Central and S America.
Occurrence Very rare vagrant to Britain.

V	—	—

Rufous-sided Towhee

Red-eyed Vireo

Black-and-white Warbler

Northern Parula

Yellow Warbler

Blackpoll Warbler
Dendroica striata L 14cm

Both sexes and all plumages show 2 pale wing bars. Breeding male has black cap and throat, white cheeks, streaked upperparts and white underparts, the flanks heavily streaked. Female has heavy streaking and greyish-green wash to head, back and flanks. First-autumn birds are greenish-yellow on head, back and flanks with dark streaking on back. Winter adults are similar to juveniles but heavily streaked on head, breast and flanks.

Voice Call a sharp *tsip*.

Habitat Woodland.

Distribution Breeds northern N America and winters S America.

Occurrence Rare vagrant to NW Europe, mainly Britain.

V	—	—

Yellowthroat
Geothlypis trichas L 13cm

Upperparts olive-brown and underparts, including undertail coverts, yellowish. Breeding male has bright-yellow throat and black face mask, bordered above with greyish-white. Female lacks male's black mask but otherwise similar. Immature birds similar to female but with duller plumage. Immature male may show suggestion of black mask.

Voice Call a harsh *tuc*.

Habitat Vagrants likely to favour scrub and wetland thickets.

Distribution Breeds across most of N America, winters from southern states southwards.

Occurrence Very rare vagrant to Britain.

V	—	—

Yellow-rumped Warbler
Dendroica coronata L 14cm

In all plumages shows yellow rump, yellow patch on sides and 2 pale wing bars. Non-breeding birds have streaked, brownish upperparts, white throat and white underparts showing streaking on breast and flanks. Birds from north-east N America have faint, pale supercilium. Breeding male has blackish-grey upperparts and breast band and white throat in birds from north-east N America.

Voice Call a sharp *tik*.

Habitat Vagrants likely to favour woodland and scrub.

Distribution Breeds across most of northern N America and winters from southern states southwards.

American Redstart
Setophaga ruticilla L 13cm

Breeding male is black with orange-red on sides, wings and sides to base of tail. Female and first-winter birds have grey-brown upperparts, white underparts and yellow patches on sides, wings and sides to base of tail. Tail often fanned to reveal colour to best effect.

Voice Call a sharp *tik*.

Habitat Woodland and scrub.

Distribution Breeds across central and eastern N America and winters in Central and S America.

Occurrence Very rare vagrant to NW Europe including Britain.

V	—	—

Bobolink
Dolichonyx oryzivorus L 18cm

Breeding male distinctive with black plumage showing buff nape and white scapulars and rump. Female has streaked, buff plumage with prominent dark stripes on sides of crown and behind eye. Juvenile is similar to female but with warmer buff plumage and less streaking on underparts.

Voice Call a sharp *pink*.

Habitat Vagrants likely to favour fields and open, grassy areas.

Distribution Breeds central N America and winters S America.

Occurrence Very rare vagrant to Europe including Britain.

V	—	—

Scarlet Tanager
Piranga olivacea L 18cm

Rather plump-looking bird with proportionately large bill. Breeding male has striking red plumage with black wings and tail. Female is uniform and unmarked buffish-yellow. Adult and immature males in winter resemble female but with contrastingly dark wings.

Voice Call a disyllabic *chip-grrrr*.

Habitat Vagrants likely to favour woodland and scrub.

Distribution Breeds north-east N America and winters S America.

Occurrence Rare vagrant to NW Europe, mainly Britain.

V	—	—

Blackpoll Warbler

Yellowthroat

Yellow-rumped Warbler
Bobolink, female

American Redstart, female
Scarlet Tanager, male

Further Reading

Campbell, B and Lack, E (eds), *A Dictionary of Birds* (T & AD Poyser, 1985).

Cramp, S and Simmonds, KEL (eds), *Handbook of the Birds of Europe, the Middle East and North Africa* (Oxford University Press, 1977– [vols I–VI published to date]).

Delin, H and Svensson, L, *Photographic Guide to the Birds of Britain and Europe* (Hamlyn, 1988).

Dymond, JN, Fraser, PA and Gantlett, SJM, *Rare Birds in Britain and Ireland* (T & AD Poyser, 1989).

Gibbons, DW, Reid, JB and Chapman, RA (eds) *The New Atlas of Breeding Birds in Britain and Ireland 1988–1991* (T & AD Poyser, 1993).

Harrison, C, *An Atlas of the Birds of the Western Palaearctic* (Collins, 1982).

Harrison, P, *Seabirds: An Identification Guide* (revised edition) (Christopher Helm, 1991).

Hayman, P, Marchant, J and Prater, AJ, *Shorebirds: An Identification Guide* (Christopher Helm, 1986).

Jonsson, L, *Birds of Europe with North Africa and the Middle East* (Christopher Helm, 1992).

Lack, P, (ed.), *The Atlas of Wintering Birds in Britain and Ireland* (T & AD Poyser, 1986).

Lewington, I, Alstrom, P and Colston, P, *A Field Guide to the Rare Birds of Britain and Europe* (Harper Collins, 1991).

Madge, S, *Wildfowl: An Identification Guide to the Ducks, Geese and Swans of the World* (Christopher Helm, 1988).

National Geographic Society, *Field Guide to the Birds of North America* (National Geographic Society, 1983).

Porter, RF, Willis, I, Christiansen, S and Nielsen, BP, *Flight Identification of European Raptors* (T & AD Poyser, 1974).

Useful Addresses

British Ornithologist's Club (BOC)
c/o British Ornithologist's Union
Zoological Society of London
Regent's Park
London NW1 4RY

British Ornithologist's Union (BOU)
c/o Zoological Society of London
Regent's Park
London NW1 4RY

British Trust for Ornithology (BTO)
The Nunnery
Nunnery Place
Thetford
Norfolk IP24 2PU

English Nature
Northminster House
Peterborough PE1 1UA

International Council for Bird Preservation (ICBP)
32 Cambridge Road
Girton
Cambridge CB3 OPJ

Irish Wildbird Conservancy
Ruttledge House
8 Longford Place
Monkstown
Co. Dublin, Ireland

Royal Society for the Protection of Birds (RSPB)
The Lodge
Sandy
Bedfordshire SG19 2DL

Scottish Ornithologist's Club (SOC)
21 Regent Terrace
Edinburgh EH7 5BT

Wildfowl and Wetlands Trust
Gatehouse
Slimbridge
Gloucestershire GL2 7BT

The Wildlife Trust (formerly RSNC)
The Green
Witham Park
Waterside South
Lincoln LN5 7JR

Index

PHOTOGRAPHIC ACKNOWLEDGEMENTS

Each photograph is referenced by a page number followed by a number indicating its position on the page working from left to right and top to bottom.

Nature Photographers: T Andrewartha 143.3, 207.3; SC Bisserot 173.4; Frank V Blackburn 75.2, 91.1, 91.3, 91.4, 187.1, 197.1, 197.2, 205.1, 213.4, 227.2, 245.2, 245.4, 251.1, 259.1, 259.2, 265.1, 265.2, 269.1, 279.3, 303.6; Mark Bolton 21.5, 23.1, 73.2, 211.2, 215.2, 243.3, 249.4, 255.2; Derek Bonsall 221.1; Kevin Carlson 31.1, 33.6, 37.3, 37.4, 73.3, 77.1, 77.4, 79.4, 83.5, 85.3, 87.1, 93.4, 103.1, 105.4, 175.3, 175.5, 203.3, 207.2, 217.1, 223.2, 223.4, 227.1, 227.3, 227.4, 227.5, 233.3, 241.2, 241.4, 245.3, 247.2, 247.3, 249.1, 249.2, 251.4, 251.5, 251.6, 253.1, 253.2, 253.3, 255.3, 257.3, 259.4, 261.2, 261.3, 261.4, 263.2, 267.1, 267.2, 267.4, 269.4, 271.3, 285.4, 287.6, 291.1, 299.1, 299.3, 299.4, 301.1, 301.2, 303.7, 311.5; Colin Carver 83.2, 121.4, 189.3, 219.1, 235.2, 239.1, 243.2, 251.2, 253.4, 255.4, 269.2, 271.4, 273.3, 273.4, 285.1, 287.2, 289.5, 293.2, 303.2; Hugh Clark 87.4, 215.1, 215.3, 217.2, 231.7; Andrew Cleave 21.3, 27.6, 29.4, 63.4, 67.1, 123.5, 139.1, 149.5, 159.1, 159.2, 159.3, 169.1, 169.3, 181.1, 237.3, 269.5, 305.2; Peter Craig-Cooper 33.2, 73.7, 111.3; RS Daniell 85.5, 117.4, 135.4, 141.4; AK Davies 177.1; RH Fisher 195.2; CH Gomersall 73.4, 93.1, 177.6, 207.1; ME Gore 35.2, 37.1, 73.1, 75.5, 77.3, 85.4, 101.1, 105.5, 133.5, 155.3, 171.4, 171.5, 189.1, 231.5, 269.6, 283.1, 289.4, 305.3; J Hancock 107.1, 235.3, 271.6; Dr MR Hill 19.2, 117.3, 131.2, 131.5, 135.3, 149.1, 187.6, 213.1, 213.2, 219.2, 221.3, 223.3, 225.5, 261.5, 267.3; EA Janes 19.3, 81.2, 95.2, 99.2, 99.3, 105.1, 121.1, 129.1, 147.1, 175.1, 183.4, 191.2, 195.3, 213.5, 233.2, 277.2, 295.1; John Karmali 37.5; Chris and Jo Knights 147.3, 171.1; B Mearns 121.2; Hugh Miles 155.4; M Müller and H Wohlmuth 33.7, 75.4, 77.2, 79.5, 81.4, 81.5, 89.4, 107.4, 115.6, 141.6, 171.3, 211.1, 221.2, 251.3, 263.4, 301.3; CK Mylne 161.2; Philip J Newman 17.1, 17.5, 43.4, 45.4, 91.2, 93.3, 95.4, 95.6, 97.1, 97.2, 97.3, 97.4, 139.4, 141.1, 149.2, 177.5, 193.3, 249.5, 261.1, 265.4; D Osborn 53.3, 139.2, 173.5; WS Paton 19.4, 41.4, 75.1, 79.2, 83.4, 85.1,89.2, 93.5, 163.2, 191.4, 193.5, 201.3, 237.2, 275.2; JF Reynolds 193.4, 203.2; Peter Roberts 79.3, 129.4, 153.4, 167.6, 169.2; J Russell 237.1; Don Smith 87.2, 89.3, 93.6, 149.6, 191.1, 191.5, 195.1, 195.4, 197.3, 211.4, 279.4, 295.5, 307.5, 309.1; Robert T Smith 19.1, 231.1, 231.2, 241.1; Paul Sterry 15.4, 17.2, 17.3, 19.5, 21.1, 21.2, 21.4, 23.3, 25.1, 25.2, 27.1, 27.2, 27.3, 27.4, 27.5, 29.1, 29.3, 29.5, 31.4, 31.5, 33.1, 33.3, 33.4, 35.1, 35.3, 35.4, 35.5, 35.7, 37.2, 38/39, 41.1, 41.2, 41.3 41.5, 43.1, 43.3, 43.5, 43.6, 45.2, 45.3, 45.5, 45.6 47.1, 47.2, 47.3, 47.4, 47.5, 47.6, 49.1, 49.2, 49.3 49.4, 49.5, 51.2, 51.3, 51.4, 51.5, 51.6, 53.1, 53.2 53.4, 55.1, 55.2, 55.3, 55.4, 55.5, 57.1, 57.2, 57.3 57.4, 57.5, 57.6, 59.1, 59.2, 59.3, 59.4, 59.5, 59.6 59.7, 61.1, 61.2, 61.3, 61.4, 61.5, 61.6, 63.1, 63.2 63.3, 63.5, 63.6, 63.7, 65.3, 65.4, 65.5, 65.6, 67.2 67.3, 67.4, 67.5, 67.6, 69.1, 69.3, 69.4, 69.5, 69.6 69.7, 79.1, 81.1, 83.1, 83.3, 85.2, 87.3, 95.1, 95.3 95.5, 101.2, 101.3, 101.4, 103.3, 107.2, 107.5 109.2, 109.3, 109.4, 109.5, 111.1, 111.2, 111.4 115.3, 115.4, 115.5, 117.2, 117.5, 119.3, 119.4 119.5, 119.6, 123.1, 123.3, 123.4, 125.1, 125.2 125.3, 127.2, 129.2, 129.3, 131.1, 131.3, 133.1 133.2, 133.3, 133.4, 135.1, 135.2, 135.5, 135 137.1, 137.2, 137.3, 137.4, 139.5, 141.2, 14 141.5, 143.2, 143.4, 143.5, 143.6, 145.1, 145.2 145.3, 147.4, 147.5, 149.3, 149.4, 153.1, 153.2 155.1, 157.1, 157.2, 157.3, 157.4, 157.5, 157.6 161.1, 161.4, 161.5, 161.6, 163.1, 163.3, 165.1 165.2, 165.3, 165.4, 167.1, 167.3, 167.4, 167.5 173.2, 173.3, 177.2, 177.3, 179.1, 179.2, 179.3 179.4, 179.5, 181.3, 181.4, 183.2, 183.3, 185.1 185.2, 187.3, 193.1, 199.1, 199.2, 199.3, 199.4 201.1, 201.2, 203.1, 203.4, 205.2, 205.3, 208/209 217.3, 219.3, 221.4, 223.1, 223.5, 225.1, 225.2 225.3, 225.4, 229.3, 231.3, 231.4, 235.1, 235.4 235.5, 237.4, 237.5, 239.2, 239.3, 239.4, 243.1 249.3, 253.5, 255.1, 263.1, 263.3, 265.3, 265.5 269.3, 269.7, 271.1, 271.2, 273.1, 273.2, 273.5 275.1, 277.3, 279.1, 279.2, 281.1, 281.2, 281.3 281.4, 283.2, 287.1, 287.3, 289.1, 289.2, 289.3 291.2, 291.4, 291.5, 293.1, 293.3, 293.4, 303.1 303.3, 303.4, 303.5, 305.1, 305.4, 305.5, 305.6 307.3, 307.4, 309.5, 311.2, 311.4; Derick Summers 301.4; EK Thompson 15.1, 55.6, 81.3; Roger Tidman 15.2, 15.3, 17.4, 17.6, 23.2, 23.4, 25.3 25.4, 29.2, 31.2, 33.5, 35.6, 43.2, 45.1, 51.1, 65.1 65.2, 69.2, 70/71, 73.5, 73.6, 75.3, 79.6, 89, 93.2 99.1, 101.6, 103.2, 105.2, 105.3, 109.1, 113.4 115.1, 115.2, 117.1, 119.1, 119.2, 121.3, 121.5 123.2, 127.1, 129.5, 129.6, 131.4, 133.6, 139.3 143.1, 145.4, 147.2, 147.6, 150/151, 153.3, 155 159.4, 159.5, 161.3, 163.4, 163.5, 165.4, 167.2 171.2, 173.1, 175.2, 175.4, 177.4, 181.2, 185 187.2, 187.4, 191.3, 193.2, 207.4, 211.3, 211.5 215.4, 217.4, 217.5, 229.1, 229.4, 231.6, 235 241.3, 243.4, 245.1, 255.5, 257.2, 257.4, 259 273.6, 277.1, 283.3, 283.4, 283.5, 285.2, 287 287.5, 289.6, 291.3, 295.3, 295.4, 297.1, 297.2 297.3, 297.4, 299.2, 301.5, 307.1, 307.2, 309.2 309.3, 311.3, 311.6; Jonathan Wilson 31.1 **Windrush Photos**: David M Cottridge 187.5 285.3, 311.1; Göran Ekstrom 125.4, 185.3, 185.5 229.2, 247.1, 271.5; A & E Morris 309.4; David Tipling 101.5, 169.4, 257.1. **RSPB**: Dusan Boucny 189.2; Jan Sevcik 205.4. **Tim Loseby**: 89.1, 295.2. **Paul Doherty**: 185.4, 257.5.